W9-AWG-248

Great American Documents

Great American Documents

Introductory Notes by
Robert A. Divine
John Robinson

Grolier Enterprises, Inc. Danbury, Connecticut

Published by Grolier Enterprises, Inc.

© 1971 and 1987 by American Heritage, a division of Forbes Inc. All rights reserved. This 1987 edition is published by agreement with American Heritage, a division of Forbes Inc., 60 Fifth Avenue, New York, NY 10011.

All rights reserved. No part of this book may be reproduced or transmitted in any form by any means electronic, mechanical, or otherwise, whether now or hereafter devised, including photocopying, recording, or by any information storage and retrieval system without express written prior permission from the Publisher.

ISBN 0-7172-8198-1

Grolier Incorporated offers a varied selection of both adult and children's book racks. For details on ordering, please write to Grolier Incorporated, Sherman Turnpike, Danbury, CT 06816, Attn: Premium Department

Printed and Manufactured in the United States of America

Contents

Foreword

As the United States celebrated the two-hundredth anniversary of the Constitution, a growing number of Americans found themselves asking what had become of the old verities that had guided them through so many difficult circumstances in the past. It was possible, of course, that they had misplaced them or forgotten them; it was also conceivable that they had been mistaken about them all along—perhaps they were, after all, only the rhetoric of the past, suited to the needs of a long-ago occasion, with no real application to the demands of a society plunging toward the twenty-first century.

These questions have been in the minds of those who compiled the selections in this book, who continue to feel that Americans are basically an idealistic lot. They have lived by many lights, not least of which was the body of words that records their aspirations and reminds them what their common enterprise is all about. In a nation whose goal of self-government was determined long ago, many of the old hopes and dreams remain—some unfulfilled or only partially achieved, but hopes and dreams nonetheless—tokens of that peculiar quirk in man that forces him to press on in private or public quest of something ever better.

This volume includes some of the fundamental documents of American history, those that have acquired a timeless quality, and that appear to have validity for present and future generations. They happen to be words *about* which many people have read or heard, yet they are not often read themselves. Written or spoken originally in response to a crisis or in pursuit of an opportunity, they speak to us from the past, forming a mosaic chronicle of what America was and is and wished to become. They are what preceding generations had to say about the common beliefs which they and we share.

Arranged chronologically, these particular documents are, on the whole, public in nature. They represent either some form of public action or a distillation of matured opinion, and as such they have pointed the direction of the nation's growth. Some have acquired a richer patina with the passing years, as did the Gettysburg Address. Certain issues to which men spoke have long been forgotten, yet there survives within the words themselves some abiding truth about the American dream. None of the documents in this book is dead; within all we may find the essence of what we are and what we aspire to.

Privileges and Prerogatives Granted to Columbus 1492

In 1485 Christopher Columbus arrived in Spain with a bold plan. An Italian sailor who had participated in the Portuguese quest for a route to Asia around the coast of Africa, Columbus reasoned that by sailing due west across the Atlantic he could reach the Indies and thus gain easy access to the lucrative Oriental trade. He first proposed to the Portuguese that they back him financially, but they refused — not because they doubted that the world was round, but because they rightly believed that Columbus had greatly underestimated the size of the earth. Undaunted, Columbus presented his plan to Spain's King Ferdinand and Queen Isabella; and although they initially expressed interest, they withheld their approval after scholars advised against the project. In 1491 Columbus made his final request to the Spanish monarchs; and this time he raised his terms, asking for a title of nobility, high office, and substantial revenue as a reward if his venture proved successful.

Ferdinand and Isabella rejected Columbus' plan in early 1492; and he set out for Paris to win French support, still confident that his scheme would succeed. As he made his way north, a royal courier intercepted him — Queen Isabella, in an act of feminine intuition, had changed her mind. Impressed by Columbus' supreme self-confidence, she had decided that the potential rewards for Spain were worth the relatively small cost of the expedition. She and her husband borrowed the required sum (on the order of fourteen thousand dollars) from the Treasury, and on April 30 they issued a formal commission to Columbus. It was on the authority of this document that he set sail on August 3, 1492, in search of a new route to the Indies — and ended up discovering a new world.   R.A.D.

F ERDINAND AND ELIZABETH, . . .

For as much of you, *Christopher Columbus*, are going by our command, with some of our vessels and men, to discover and subdue some Islands and Continent in the ocean, and it is hoped that by God's assistance, some of the said Islands and Continent in the ocean will be discovered and conquered by your means and conduct, therefore it is but just and reasonable, that since you expose yourself to such danger to serve us, you should be rewarded for it. And we being willing to honour and favour you for the reasons aforesaid; Our will is, That you, *Christopher Columbus,* after discovering and conquering the said Islands and Continent in the said ocean, or any of them, shall be our Admiral of the said Islands and Continent you shall so discover and conquer; and that you be our Admiral, Vice-Roy, and Governour in them, and that for the future, you may call and stile yourself, D. *Christopher Columbus,* and that your sons and successors in the said employment, may call themselves Dons, Admirals, Vice-Roys, and Governours of them; and that you may exercise the office of Admiral, with the charge of Vice-Roy and Governour of the said Islands and Continent, which you and your Lieutenants shall conquer, and freely decide all causes, civil and criminal, appertaining to the said employment of Admiral, Vice-Roy, and Governour, as you shall think fit in justice, and as the Admirals of our kingdoms use to do; and that you have power to punish offenders; and you and your Lieutenants exercise the employments of Admiral, Vice-Roy, and Governour, in all things belonging to the said offices, or any of them; and that you enjoy the perquisites and salaries belonging to the said employments, and to each of them, in the same manner as the High Admiral of our kingdoms does. And by this our letter, or a copy of it signed by a *Public Notary:* We command Prince *John,* our most dearly beloved Son, the Infants, Dukes, Prelates, Marquesses, Great Masters and Military Orders, Priors, Commendaries, our Counsellors, Judges, and other Officers of Justice whatsoever, belonging to our Household, Courts, and Chancery, and Constables of Castles, Strong Houses, and others, and all Corporations, Bayliffs, Governours, Judges, Commanders, Sea Officers; and the Aldermen, Common Council, Officers, and Good People of all Cities, Lands, and Places in our Kingdoms and Dominions, and in those you shall conquer and subdue, and the captains, masters, mates, and other officers and sailors, our natural subjects now being, or that shall be for the time to come, and any of them, that when you shall have discovered the said Islands and Continent in the ocean; and you, or any that shall have your commission, shall have taken the usual oath in such cases, that they for the future, look upon you as long as you live, and after you, your son and heir, and so from one heir to another forever, as our Admiral on our said Ocean, and as Vice-Roy and Governour of the said Islands and Continent, by you, *Christopher Columbus,* discovered and conquered; and that they treat you and your Lieutenants, by you appointed, for executing the employments of Admiral, Vice-Roy, and Governour, as such in all respects, and give you all the perquisites and other things belonging and appertaining to the said offices; and allow, and cause to be allowed you, all the honours, graces, concessions, prehaminences, prerogatives, immunities, and other things, or any of them which are due to you, by virtue of your commands of Admiral, Vice-Roy, and Governour, and to be observed completely, so that nothing be diminished; and that they make no objection to this, or any part of it, nor suffer it to be made; forasmuch as we from this time forward, by this our letter, bestow on you the employments of Admiral, Vice-Roy, and perpetual Governour forever; and we put you into possession of the said offices, and of every of them, and full power to use and exercise them, and to receive the perquisites and salaries belonging to them, or any of them, as was said above. Concerning all which things, if it be requisite, and you shall desire it, We command our Chancellour, Notaries, and other Officers, to pass, seal, and deliver to you, our Letter of Privilege, in such form and legal manner, as you shall require or stand in need of. And that none of them presume to do any thing to the contrary, upon pain of our displeasure, and fortfeiture of 30 ducats for each offence. And we command him, who shall show them this our Letter, that he summon them to appear before us at our Court, where we shall then be, within fifteen days after such summons, under the said penalty. Under which same, we also command any Public Notary whatsoever, that he give to him that shows it him, a certificate under his seal, that we may know how our command is obeyed.

GIVEN at *Granada,* on the 30th of April, in the year of our Lord, 1492.—

I, THE KING, I, THE QUEEN

The Mayflower Compact 1620

In 1606, a year before the founding of Jamestown in Virginia, a group of Separatists from the Church of England left their native land to settle in Holland. Despairing of purifying the Established Church of Catholic ritual and doctrine, they sought to practice their own form of religion in peace. While they enjoyed religious freedom among the Dutch, many of them became disenchanted with life in Europe and began to explore the possibility of migrating to America. They received a patent from the Virginia Company in England and found a group of London merchants who were willing to finance their venture for commercial reasons. In 1620 some thirty-five Pilgrims, as they came to be called, sailed from Holland to Southampton, where they were joined by sixty-seven English emigrants—many of whom were not Separatists—and in September they set out for the New World in the *Mayflower*.

Heavy storms drove the *Mayflower* off course and when the Pilgrims finally sighted land, they found themselves off the coast of Cape Cod. Exhausted by the rough journey, the leaders decided to settle in New England, knowing that they were far to the north of the land granted to them. When some of the English emigrants, realizing they were now outside the legal jurisdiction of the Virginia Company, indicated that they planned to go their own way once on shore, the Pilgrims acted swiftly to preserve unity. Drawing on their church experience, they drew up a compact which all but three of the men on board the *Mayflower* signed on November 21, 1620, while the ship was anchored in Provincetown harbor. The Mayflower Compact, designed to maintain order at a crucial moment, became in time the constitution for the Plymouth Plantation and a vital precedent for the American tradition of self-government.   R.A.D.

In The Name of God, Amen. We, whose names are underwritten, the Loyal Subjects of our dread Sovereign Lord King *James,* by the Grace of God, of *Great Britain, France,* and *Ireland,* King, *Defender of the Faith,* &c. Having undertaken for the Glory of God, and Advancement of the Christian Faith, and the Honour of our King and Country, a Voyage to plant the first colony in the northern Parts of Virginia; Do by these Presents, solemnly and mutually in the Presence of God and one another, covenant and combine ourselves together into a civil Body Politick, for our better Ordering and Preservation, and Furtherance of the Ends aforesaid; And by Virtue hereof do enact, constitute, and frame, such just and equal Laws, Ordinances, Acts, Constitutions, and Offices, from time to time, as shall be thought most meet and convenient for the general Good of the Colony; unto which we promise all due Submission and Obedience. In WITNESS whereof we have hereunto subscribed our names at *Cape Cod* the eleventh of *November,* in the Reign of our Sovereign Lord King *James* of *England, France,* and *Ireland,* the eighteenth and of *Scotland,* the fifty-fourth. *Anno Domini,* 1620

	Mr. Stephen Hopkins
Mr. John Carver	Digery Priest
Mr. William Bradford	Thomas Williams
Mr. Edward Winslow	Gilbert Winslow
Mr. William Brewster	Edmund Margesson
Isaac Allerton	Peter Brown
Miles Standish	Richard Bitteridge
John Alden	George Soule
John Turner	Edward Tilly
Francis Eaton	John Tilly
James Chilton	Francis Cooke
John Craxton	Thomas Rogers
John Billington	Thomas Tinker
Joses Fletcher	John Ridgate
John Goodman	Edward Fuller
Mr. Samuel Fuller	Richard Clark
Mr. Christopher Martin	Richard Gardiner
Mr. William Mullins	Mr. John Allerton
Mr. William White	Thomas English
Mr. Richard Warren	Edward Doten
John Howland	Edward Liester

Massachusetts School Law of 1647

Increasing religious intolerance in England led many Puritans to follow the Pilgrims to the New World. In 1630 a group of Puritans founded the Massachusetts Bay Colony at Boston, which soon outstripped the small Pilgrim settlement at Plymouth. From the outset, the Puritans were inspired by a vision of creating a religious commonwealth in which they would carry out God's will on earth. Many of the leaders were university graduates, who realized the importance of education for a religious community that based its faith on the Bible. In 1636 they founded Harvard College; and although the first head was quickly dismissed when he beat his students unmercifully, fed them tainted beef, and ran off with the college's funds, Harvard flourished under his successors, training ministers for the colony's churches and producing men of learning who developed a respect for knowledge for its own sake. The university could thrive only if it had a steady influx of qualified students; so in 1642 the Massachusetts General Court passed a law requiring the colonists to teach their children to read. A number of towns established schools for this purpose, and in 1647 Massachusetts enacted a more sweeping law that established the first system of public education in the American colonies.   R.A.D.

13

It being one chiefe proiect of ye ould deluder, Satan, to keepe men from the knowledge of ye Scriptures, as in form^r times by keeping y^m in an unknowne tongue, so in these latt^r times by perswading from ye use of tongues, y^t so at least ye true sence & meaning of ye originall might be clouded by false glosses of saint seeming deceivers, y^t learning may not be buried in ye grave of o^r fath^{rs} in ye church and commonwealth, the Lord assisting o^r endeavo^{r}s, —

It is therefore ord^{r}ed, y^t ev^{r}y towneship in this iurisdiction, aft^r ye Lord hath increased y^m number to 50 houshold^{rs}, shall then forthwth appoint one wth in their towne to teach all such children as shall resort to him to write & reade, whose wages shall be paid eith^r by ye parents or mast^{rs} of such children, or by ye inhabitants in gen^{r}all, by way of supply, as ye maior part of those y^t ord^r ye prudentials ye towne shall appoint; provided, those y^t send their children be not oppressed by paying much more y^m they can have y^m taught for in oth^r townes; & it is furth^r ordered, y^t where any towne shall increase to ye numb^r of 100 families or househould^{rs}, they shall set up a grammer schoole, ye m^r thereof being able to instruct youth so farr as they shall be fitted for ye university, provided, y^t if any towne neglect ye performance hereof above one yeare, y^t every such towne shall pay 5 pounds to ye next schoole till they shall performe this order.

Jonathan Edwards: Sinners in the Hands of an Angry God 1741

In the eighteenth century, the impact of Newtonian science and the day-to-day involvement with material challenges gradually weakened the grip of Puritanism on New England. The initial impulse to create a Zion in the wilderness waned as life became more secular. Then in the 1730's, an astonishing outburst of religious enthusiasm swept through all thirteen colonies. This Great Awakening, the first American religious revival, was a mass phenomenon in which large numbers of people, reacting against Puritan austerity, expressed their feelings about God with freedom and even abandon.

Jonathan Edwards began the religious revival while he was serving as pastor of a Congregational church in Northampton, Massachusetts. A graduate of Yale, Edwards was a brilliant theologian who developed an intense belief in the majesty of God and the sinfulness of man. In Northampton he sought to convert his followers to a higher level of religious commitment by terrifying them with visions of damnation. Reaction to his extreme emotionalism ultimately drove him from the pulpit, and he spent his last years ministering to Indians on the Massachusetts frontier.

Edwards preached his most famous sermon in Enfield, Connecticut, on July 8, 1741. As he roused his listeners to emotional fervor, the church reverberated with the moans and cries of those seeking salvation.   R.A.D.

The bow of God's wrath is bent, and the arrow made ready on the string, and justice bends the arrow at your heart, and strains the bow, and it is nothing but the mere pleasure of God, and that of an angry God, without any promise or obligation at all, that keeps the arrow one moment from being made drunk with your blood. Thus all you that never passed under a great change of heart, by the mighty power of the Spirit of God upon your souls; all you that were never born again, and made new creatures, and raised from being dead in sin, to a state of new, and before altogether unexperienced light and life, are in the hands of an angry God. However you may have reformed your life in many things, and may have had religious affections, and may keep up a form of religion in your families and closets, and in the house of God, it is nothing but his mere pleasure that keeps you from being this moment swallowed up in everlasting destruction. However unconvinced you may now be of the truth of what you hear, by and by you will be fully convinced of it. Those that are gone from being in the like circumstances with you, see that it was so with them, for destruction came suddenly upon most of them; when they expected nothing of it, and while they were saying, Peace and safety: now they see, that those things on which they depended for peace and safety, were nothing but thin air and empty shadows.

The God that holds you over the pit of hell, much as one holds a spider, or some loathsome insect over the fire, abhors you, and is dreadfully provoked: his wrath towards you burns like fire; he looks upon you as worthy of nothing else, but to be cast into the fire; he is of purer eyes than to bear to have you in his sight; you are ten thousand times more abominable in his eyes, than the most hateful venomous serpent is in ours. You have offended him infinitely more than ever a stubborn rebel did his prince; and yet it is nothing but his hand that holds you from falling into the fire every moment. It is to be ascribed to nothing else, that you did not go to hell the last night; that you was suffered to awake again in this world, after you closed your eyes to sleep. And there is no other reason to be given, why you have not dropped into hell since you arose in the morning, but that God's hand has held you up. There is no other reason to be given why you have not gone to hell, since you have sat here in the house of God, provoking his pure eyes by your sinful wicked manner of attending his solemn worship. Yea, there is nothing else that is to be given as a reason why you do not this very moment drop down into hell.

O sinner! Consider the fearful danger you are in: it is a great furnace of wrath, a wide and bottomless pit, full of the fire of wrath, that you are held over in the hand of that God, whose wrath is provoked and incensed as much against you, as against many of the damned in hell. You hang by a slender thread, with the flames of divine wrath flashing about it, and ready every moment to singe it, and burn it asunder; and you have no interest in any Mediator, and nothing to lay hold of to save yourself, nothing to keep off the flames of wrath, nothing of your own, nothing that you ever have done, nothing that you can do, to induce God to spare you one moment.

Benjamin Franklin: The Albany Plan of Union 1754

If the thirteen colonies were slow to develop a sense of unity, it was because the colonists thought of themselves as Englishmen, not Americans, and were far more concerned with local needs than with inter-colonial issues. It was the problem of defense which forced them to begin considering their common interests. In the early 1750's, the French began moving into the Ohio Valley region, winning the loyalty of the Indian tribes and building a series of forts. After a detachment of Virginia militia had clashed with the French on the frontier, British officials called colonial representatives together at Albany in the spring of 1754 to negotiate with the friendly Iroquois Indians and to consult on plans for joint military efforts.

Seven colonies sent delegates to Albany, and Benjamin Franklin, representing Pennsylvania, soon dominated the conference. Already famous for his civic, literary, and scientific achievements, Franklin had become an advocate of colonial unity as a result of his service as Deputy Postmaster General for all North America. In 1751 he wrote an essay projecting the expansion of the American colonies westward; and when he traveled to Albany, he brought with him an outline of "a Scheme for Uniting the Northern Colonies." At Albany, Franklin drafted a formal plan of union which the other delegates approved unanimously. However, the colonial assemblies, which were jealous of their authority, later rejected the plan. The result, in the French and Indian War, was a lack of coordination which greatly hampered the British effort.

Franklin later commented that adoption of his Albany plan might well have prevented the Revolution by providing a framework for resolving differences between England and the colonies. "But such mistakes are not new," he added philosophically; "history is full of the errors of states and princes. . . ."

R.A.D.

It is proposed that humble application be made for an act of
Parliament of Great Britain, by virtue of which one general
government may be formed in America, including all the said
colonies, within and under which government each colony may
retain its present constitution, except in the particulars wherein a
change may be directed by the said act, as hereafter follows.

1. That the said general government be administered by a President-General, to be appointed and supported by the crown; and a
Grand Council, to be chosen by the representatives of the people of
the several Colonies met in their respective assemblies.

2. That within——months after the passing such act, the House
of Representatives that happen to be sitting within that time, or
that shall be especially for that purpose convened, may and shall
choose members for the Grand Council, in the following proportion, that is to say,

Massachusetts Bay	7
New Hampshire	2
Connecticut	5
Rhode Island	2
New York	4
New Jersey	3
Pennsylvania	6
Maryland	4
Virginia	7
North Carolina	4
South Carolina	4
	48

3. ——who shall meet for the first time at the city of Philadelphia, being called by the President-General as soon as conveniently
may be after his appointment.

4. That there shall be a new election of the members of the
Grand Council every three years; and, on the death or resignation
of any member, his place should be supplied by a new choice at the
next sitting of the Assembly of the Colony he represented.

5. That after the first three years, when the proportion of
money arising out of each Colony to the general treasury can be
known, the number of members to be chosen for each Colony
shall, from time to time, in all ensuing elections, be regulated by
that proportion, yet so as that the number to be chosen by any one

Province be not more than seven, nor less than two.

6. That the Grand Council shall meet once in every year, and oftener if occasion require, at such time and place as they shall adjourn to at the last preceding meeting, or as they shall be called to meet at by the President-General on any emergency; he having first obtained in writing the consent of seven of the members to such call, and sent duly and timely notice to the whole.

7. That the Grand Council have power to choose their speaker; and shall neither be dissolved, prorogued, nor continued sitting longer than six weeks at one time, without their own consent or the special command of the crown.

8. That the members of the Grand Council shall be allowed for their service ten shillings sterling per diem, during their session and journey to and from the place of meeting; twenty miles to be reckoned a day's journey.

9. That the assent of the President-General be requisite to all acts of the Grand Council, and that it be his office and duty to cause them to be carried into execution.

10. That the President-General, with the advice of the Grand Council, hold or direct all Indian treaties, in which the general interest of the Colonies may be concerned; and make peace or declare war with Indian nations.

11. That they make such laws as they judge necessary for regulating all Indian trade.

12. That they make all purchases from Indians, for the crown, of lands not now within the bounds of particular Colonies, or that shall not be within their bounds when some of them are reduced to more convenient dimensions.

13. That they make new settlements on such purchases, by granting lands in the King's name, reserving a quitrent to the crown for the use of the general treasury.

14. That they make laws for regulating and governing such new settlements, till the crown shall think fit to form them into particular governments.

15. That they raise and pay soldiers and build forts for the defence of any of the Colonies, and equip vessels of force to guard the coasts and protect the trade on the ocean, lakes, or great rivers; but they shall not impress men in any Colony, without the consent of the Legislature.

16. That for these purposes they have power to make laws, and

lay and levy such general duties, imposts, or taxes, as to them shall appear most equal and just (considering the ability and other circumstances of the inhabitants in the several Colonies), and such as may be collected with the least inconvenience to the people; rather discouraging luxury, than loading industry with unnecessary burdens.

17. That they may appoint a General Treasurer and Particular Treasurer in each government when necessary; and, from time to time, may order the sums in the treasuries of each government into the general treasury; or draw on them for special payments, as they find most convenient.

18. Yet no money to issue but by joint orders of the President-General and Grand Council; except where sums have been appropriated to particular purposes, and the President-General is previously empowered by an act to draw such sums.

19. That the general accounts shall be yearly settled and reported to the several Assemblies.

20. That a quorum of the Grand Council, empowered to act with the President-General, do consist of twenty-five members; among whom there shall be one or more from a majority of the Colonies.

21. That the laws made by them for the purposes aforesaid shall not be repugnant, but, as near as may be, agreeable to the laws of England, and shall be transmitted to the King in Council for approbation, as soon as may be after their passing; and if not disapproved within three years after presentation, to remain in force.

22. That, in case of the death of the President-General, the Speaker of the Grand Council for the time being shall succeed, and be vested with the same powers and authorities, to continue till the King's pleasure be known.

23. That all military commission officers, whether for land or sea service, to act under this general constitution, shall be nominated by the President-General; but the approbation of the Grand Council is to be obtained, before they receive their commissions. And all civil officers are to be nominated by the Grand Council, and to receive the President-General's approbation before they officiate.

24. But, in case of vacancy by death or removal of any officer, civil or military, under this constitution, the Governor of the Prov-

ince in which such vacancy happens may appoint, till the pleasure of the President-General and Grand Council can be known.

25. That the particular military as well as civil establishments in each Colony remain in their present state, the general constitution notwithstanding; and that on sudden emergencies any Colony may defend itself, and lay the accounts of expense thence arising before the President-General and General Council, who may allow and order payment of the same, as far as they judge such accounts just and reasonable.

Resolutions of the Stamp Act Congress 1765

The sweeping English victory in the French and Indian War led to tension and conflict between colonies and mother country. Acquisition of Canada from France and the heavy debts incurred in the war forced the British to reorganize their empire in North America. George Grenville, the Chancellor of the Exchequer, secured the passage of two parliamentary acts designed to make the colonies assume a portion of England's severe financial burden. The first, popularly known as the Sugar Act, imposed new duties on the importation of such luxuries as sugar and wine and tightened up the customs service. The Stamp Act, the second revenue measure, went much further, imposing for the first time an internal tax on the American colonies. It sought to raise £60,000 a year by requiring the colonists to buy revenue stamps for all business transactions, legal documents, and newspapers.

To Grenville's surprise and dismay, Americans reacted strongly against these laws, especially the Stamp Act. Conservative lawyers and merchants joined with radical agitators to protest the infringement of their traditional right to be taxed only by their own colonial assemblies. Violence occurred in New York, Charleston, and Boston when mobs of patriots attacked the homes of stamp agents, confiscated and burned the stamps, and intimidated citizens who tried to comply with the law. More moderate colonial leaders gathered in New York in October, 1765, to hold a Stamp Act Congress. After defeating motions from a radical minority which denied the power of the Parliament to legislate for the colonies, the majority approved a set of resolutions drafted by John Dickinson, a moderate Philadelphia lawyer. These resolutions were sent to England, together with an address to the King, a memorial to the House of Lords, and a petition to the House of Commons. Parliament repealed the Stamp Act in 1766, but it specifically denied the claim to no taxation without representation and thus continued on a collision course with the colonists.

R.A.D.

The members of this Congress, sincerely devoted with the warmest sentiments of affection and duty to His Majesty's person and Government, inviolably attached to the present happy establishment of the Protestant succession, and with minds deeply impressed by a sense of the present and impending misfortunes of the British colonies on this continent; having considered as maturely as time will permit the circumstances of the said colonies, esteem it our indispensable duty to make the following declarations of our humble opinion respecting the most essential rights and liberties of the colonists, and of the grievances under which they labour, by reason of several late Acts of Parliament.

I. That His Majesty's subjects in these colonies owe the same allegiance to the Crown of Great Britain that is owing from his subjects born within the realm, and all due subordination to that august body the Parliament of Great Britain.

II. That His Majesty's liege subjects in these colonies are intitled to all the inherent rights and liberties of his natural born subjects within the kingdom of Great Britain.

III. That it is inseparably essential to the freedom of a people, and the undoubted right of Englishmen, that no taxes be imposed on them but with their own consent, given personally or by their representatives.

IV. That the people of these colonies are not, and from their local circumstances cannot be, represented in the House of Commons in Great Britain.

V. That the only representatives of the people of these colonies are persons chosen therein by themselves, and that no taxes ever have been, or can be constitutionally imposed on them, but by their respective legislatures.

VI. That all supplies to the Crown being free gifts of the people, it is unreasonable and inconsistent with the principles and spirit of the British Constitution, for the people of Great Britain to grant to His Majesty the property of the colonists.

VII. That trial by jury is the inherent and invaluable right of every British subject in these colonies.

VIII. That the late Act of Parliament, entitled *An Act for granting and applying certain stamp duties, and other duties, in the British colonies and plantations in America, etc.,* by imposing taxes on the inhabitants of these colonies; and the said Act, and several other Acts, by extending the jurisdiction of the courts of Admiralty beyond its ancient limits, have a manifest tendency to subvert the rights and liberties of the colonists.

IX. That the duties imposed by several late Acts of Parliament, from the peculiar circumstances of these colonies, will be extremely burthensome and grievous; and from the scarcity of specie, the payment of them absolutely impracticable.

X. That as the profits of the trade of these colonies ultimately center in Great Britain, to pay for the manufactures which they are obliged to take from thence, they eventually contribute very largely to all supplies granted there to the Crown.

XI. That the restrictions imposed by several late Acts of Parliament on the trade of these colonies will render them unable to purchase the manufactures of Great Britain.

XII. That the increase, prosperity, and happiness of these colonies depend on the full and free enjoyments of their rights and liberties, and an intercourse with Great Britain mutually affectionate and advantageous.

XIII. That it is the right of the British subjects in these colonies to petition the King or either House of Parliament.

Lastly, That it is the indispensable duty of these colonies to the best of sovereigns, to the mother country, and to themselves, to endeavour by a loyal and dutiful address to His Majesty, and humble applications to both Houses of Parliament, to procure the repeal of the Act for granting and applying certain stamp duties, of all clauses of any other Acts of Parliament, whereby the jurisdiction of the Admiralty is extended as aforesaid, and of the other late Acts for the restriction of American commerce.

Thomas Paine: Common Sense 1776

In November, 1774, Thomas Paine arrived in Philadelphia from England. Paine, thirty-six, was a former corset-maker and exciseman who had failed at everything he had undertaken; and he came to America with little more than a letter of introduction from Benjamin Franklin, who had met him in London and had been impressed with "those wonderful eyes of his." With this entrée, Paine quickly became the editor of *The Pennsylvania Magazine* and displayed a rare ability to give expression to the feelings of many thoughtful Americans.

After the controversy between the colonies and England led to fighting at Lexington and Concord in the spring of 1775, Paine was in the vanguard of those calling for a complete break with the mother country. Aware of the reluctance of many Americans to take the final step, he eloquently stated the case for independence in his pamphlet *Common Sense,* published in January, 1776. Within three months, more than one hundred thousand copies circulated through the colonies and his arguments helped convert thousands of uncertain Americans to the cause of independence. Paine later went to Paris during the French Revolution to plead the cause of freedom again. Eventually he returned to the United States, settling in New York where he died impoverished and in obscurity in 1809. Paine best summed up his life when he declared, "My country is the world; to do good, my religion."

R.A.D.

In the following pages I offer nothing more than simple facts, plain arguments, and common sense: and have no other preliminaries to settle with the reader than that he will divest himself of prejudice and prepossession, and suffer his reason and his feelings to determine for themselves: that he will put on, or rather that he will not put off, the true character of a man, and generously enlarge his views beyond the present day.

Volumes have been written on the subject of the struggle between England and America. Men of all ranks have embarked in the controversy, from different motives, and with various designs; but all have been ineffectual, and the period of debate is closed. Arms as the last resource decide the contest; the appeal was the choice of the King, and the Continent has accepted the challenge. . . .

The Sun never shined on a cause of greater worth. 'Tis not the affair of a City, a County, a Province, or a Kingdom; but of a Continent—of at least one eighth part of the habitable Globe. 'Tis not the concern of a day, a year, or an age; posterity are virtually involved in the contest, and will be more or less affected even to the end of time by the proceedings now. Now is the seed-time of Continental union, faith, and honor. The least fracture now will be like a name engraved with the point of a pin on the tender rind of a young oak; the wound would enlarge with the tree, and posterity read it in full grown characters.

By referring the matter from argument to arms, a new era for politics is struck—a new method of thinking hath arisen. All plans, proposals, *etc.*, prior to the nineteenth of April, *i.e.*, to the commencement of hostilities [at Lexington], are like the almanacs of the last year; which though proper then, are superseded and useless now. Whatever was advanced by the advocates on either side of the question then, terminated in one and the same point, *viz.*, a union with Great Britain; the only difference between the parties was the method of effecting it; the one proposing force, the other friendship; but it hath so far happened that the first hath failed, and the second hath withdrawn her influence.

As much hath been said of the advantages of reconciliation, which, like an agreeable dream, hath passed away and left us as we were, it is but right that we should examine the contrary side of the argument, and inquire into some of the many material injuries which these Colonies sustain, and always will sustain, by being connected with and dependent on Great Britain. To examine that connection and dependence, on the principles of nature and common sense, to see what we have to trust to, if separated, and what we are to expect, if dependent.

I have heard it asserted by some, that as America has flourished under her former connection with Great Britain, the same connection is necessary towards her future happiness, and will always have the same effect. Nothing can be more fallacious than this kind of argument. We may as well assert that because a child has thrived upon milk, that it is never to have meat, or that the first twenty years of our lives is to become a precedent for the next twenty. But even this is admitting more than is true; for I answer roundly, that America would have flourished as much, and probably much more, had no European power taken any notice of her. The commerce by which she hath enriched herself are the necessaries of life, and will always have a market while eating is the custom of Europe.

But she has protected us, say some. That she hath engrossed us is true, and defended the Continent at our expense as well as her own, is admitted; and she would have defended Turkey from the same motive, *viz.*, for the sake of trade and dominion.

Alas! we have been long led away by ancient prejudices and made large sacrifices to superstition. We have boasted the protection of Great Britain, without considering that her motive was *interest* not *attachment;* and that she did not protect us from *our enemies* on *our account;* but from *her enemies* on *her own account,* from those who had no quarrel with us on any *other account,* and who will always be our enemies on the *same account.* Let Britain waive her pretensions to the Continent, or the Continent throw off the dependence, and we should be at peace with France and Spain, were they at war with Britain. The miseries of Hanover's last war ought to warn us against connections.

It hath lately been asserted in parliament that the Colonies have no relation to each other but through the Parent Country, *i.e.*, that Pennsylvania and the Jerseys, and so on for the rest, are sister Colonies by the way of England; this is certainly a very roundabout way of proving relationship, but it is the nearest and only true way of proving enmity—or enemyship, if I may so call it. France and Spain never were, nor perhaps ever will be, our enemies as *Americans,* but as our being the *subjects of Great Britain.*

But Britain is the parent country, say some. Then the more shame upon her conduct. Even brutes do not devour their young, nor savages make war upon their families; wherefore, the assertion, if true, turns to her reproach; but it happens not to be true, or only partly so, and the phrase *parent* or *mother country* hath been jesuitically adopted by the King and his parasites, with a low papistical design of gaining an unfair bias on the credulous weakness of our minds. Europe, and not England, is the parent country of America. This new World hath been the asylum for the persecuted lovers of civil and religious liberty from *every part* of Europe. Hither have they fled, not from the tender embraces of the mother, but from the cruelty of the monster; and it is so far true of England, that the same tyranny which drove the first emigrants from home, pursues their descendants still.

In this extensive quarter of the globe, we forget the narrow limits of three hundred and sixty miles (the extent of England) and carry our friendship on a larger scale; we claim brotherhood with every European Christian, and triumph in the generosity of the sentiment.

It is pleasant to observe by what regular gradations we surmount the force of local prejudices, as we enlarge our acquaintance with the World. A man born in any town in England divided into parishes, will naturally associate most with his fellow parishioners (because their interests in many cases will be common) and distinguish him by the name of *neighbor;* if he meet him but a few miles from home, he drops the narrow idea of a street, and salutes him by the name of *townsman;* if he travel out of the county and meet him in any other he forgets the minor divisions of street and town, and calls him *countryman, i.e., countyman:* but if in their foreign excursions they should associate in France, or any other part of *Europe,* their local remembrance would be enlarged into that of *Englishmen.* And by a just parity of reasoning, all Europeans meeting in America, or any other quarter of the globe, are *countrymen;* for England, Holland, Germany, or Sweden, when compared with the whole, stand in the same places on the larger scale, which the divisions of street, town, and county do on the smaller ones; distinctions too limited for Continental minds. Not one third of the inhabitants, even of this province [Pennsylvania], are of English descent. Wherefore, I reprobate the phrase of Parent or Mother Country applied to England only, as being false, selfish, narrow, and ungenerous.

But, admitting that we were all of English descent, what does it amount to? Nothing. Britain, being now an open enemy, extinguishes every other name and title: to say that reconciliation is our duty, is truly farcical. The first king of England, of the present line (William the Conqueror) was a Frenchman, and half the peers of England are descendants from the same country; wherefore, by the same method of reasoning, England ought to be governed by France.

Much hath been said of the united strength of Britain and the Colonies, that in conjunction they might bid defiance to the world: But this is mere presumption; the fate of war is uncertain, neither do the expressions mean any thing; for this continent would never suffer itself to be drained of inhabitants, to support the British arms in either Asia, Africa, or Europe.

Besides, what have we to do with setting the world at defiance? Our plan is commerce, and that, well attended to, will secure us the peace and friendship of all Europe; because it is the interest of all Europe to have America a free port. Her trade will always be a protection, and her barrenness of gold and silver secure her from invaders.

I challenge the warmest advocate for reconciliation to show a single advantage that this continent can reap by being connected with Great Britain. I repeat the challenge; not a single advantage is derived. Our corn will fetch its price in any market in Europe, and our imported goods must be paid for, buy them where we will.

But the injuries and disadvantages which we sustain by that connection are without number; and our duty to mankind at large, as well as to ourselves, instruct us to renounce the alliance: because, any submission to, or dependence on, Great Britain, tends directly to involve this Continent in European wars and quarrels, and set us at variance with nations who would otherwise seek our friendship, and against whom we have neither anger nor complaint. As Europe is our market for trade, we ought to form no partial connection with any part of it. It is the true interest of America to steer clear of European contentions, which she never can do while, by her dependence on Britain, she is made the makeweight in the scale of British politics. . . . A government of our own is our natural right: and when a man seriously reflects on the precariousness of human affairs, he will become convinced that it is infinitely wiser and safer to form a constitution of our own in a cool deliberate manner, while we have it in our power, than to trust such an interesting event to time and chance. If we omit it now, some Massanello* may hereafter arise, who, laying hold of popular disquietudes, may collect together the desperate and the discontented, and by assuming to themselves the powers of government, finally sweep away the liberties of the Continent like a deluge. Should the government of America return again into the hands of Britain, the tottering situation of things will be a temptation for some desperate adventurer to try his fortune; and in such a case, what relief can Britain give? Ere she could hear the news, the fatal business might be done; and ourselves suffering like the wretched Britons under the oppression of the Conqueror. Ye that oppose independence now, ye know not what ye do: ye are opening a door to eternal tyranny, by keeping vacant the seat of government. There are thousands and tens of thousands, who would think it glorious to expel from the Continent that barbarous and hellish power, which hath stirred up the Indians and the Negroes to destroy us; the cruelty hath a double guilt, it is dealing brutally by us, and treacherously by them.

To talk of friendship with those in whom our reason forbids us to have faith, and our affections wounded through a thousand pores instruct us to detest, is madness and folly. Every day wears out the little remains of kindred between us and them; and can there be any reason to hope, that as the relationship expires, the affection will increase, or that we shall agree better when we have ten times more and greater concerns to quarrel over than ever?

Ye that tell us of harmony and reconciliation, can ye restore to us the time that is past? Can ye give to prostitution its former innocence? neither can ye reconcile Britain and America. The last cord now is broken, the people of England are presenting addresses against us. There are injuries which nature cannot forgive; she would cease to be nature if she did. As well can the lover forgive the ravisher of his mistress, as the Continent forgive the murders of Britain. The Almighty hath implanted in us these unextin-

---

*Thomas Anello, otherwise Massanello, a fisherman of Naples, who after spiriting up his countrymen in the public market place against the oppression of the Spaniards, to whom the place was then subject, prompted them to revolt, and in the space of a day became King. [*Paine's note.*]

guishable feelings for good and wise purposes. They are the Guardians of his Image in our hearts. They distinguish us from the herd of common animals. The social compact would dissolve, and justice be extirpated from the earth, or have only a casual existence, were we callous to the touches of affection. The robber and the murderer would often escape unpunished, did not the injuries which our tempers sustain provoke us into justice.

O! ye that love mankind! Ye that dare oppose not only the tyranny but the tyrant, stand forth! Every spot of the old world is overrun with oppression. Freedom hath been hunted round the Globe. Asia and Africa have long expelled her. Europe regards her like a stranger, and England hath given her warning to depart. O! receive the fugitive, and prepare in time an asylum for mankind.

THE NATION'S ORIGINS

The Granger Collection

The voyages of Columbus opened up the Western Hemisphere to exploration by European mariners. This 1526 map by Juan Vespucci shows the Caribbean and the west coast of South America as they were known to Europeans three decades later.

The Granger Collection

On board the Mayflower, the ship that brought them to America, the Pilgrims drew up the Compact that bound them together as a political community and became the constitution of the Plymouth Colony.

The God-fearing settlers of early New England are portrayed in George H. Boughton's painting, "Pilgrims Going to Church." They founded their school system to provide for an educated ministry.

The Bettmann Archive

Hingham's Old Ship Church (1681) is the only surviving example of a 17th-century Massachusetts meeting house. The meeting house, used for both worship and town government, was the center of community life.

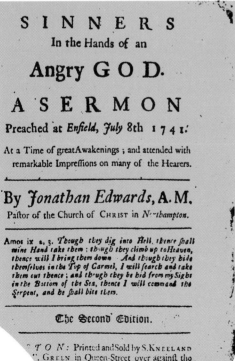

The title page of a printed copy of revivalist preacher Jonathan Edwards' most famous sermon includes a biblical passage describing the sinner's inability to escape God's wrath.

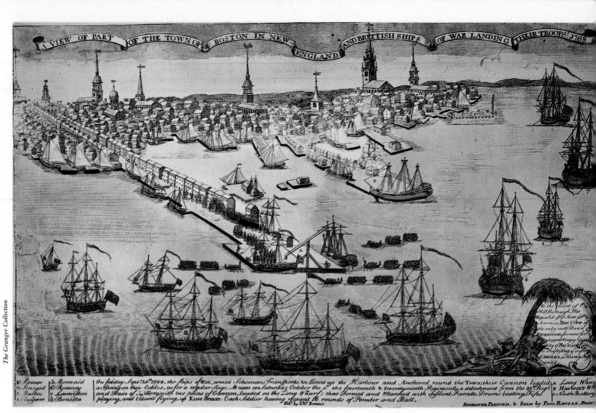

The Granger Collection

An engraving by Paul Revere shows 4,000 British troops landing at Boston in 1768 to occupy the city. This kind of intimidation inspired the Declaration of Independence's protest against "quartering large bodies of armed troops among us."

The Battle of Lexington (April 19, 1775), shown here in an engraving by Alonzo Chappel, marked the beginning of the American Revolution.

The Bettmann Archive

The Bettmann Archive

What began at Lexington ended with the French and American victory over the British at Yorktown, Va., in 1781. This painting by Louis Van Blarenberghe shows the allied commanders, Washington and Rochambeau, with their staffs during the siege of Yorktown.

COMMON SENSE;

ADDRESSED TO THE

INHABITANTS

O F

AMERICA,

On the following interesting

SUBJECTS.

I. Of the Origin and Design of Government in general, with concise Remarks on the English Constitution.

II. Of Monarchy and Hereditary Succession.

III. Thoughts on the present State of American Affairs.

IV. Of the present Ability of America, with some miscellaneous Reflections.

Man knows no Master save creating Heaven,
Or those whom choice and common good ordain.
                                        Thomson.

PHILADELPHIA;
Printed, and Sold, by R. BELL, in Third-Street.
MDCCLXXVI.

The Granger Collection

Thomas Paine's pamphlet Common Sense, published anonymously in 1776, helped sway American opinion in favor of independence.

©J. L. G. Ferris/Archives of '76, Bay Village, Ohio

In a painting by J. L. G. Ferris, Thomas Jefferson shows the draft of the Declaration of Independence to his colleagues, John Adams and Benjamin Franklin.

Congress OF THE United States

begun and held at the City of New-York, on
Wednesday the Fourth of March, one thousand seven hundred and eighty nine

THE *Conventions of a number of the States, having at the time of their adopting the Constitution, expressed a desire, in order to prevent misconstruction or abuse of its powers, that further declaratory and restrictive clauses should be added: And as extending the ground of public confidence in the Government, will best ensure the beneficent ends of its institution.*

RESOLVED *by the Senate and House of Representatives of the United States of America, in Congress assembled, two thirds of both Houses concurring, that the following Articles be proposed to the Legislatures of the several States, as amendments to the Constitution of the United States, all, or any of which Articles, when ratified by three fourths of the said Legislatures, to be valid to all intents and purposes, as part of the said Constitution; viz.*

ARTICLES *in addition to, and Amendment of the Constitution of the United States of America, proposed by Congress, and ratified by the Legislatures of the several States, pursuant to the fifth Article of the original Constitution.*

Article the first.... After the first enumeration required by the first Article of the Constitution, there shall be one Representative for every thirty thousand, until the number shall amount to one hundred, after which, the proportion shall be so regulated by Congress, that there shall be not less than one hundred Representatives, nor less than one Representative for every forty thousand persons, until the number of Representatives shall amount to two hundred, after which the proportion shall be so regulated by Congress, that there shall not be less than two hundred Representatives, nor more than one Representative for every fifty thousand persons.

Article the second.... No law, varying the compensation for the services of the Senators and Representatives, shall take effect, until an election of Representatives shall have intervened.

Article the third.... Congress shall make no law respecting an establishment of religion, or prohibiting the free exercise thereof; or abridging the freedom of speech, or of the press; or the right of the people peaceably to assemble, and to petition the Government for a redress of grievances.

Article the fourth.... A well regulated Militia, being necessary to the security of a free State, the right of the people to keep and bear arms, shall not be infringed.

Article the fifth.... No Soldier shall, in time of peace be quartered in any house, without the consent of the owner, nor in time of war, but in a manner to be prescribed by law.

Article the sixth.... The right of the people to be secure in their persons, houses, papers, and effects, against unreasonable searches and seizures, shall not be violated, and no Warrants shall issue, but upon probable cause, supported by oath or affirmation, and particularly describing the place to be searched, and the persons or things to be seized.

Article the seventh.... No person shall be held to answer for a capital, or otherwise infamous crime, unless on a presentment or indictment of a Grand Jury, except in cases arising in the land or naval forces, or in the Militia, when in actual service in time of War or public danger; nor shall any person be subject for the same offence to be twice put in jeopardy of life or limb; nor shall be compelled in any criminal case to be a witness against himself, nor be deprived of life, liberty, or property, without due process of law; nor shall private property be taken for public use, without just compensation.

Article the eighth.... In all criminal prosecutions, the accused shall enjoy the right to a speedy and public trial, by an impartial jury of the State and district wherein the crime shall have been committed, which district shall have been previously ascertained by law, and to be informed of the nature and cause of the accusation; to be confronted with the witnesses against him; to have compulsory process for obtaining witnesses in his favor, and to have the assistance of counsel for his defence.

Article the ninth.... In suits at common law, where the value in controversy shall exceed twenty dollars, the right of trial by jury shall be preserved, and no fact tried by a jury, shall be otherwise re-examined in any court of the United States, than according to the rules of the common law.

Article the tenth.... Excessive bail shall not be required, nor excessive fines imposed, nor cruel and unusual punishments inflicted.

Article the eleventh.... The enumeration in the Constitution, of certain rights, shall not be construed to deny or disparage others retained by the people.

Article the twelfth.... The powers not delegated to the United States by the Constitution, nor prohibited by it to the States, are reserved to the States respectively, or to the people.

ATTEST,

Frederick Augustus Muhlenberg, Speaker of the House of Representatives.

John Adams, Vice-President of the United States, and President of the Senate.

John Beckley, Clerk of the House of Representatives.
Sam. A. Otis Secretary of the Senate.

The Granger Collection

The U. S. Constitution, the first written constitution adopted by a modern nation, was praised by the 19th-century British statesman William Ewart Gladstone as "the most wonderful work ever struck off at a given time by the brain and purpose of man."

The Granger Collection

Shown here is the original twelve-amendment bill of rights presented to the states for ratification in 1789. The original amendments one and two—which concerned the number and payment of senators and representatives—were not ratified.

The Granger Collection

BARON STEUBEN.   GOV. ARTHUR ST. CLAIR.   SECRETARY SAMUEL A. OTIS.   ROGER SHERMAN.   GOV. GEORGE CLINTON.
CHANCELLOR ROBERT R. LIVINGSTON.   GEORGE WASHINGTON.   JOHN ADAMS.   GEN'L HENRY KNOX.

Taking office under the new Constitution, George Washington is inaugurated as president on the balcony of Federal Hall in New York City, April 30, 1789.

The Declaration of Independence 1776

Stimulated by Paine's persuasive arguments, the sentiment for independence grew steadily throughout the colonies in 1776. In early June, Richard Henry Lee, a Virginian, rose in the Second Continental Congress and moved that "these United Colonies are, and of right ought to be, Free and Independent States." To satisfy a reluctant minority, the Congress agreed to postpone for three weeks a final vote on Lee's resolution. Meanwhile, the delegates appointed a five-man committee headed by Thomas Jefferson to prepare a statement of independence.

Jefferson was a surprising choice for this momentous assignment. At thirty-three, he was one of the youngest members of the Congress and relatively unknown. In the Virginia House of Burgesses, he had been a leader in the struggle against British oppression. A shy man in public, he had seldom spoken out in the congressional debates, but he quietly earned the respect of his colleagues as a legislative draftsman. John Adams, a far more prominent colonial leader at that time, developed a genuine admiration for Jefferson's skill as a writer; and when the Virginian asked him to draft the declaration, Adams demurred, saying, "You can write ten times better than I can." In early June, Jefferson retired to his quarters in a Philadelphia boarding house and completed the first draft of the declaration. Adams and Benjamin Franklin, another member of the committee, made a few slight changes; Jefferson gave the document a thorough revision, and the committee approved it without further alteration and sent it on to Congress on June 28. A week later on July 2, the delegates approved Lee's motion for independence and then spent two-and-a-half days debating the declaration. In the process, they made extensive changes in the text, removing extraneous sections and generally tightening up the arguments. Finally, on the evening of July 4, 1776, the Continental Congress formally adopted the Declaration of Independence.

Jefferson's role as author was not widely known for several years, and he always was careful not to claim that the ideas were original with him. He gave expression to the prevailing liberalism of his age, stating the concepts of natural rights in arresting and extremely felicitous language. "I did not consider it any part of my charge to invent new ideas," Jefferson later explained, "but to place before mankind the common sense of the subject, in terms so plain and firm as to command their assent. . . . It was intended to be an expression of the American mind."

R.A.D.

THE UNANIMOUS DECLARATION OF THE
THIRTEEN UNITED STATES OF AMERICA,

When in the Course of human events, it becomes necessary for one people to dissolve the political bands which have connected them with another, and to assume among the Powers of the earth, the separate and equal station to which the Laws of Nature and of Nature's God entitle them, a decent respect to the opinions of mankind requires that they should declare the causes which impel them to the separation.

We hold these truths to be self-evident, that all men are created equal, that they are endowed by their Creator with certain unalienable Rights, that among these are Life, Liberty and the pursuit of Happiness. That to secure these rights, Governments are instituted among Men, deriving their just powers from the consent of the governed, That whenever any Form of Government becomes destructive of these ends, it is the Right of the People to alter or to abolish it, and to institute new Government, laying its foundation on such principles and organizing its powers in such form, as to them shall seem most likely to effect their Safety and Happiness. Prudence, indeed, will dictate that Governments long established should not be changed for light and transient causes; and accordingly all experience hath shown, that mankind are more disposed to suffer, while evils are sufferable, than to right themselves by abolishing the forms to which they are accustomed. But when a long train of abuses and usurpations, pursuing invariably the same Object evinces a design to reduce them under absolute Despotism, it is their right, it is their duty, to throw off such Government, and to provide new Guards for their future security.—Such has been the patient sufferance of these Colonies; and such is now the necessity which constrains them to alter their former Systems of Government. The history of the present King of Great Britain is a history of repeated injuries and usurpations, all having in direct object the establishment of an absolute Tyranny over these States. To prove this, let Facts be submitted to a candid world.

He has refused his Assent to Laws, the most wholesome and necessary for the public good.

He has forbidden his Governors to pass Laws of immediate and pressing importance, unless suspended in their operation till his Assent should be obtained; and when so suspended, he has utterly neglected to attend to them.

He has refused to pass other Laws for the accommodation of large districts of people, unless those people would relinquish the right of Representation in the Legislature, a right inestimable to them and formidable to tyrants only.

He has called together legislative bodies at places unusual, uncomfortable, and distant from the depository of their Public Records, for the sole purpose of fatiguing them into compliance with his measures.

He has dissolved Representative Houses repeatedly, for opposing with manly firmness his invasions on the rights of the people.

He has refused for a long time, after such dissolutions, to cause others to be elected; whereby the Legislative Powers, incapable of Annihilation, have returned to the People at large for their exercise; the State remaining in the mean time exposed to all the dangers of invasion from without, and convulsions within.

He has endeavoured to prevent the population of these States; for that purpose obstructing the Laws of Naturalization of Foreigners; refusing to pass others to encourage their migration hither, and raising the conditions of new Appropriations of Lands.

He has obstructed the Administration of Justice, by refusing his Assent to Laws for establishing Judiciary Powers.

He has made Judges dependent on his Will alone, for the tenure of their offices, and the amount and payment of their salaries.

He has erected a multitude of New Offices, and sent hither swarms of Officers to harass our People, and eat out their substance.

He has kept among us, in times of peace, Standing Armies without the Consent of our legislature.

He has affected to render the Military independent of and superior to the Civil Power.

He has combined with others to subject us to a jurisdiction foreign to our constitution, and unacknowledged by our laws; giving his Assent to their acts of pretended legislation:

For quartering large bodies of armed troops among us:

For protecting them, by a mock Trial, from Punishment for any Murders which they should commit on the Inhabitants of these States:

For cutting off our Trade with all parts of the world:

For imposing taxes on us without our Consent:

For depriving us in many cases, of the benefits of Trial by Jury:

For transporting us beyond Seas to be tried for pretended offences:

For abolishing the free System of English Laws in a neighbouring Province, establishing therein an Arbitrary government, and enlarging its Boundaries so as to render it at once an example and fit instrument for introducing the same absolute rule into these Colonies:

For taking away our Charters, abolishing our most valuable Laws, and altering fundamentally the Forms of our Governments:

For suspending our own Legislature, and declaring themselves invested with Power to legislate for us in all cases whatsoever.

He has abdicated Government here, by declaring us out of his Protection and waging War against us.

He has plundered our seas, ravaged our Coasts, burnt our towns, and destroyed the lives of our people.

He is at this time transporting large armies of foreign mercenaries to compleat the works of death, desolation and tyranny, already begun with circumstances of Cruelty & perfidy scarcely paralleled in the most barbarous ages, and totally unworthy the Head of a civilized nation.

He has constrained our fellow Citizens taken Captive on the high Seas to bear Arms against their Country, to become the executioners of their friends and Brethren, or to fall themselves by their Hands.

He has excited domestic insurrections amongst us, and has endeavoured to bring on the inhabitants of our frontiers, the merciless Indian Savages, whose known rule of warfare, is an undistinguished destruction of all ages, sexes and conditions.

In every stage of these Oppressions We have Petitioned for Redress in the most humble terms: Our repeated Petitions have been answered only by repeated injury. A Prince, whose character is thus marked by every act which may define a Tyrant, is unfit to be the ruler of a free People.

Nor have We been wanting in attention to our Brittish brethren. We have warned them from time to time of attempts by their legislature to extend an unwarrantable jurisdiction over us. We have reminded them of the circumstances of our emigration and settlement here. We have appealed to their native justice and magnanimity, and we have conjured them by the ties of our common kindred to disavow these usurpations, which, would inevitably interrupt our connections and correspondence. They too have been deaf to the voice of justice and of consanguinity. We must, therefore, acquiesce in the necessity, which denounces our Separation, and hold them, as we hold the rest of mankind, Enemies in War, in Peace Friends.

We, therefore, the Representatives of the united States of America, in General Congress, Assembled, appealing to the Supreme Judge of the world for the rectitude of our intentions, do, in the Name, and by Authority of the good People of these Colonies, solemnly publish and declare, That these United Colonies are, and of Right ought to be Free and Independent States; that they are Absolved from all Allegiance to the British Crown, and that all political connection between them and the State of Great Britain, is and ought to be totally dissolved; and that as Free and Independent States, they have full Power to levy War, conclude Peace, contract Alliances, establish Commerce, and to do all other Acts and Things which Independent States may of right do. And for the support of this Declaration, with a firm reliance on the Protection of Divine Providence, we mutually pledge to each other our Lives, our Fortunes and our sacred Honor.

Connecticut
SAM'EL HUNTINGTON
ROGER SHERMAN
WM. WILLIAMS
OLIVER WOLCOTT

Delaware
THO. M'KEAN
GEO. READ
CAESAR RODNEY

Georgia
BUTTON GWINNETT
LYMAN HALL
GEO. WALTON

Maryland
CHARLES CARROLL
of Carrollton
SAMUEL CHASE
WM. PACA
THOS. STONE

Massachusetts Bay
JOHN ADAMS
SAML. ADAMS
ELBRIDGE GERRY
JOHN HANCOCK
ROBT. TREAT PAINE

New Hampshire
JOSIAH BARTLETT
MATTHEW THORNTON
WM. WHIPPLE

New Jersey
ABRA. CLARK
JOHN HART
FRAS. HOPKINSON
RICHD. STOCKTON
JNO. WITHERSPOON

New York
WM. FLOYD
FRANS. LEWIS
PHIL. LIVINGSTON
LEWIS MORRIS

North Carolina
JOSEPH HEWES
WM. HOOPER
JOHN PENN

Pennsylvania
GEO. CLYMER
BENJA. FRANKLIN
ROBT. MORRIS
JOHN MORTON
GEO. ROSS
BENJAMIN RUSH
JAS. SMITH
GEO. TAYLOR
JAMES WILSON

Rhode Island
WILLIAM ELLERY
STEP. HOPKINS

South Carolina
THOS. HEYWARD, JUNR.
THOMAS LYNCH, JUNR.
ARTHUR MIDDLETON
EDWARD RUTLEDGE

Virginia
CARTER BRAXTON
BENJA. HARRISON
TH. JEFFERSON
FRANCIS LIGHTFOOT LEE
RICHARD HENRY LEE
THS. NELSON, JR.
GEORGE WYTHE

Hector St. John de Crèvecoeur: What is an American? 1782

The Revolution not only won independence for the colonists, it helped create a sense of national identity. In the common struggle against England, Americans found strength and inspiration in the realization that they were forging a new country. After the war, a new national culture began to emerge, as expressed in the poems of Philip Freneau, the paintings of John Trumbull, and the patriotic textbooks of Noah Webster. Men like Franklin, Jefferson, and, above all, George Washington became national heroes as Americans began to think of themselves as a distinct people, different from Europeans and the rest of mankind.

Hector St. John de Crèvecoeur gave the classic description of Americanization in an essay published in 1782. A Frenchman by birth, Crèvecoeur had come to Canada in the 1750's and then had moved to upstate New York. He married an American girl, purchased a farm in Orange County, and settled down to a quiet rural life on the American frontier. He tried to avoid taking part in the Revolution; but his neighbors, suspecting him of Tory sympathies, drove him from his farm. Finally he went to England, where he published a collection of twelve essays entitled *Letters from an American Farmer*. Crèvecoeur later returned to the United States only to find his farmhouse destroyed, his wife dead, and his children scattered. He served for several years as the French consul in New York and then spent his last days in his native France. His essays survived the tragedies of his own life, voicing the optimism Americans felt after the Revolution.

R.A.D.

What then is the American, this new man? He is either an European, or the descendant of an European; hence that strange mixture of blood, which you will find in no other country. I could point out to you a man, whose grandfather was an Englishman, whose wife was Dutch, whose son married a French woman, and whose present four sons have now four wives of different nations. *He* is an American, who, leaving behind him all his ancient prejudices and manners, receives new ones from the new mode of life he has embraced, the new government he obeys, and the new rank he holds. He becomes an American by being received in the broad lap of our great *Alma Mater*. Here individuals of all nations are melted into a new race of men, whose labours and posterity will one day cause great change in the world. Americans are the western pilgrims, who are carrying along with them that great mass of arts, sciences, vigour, and industry, which began long since in the east; they will finish the great circle. The Americans were once scattered all over Europe; here they are incorporated into one of the finest systems of population which has ever appeared, and which will hereafter become distinct by the power of the different climates they inhabit. The American ought therefore to love this country much better than that wherein either he or his forefathers were born. Here the rewards of his industry follow with equal steps the progress of his labour; his labour is founded on the basis of nature, *self-interest;* can it want a stronger allurement? Wives and children, who before in vain demanded of him a morsel of bread, now, fat and frolicsome, gladly help their father to clear those fields whence exuberant crops are to arise to feed and to clothe them all; without any part being claimed, either by a despotic prince, a rich abbot, or a mighty lord. Here religion demands but little of him; a small voluntary salary to the minister, and gratitude to God; can he refuse these? The American is a new man, who acts upon new principles; he must therefore entertain new ideas, and form new opinions. From involuntary idleness, servile dependance, penury, and useless labour, he has passed to toils of a very different nature, rewarded by ample subsistence. — This is an American.

The Northwest Ordinance 1787

The new American nation faced a colonial problem in the West. Under the Articles of Confederation, the states gradually ceded their claims to land west of the Appalachians to the central government. Settlers had been developing communities in Kentucky and Tennessee during the Revolution, and the Congress made no attempt to assert its authority over them; but the land north of the Ohio River was unsettled national domain, and here the new government initiated policies which set the pattern for future western development.

In 1785, following Jefferson's recommendations, Congress began a system of surveying the land in six-mile-square sections and offering it to settlers in 640-acre plots. Two years later, Congress debated the even more basic issue of government in the West: meeting in New York, a session attended by only eighteen members, representing just eight states, enacted the Northwest Ordinance. Congress had been influenced by eastern land speculators who feared excessive self-government by western settlers, and this act was a modification of a liberal measure drafted by Jefferson in 1784. Although the Northwest Ordinance limited the extent of self-government in the West, especially in the early stages, it did permit new states to form and enter the Union on equal terms with the original thirteen. By refusing to treat the West as a colonial region to be exploited by the East, the Congress opened the way for the rapid expansion of the United States into a continental nation. R.A.D.

Section 1. *Be it ordained by the United States in Congress assembled,* That the said Territory for the purpose of temporary government, be one district, subject, however, to be divided into two districts, as future circumstances may, in the opinion of Congress, make it expedient. . . .

Sec. 3. *Be it ordained by the authority aforesaid,* That there shall be appointed, from time to time, by Congress, a governor, whose commission shall continue in force for the term of three years, unless sooner revoked by Congress; he shall reside in the district, and have a freehold estate therein, in one thousand acres of land, while in the exercise of his office.

Sec. 4. There shall be appointed from time to time, by Congress, a secretary, whose commission shall continue in force for four years, unless sooner revoked; he shall reside in the districts, and have a freehold estate therein, in five hundred acres of land, while in the exercise of his office. It shall be his duty to keep and preserve the acts and laws passed by the legislature, and the public records of the district, and the proceedings of the governor in his executive department, and transmit authentic copies of such acts and proceedings every six months to the Secretary of Congress. There shall also be appointed a court, to consist of three judges, any two of whom to form a court, who shall have a common-law jurisdiction and reside in the district, and have each therein a freehold estate, in five hundred acres of land, while in the exercise of their offices; and their commissions shall continue in force during good behavior.

Sec. 5. The governor and judges, or a majority of them, shall adopt and publish in the district such laws of the original states, criminal and civil, as may be necessary, and best suited to the circumstances of the district, and report them to Congress from time to time, which laws shall be in force in the district until the organization of the general assembly therein, unless disapproved of by Congress; but afterward the legislature shall have authority to alter them as they shall think fit. . . .

Sec. 9. So soon as there shall be five thousand free male inhabitants, of full age, in the district, upon giving proof thereof to the governor, they shall receive authority, with time and place, to elect representatives from their counties or townships, to represent them in the general assembly: *Provided,* That for every five hundren free male inhabitants there shall be one representative, and so on, progressively, with the number of free male inhabitants, shall the right of representation increase, until the number of representatives shall amount to twenty-five; after which the number and proportion of representatives shall be regulated by the legislature: *Provided,* That no person be eligible or qualified to act as a representative unless he shall have been a citizen of one of the United States three years, and be a resident in the district, or unless he shall have resided in the district three years; and, in either case, shall likewise hold in his own right, in fee-simple, two hundred acres of land within the same: *Provided also,* That a freehold in fifty acres of land in the district, having been a citizen of one of the states, and being resident in the district, or the like freehold and two years' residence in the district, shall be necessary to qualify a man as an elector of a representative.

Sec. 10. The representatives thus elected shall serve for the term of two years; and in case of the death of a representative, or removal from office, the governor shall issue a writ to the county or township, for which he was a member, to elect another in his stead, to serve for the residue of the term.

Sec. 11. The general assembly, or legislature, shall consist of the governor, legislative council, and a house of representatives. The legislative council shall consist of five members, to continue in office five years, unless sooner removed by Congress; any three of them to be a quorum; and the members of the council shall be nominated and appointed in the following manner, to wit: As soon as representatives shall be elected the governor shall appoint a time and place for them to meet together, and when met they shall nominate ten persons, resident in the district, and each possessed of a freehold in five hundred acres of land, and return their names to Congress, five of whom Congress shall appoint and commission to serve as aforesaid; and whenever a vacancy shall happen in the Council, by death or removal from office, the house of representatives shall nominate two persons, qualified as aforesaid, for each vacancy, and return their names to Congress, one of whom Congress shall appoint and commission for the residue of the term; and every five years, four months at least before the expiration of the time of service of the members of the council, the said house shall nominate ten persons, qualified as aforesaid, and return their names to Congress, five of whom Congress shall appoint and commission to serve as members of the council five years, unless sooner removed. And the governor, legislative council, and house of representatives shall have authority to make laws in all cases for the good government of the district, not repugnant to the principles and articles in this ordinance established and declared. And all bills, having passed by a majority in the house, and by a majority in the council, shall be referred to the governor for his assent; but no bill, or legislative act whatever, shall be of any force without his assent. The governor shall have power to convene, prorogue, and dissolve the general assembly when in his opinion, it shall be expedient. . . .

Sec. 14. It is hereby ordained and declared, by the authority aforesaid, that the following articles shall be considered as articles of compact between the original states and the people and states in the said territory, and forever remain unalterable, unless by common consent, to wit:

Article I

No person, demeaning himself in a peaceable and orderly manner, shall ever be molested on account of his mode of worship, or religious sentiments, in the said territory.

Article II

The inhabitants of the said territory shall always be entitled to the benefits of the writs of habeas corpus and of the trial by jury, of a proportionate representation of the people in the legislature, and of judicial proceedings according to the course of the common law. All persons shall be bailable, unless for capital offenses, where the proof shall be evident, or the presumption great. All fines shall be moderate; and no cruel or unusual punishment shall be inflicted. No man shall be deprived of his liberty or property, but by the judgment of his peers, or the law of the land, and, should the public exigencies make it necessary, for the common preservation, to take any person's property, or to demand his particular services, full compensation shall be made for the same. And, in the just preservation of rights and property, it is understood and declared that no law ought ever to be made or have force in the said territory that shall, in any manner whatever, interfere with or affect private contracts, or engagements, bona fide, and without fraud previously formed.

Article III

Religion, morality, and knowledge being necessary to good government and the happiness of mankind, schools and the means of education shall forever be encouraged. The utmost good faith shall always be observed toward the Indians; their lands and property shall never be taken from them without their consent; and in their property, rights, and liberty they never shall be invaded or disturbed unless in just and lawful wars authorized by Congress; but laws founded in justice and humanity shall, from time to time, be made, for preventing wrongs being done to them and for preserving peace and friendship with them.

Article IV

The said territory, and the states which may be formed therein, shall forever remain a part of this confederacy of the United States of America, subject to the Articles of Confederation, and to such alterations therein as shall be constitutionally made; and to all the acts and ordinances of the United States in Congress assembled, conformable thereto. The inhabitants and settlers in the said territory shall be subject to pay a part of the federal debts contracted, or to be contracted, and a proportional part of the expenses of government to be apportioned on them by Congress, according to the same common rule and measure by which apportionments thereof shall be made on the other states; and the taxes for paying their proportion shall be laid and levied by the authority and direction of the legislatures of the district, or districts, or new states, as in the original states, within the time agreed upon by the United States in Congress assembled. The legislatures of those districts, or new states, shall never interfere with the primary disposal of the soil by the United States in Congress assembled, nor with any regulations Congress may find necessary for securing the title in such soil to the bona fide purchasers. No tax shall be imposed on lands the property of the United States; and in no case shall nonresident proprietors be taxed higher than residents. The navigable waters leading into the Mississippi and Saint Lawrence, and the carrying places between the same, shall be common highways, and forever free, as well to the inhabitants of the said territory as to the citizens of the United States, and those of any other states that may be admitted into the confederacy, without any tax, impost, or duty therefor.

Article V

There shall be formed in the said territory not less than three nor more than five states. . . . And whenever any of the said states shall have sixty thousand free inhabitants therein, such state shall be admitted by its delegates into the Congress of the United States, on an equal footing with the original states, in all respects whatever; and shall be at liberty to form a permanent constitution and state government: *Provided,* The constitution and government, so to be formed, shall be republican, and in conformity to the principles contained in these articles, and, so far as it can be consistent with the general interest of the confederacy, such admission shall be allowed at an earlier period, and when there may be a less number of free inhabitants in the state than sixty thousand.

Article VI

There shall be neither slavery nor involuntary servitude in the said territory, otherwise than in the punishment of crimes, whereof the party shall have been duly convicted: *Provided always,* That any person escaping into the same, from whom labor or service is lawfully claimed in any one of the original states, such fugitive may be lawfully reclaimed, and conveyed to the person claiming his or her labor or service as aforesaid. . . .

Done by the United States, in Congress assembled, the 13th day of July, in the year of our Lord 1787, and of their sovereignty and independence the twelfth.

The Constitution of the United States 1787

Despite its success in solving the western problem, the Confederation government proved too weak to deal with a serious economic decline in the 1780's. After the Revolution, British merchants flooded the American market with an abundance of cheap goods. Eager Americans bought all that the British sent, but the inability of the United States to generate an equal quantity of exports led to an unfavorable balance of trade, a growing shortage of hard money, and a depressed American economy. A protective tariff seemed the logical remedy, but the Articles of Confederation gave the states exclusive power to tax imports. In 1786 delegates from a number of states gathered at Annapolis to discuss their common trade problems; and when the conference bogged down, Alexander Hamilton, a young New York lawyer who advocated centralization, suggested that a convention be held in Philadelphia in 1787 to correct "such defects as may be discovered to exist" in the Articles of Confederation.

The delegates adopted Hamilton's motion, the Continental Congress approved, and the stage was thus set for the Constitutional Convention.

On May 25, 1787, twenty-nine men representing nine states assembled in Philadelphia. They were a remarkable group, young in age yet experienced far beyond their years by their roles in the Revolution. They unanimously elected George Washington as their presiding officer, and then, ignoring their original charge to revise the Articles of Confederation, plunged boldly ahead and drafted an entirely new frame of government.

The resulting Constitution, the product of four months of secret deliberation, was a bundle of compromises—between large and small state influence, between executive and legislative power, between federal and state authority. Yet it possessed a logic that transcended its pragmatic origins and provided the young nation with a balanced and enduring system of government. R.A.D.

W̶E THE PEOPLE of the United States, in Order to form a more perfect Union, establish Justice, insure domestic Tranquility, provide for the common defence, promote the general Welfare, and secure the Blessings of Liberty to ourselves and our Posterity, do ordain and establish this Constitution for the United States of America.

ART. I

Sec. 1. All legislative Powers herein granted shall be vested in a Congress of the United States, which shall consist of a Senate and House of Representatives.

Sec. 2. The House of Representatives shall be composed of Members chosen every second Year by the People of the several States, and the Electors in each State shall have the Qualifications requisite for Electors of the most numerous Branch of the State Legislature.

No Person shall be a Representative who shall not have attained to the Age of twenty five Years, and been seven Years a Citizen of the United States, and who shall not, when elected, be an Inhabitant of that State in which he shall be chosen.

Representatives and direct Taxes shall be apportioned among the several States which may be included within this Union, according to their respective Numbers, which shall be determined by adding to the whole Number of free Persons, including those bound to Service for a Term of Years, and excluding Indians not taxed, three fifths of all other Persons. The actual Enumeration shall be made within three Years after the first Meeting of the Congress of the United States, and within every subsequent Term of ten Years, in such Manner as they shall by Law direct. The Number of Representatives shall not exceed one for every thirty Thousand, but each State shall have at Least one Representative; and until such enumeration shall be made, the State of New Hampshire shall be entitled to chuse three, Massachusetts eight, Rhode-Island and Providence Plantations one, Connecticut five, New-York six, New Jersey four, Pennsylvania eight, Delaware one, Maryland six, Virginia ten, North Carolina five, South Carolina five, and Georgia three.

When vacancies happen in the Representation from any State, the Executive Authority thereof shall issue Writs of Election to fill such Vacancies.

The House of Representatives shall chuse their Speaker and other Officers; and shall have the sole Power of Impeachment.

Sec. 3. The Senate of the United States shall be composed of two Senators from each State, chosen by the Legislature thereof, for six Years; and each Senator shall have one Vote.

Immediately after they shall be assembled in Consequence of the first Election, they shall be divided as equally as may be into three Classes. The Seats of the Senators of the first Class shall be vacated at the Expiration of the second Year, of the second Class at the Expiration of the fourth Year, and of the third Class at the Expiration of the sixth Year, so that one third may be chosen every second Year; and if Vacancies happen by Resignation, or otherwise, during the Recess of the Legislature of any State, the Executive thereof may make temporary Appointments until the next Meeting of the Legislature, which shall then fill such Vacancies.

No Person shall be a Senator who shall not have attained to the Age of thirty Years, and been nine Years a Citizen of the United States, and who shall not, when elected, be an Inhabitant of that State for which he shall be chosen.

The Vice President of the United States shall be President of the Senate, but shall have no Vote, unless they be equally divided.

The Senate shall chuse their other Officers, and also a President pro tempore, in the Absence of the Vice President, or when he shall exercise the Office of President of the United States.

The Senate shall have the sole Power to try all Impeachments. When sitting for that Purpose, they shall be on Oath or Affirmation. When the President of the United States is tried, the Chief Justice shall preside: And no Person shall be convicted without the Concurrence of two thirds of the Members present.

Judgment in Cases of Impeachment shall not extend further than to removal from Office, and disqualification to hold and enjoy any Office of honor, Trust or Profit under the United States: but the Party convicted shall nevertheless be liable and subject to Indictment, Trial, Judgment and Punishment, according to Law.

Sec. 4. The Times, Places and Manner of holding Elections for Senators and Representatives, shall be prescribed in each State by the Legislature thereof; but the Congress may at any time by Law make or alter such Regulations, except as to the Places of chusing Senators.

The Congress shall assemble at least once in every Year, and such Meeting shall be on the first Monday in December, unless they shall by Law appoint a different Day.

Sec. 5. Each House shall be the Judge of the Elections, Returns and Qualifications of its own Members, and a Majority of each shall constitute a Quorum to do Business; but a smaller Number may adjourn from day to day, and may be authorized to compel the Attendance of absent Members, in such Manner, and under such Penalties as each House may provide.

Each House may determine the Rules of its Proceedings, punish its Members for disorderly Behaviour, and, with the Concurrence of two thirds, expel a Member.

Each House shall keep a Journal of its Proceedings, and from time to time publish the same, excepting such Parts as may in their Judgment require Secrecy; and the Yeas and Nays of the Members of either House on any question shall, at the Desire of one fifth of those Present, be entered on the Journal.

Neither House, during the Session of Congress, shall, without the Consent of the other, adjourn for more than three days, nor to any other Place than that in which the two Houses shall be sitting.

Sec. 6. The Senators and Representatives shall receive a Compensation for their Services, to be ascertained by Law, and paid out of the Treasury of the United States. They shall in all Cases, except Treason, Felony and Breach of the Peace, be privileged from Arrest during their Attendance at the Session of their respective Houses, and in going to and returning from the same; and for any Speech or Debate in either House, they shall not be questioned in any other Place.

No Senator or Representative shall, during the Time for which he was elected, be appointed to any civil Office under the Authority of the United States which shall have been created, or the Emoluments whereof shall have been encreased during such time; and no Person holding any Office under the United States, shall be a Member of either House during his Continuance in Office.

Sec. 7. All Bills for raising Revenue shall originate in the House of Representatives; but the Senate may propose or concur with Amendments as on other Bills.

Every Bill which shall have passed the House of Representatives and the Senate, shall, before it become a Law, be presented to the President of the United States; If he approve he shall sign it, but if not he shall return it, with his Objections to that House in which it shall have originated, who shall enter the Objections at large on their Journal, and proceed to reconsider it. If after such Reconsideration two thirds of that House shall agree to pass the Bill, it shall be sent, together with the Objections, to the other House, by which it shall likewise be reconsidered, and if approved by two thirds of that House, it shall become a Law. But in all such Cases the Votes of both Houses shall be determined by Yeas and Nays, and the Names of the Persons voting for and against the Bill shall be entered on the Journal of each House respectively. If any Bill shall not be returned by the President within ten Days (Sundays excepted) after it shall have been presented to him, the Same shall be a Law, in like Manner as if he had signed it, unless the Congress by their Adjournment prevent its Return, in which Case it shall not be a Law.

Every Order, Resolution, or Vote to which the Concurrence of the Senate and House of Representatives may be necessary (except on a question of Adjournment) shall be presented to the President of the United States; and before the Same shall take Effect, shall be approved by him, or being disapproved by him, shall be repassed by two thirds of the Senate and House of Representatives, according to the Rules and Limitations prescribed in the Case of a Bill.

Sec. 8. The Congress shall have Power To lay and collect Taxes, Duties, Imposts and Excises, to pay the Debts and provide for the common Defence and general Welfare of the United States; but all Duties, Imposts and Excises shall be uniform throughout the United States;

To borrow Money on the credit of the United States;

To regulate Commerce with foreign Nations, and among the several States, and with the Indian Tribes;

To establish an uniform Rule of Naturalization, and uniform Laws on the subject of Bankruptcies throughout the United States;

To coin Money, regulate the Value thereof, and of foreign Coin, and fix the Standard of Weights and Measures;

To provide for the Punishment of counterfeiting the Securities and current Coin of the United States;

To establish Post Offices and post Roads;

To promote the Progress of Science and useful Arts, by securing for limited Times to Authors and Inventors the exclusive

Right to their respective Writings and Discoveries;

To constitute Tribunals inferior to the supreme Court;

To define and punish Piracies and Felonies committed on the high Seas, and Offences against the Law of Nations;

To declare War, grant Letters of Marque and Reprisal, and make Rules concerning Captures on Land and Water;

To raise and support Armies, but no Appropriation of Money to that Use shall be for a longer Term than two Years;

To provide and maintain a Navy;

To make Rules for the Government and Regulation of the land and naval Forces;

To provide for calling forth the Militia to execute the Laws of the Union, suppress Insurrections and repel Invasions;

To provide for organizing, arming, and disciplining the Militia, and for governing such Part of them as may be employed in the Service of the United States, reserving to the States respectively, the Appointment of the Officers, and the Authority of training the Militia according to the discipline prescribed by Congress;

To exercise exclusive Legislation in all Cases whatsoever, over such District (not exceeding ten Miles square) as may, by Cession of particular States, and the Acceptance of Congress, become the Seat of the Government of the United States, and to exercise like Authority over all Places purchased by the Consent of the Legislature of the State in which the Same shall be, for the Erection of Forts, Magazines, Arsenals, dock-Yards, and other needful Buildings; — And

To make all Laws which shall be necessary and proper for carrying into Execution the foregoing Powers, and all other Powers vested by this Constitution in the Government of the United States, or in any Department or Officer thereof.

Sec. 9. The Migration or Importation of such Persons as any of the States now existing shall think proper to admit, shall not be prohibited by the Congress prior to the Year one thousand eight hundred and eight, but a Tax or duty may be imposed on such Importation, not exceeding ten dollars for each Person.

The Privilege of the Writ of Habeas Corpus shall not be suspended, unless when in Cases of Rebellion or Invasion the public Safety may require it.

No Bill of Attainder or ex post facto Law shall be passed.

No Capitation, or other direct, Tax shall be laid, unless in

Proportion to the Census or Enumeration herein before directed to be taken.

No Tax or Duty shall be laid on Articles exported from any State.

No Preference shall be given by any Regulation of Commerce or Revenue to the Ports of one State over those of another: nor shall Vessels bound to, or from, one State, be obliged to enter, clear, or pay Duties in another.

No Money shall be drawn from the Treasury, but in Consequence of Appropriations made by Law; and a regular Statement and Account of the Receipts and Expenditures of all public Money shall be published from time to time.

No Title of Nobility shall be granted by the United States: And no Person holding any Office of Profit or Trust under them, shall, without the Consent of the Congress, accept of any present, Emolument, Office, or Title, of any kind whatever, from any King, Prince or foreign State.

Sec. 10. No State shall enter into any Treaty, Alliance, or Confederation; grant Letters of Marque and Reprisal; coin Money; emit Bills of Credit; make any Thing but gold and silver Coin a Tender in Payment of Debts; pass any Bill of Attainder, ex post facto Law, or Law impairing the Obligation of Contracts, or grant any Title of Nobility.

No State shall, without the Consent of the Congress, lay any Imposts or Duties on Imports or Exports, except what may be absolutely necessary for executing it's inspection Laws: and the net Produce of all Duties and Imposts, laid by any State on Imports or Exports, shall be for the Use of the Treasury of the United States; and all such Laws shall be subject to the Revision and Controul of the Congress.

No State shall, without the Consent of Congress, lay any Duty of Tonnage, keep Troops, or Ships of War in time of Peace, enter into any Agreement or Compact with another State, or with a foreign Power, or engage in War, unless actually invaded, or in such imminent Danger as will not admit of delay.

ART. II

Sec. 1. The executive Power shall be vested in a President of the United States of America. He shall hold his Office during the Term of four Years, and, together with the Vice President, chosen for the same Term, be elected, as follows

Each State shall appoint, in such Manner as the Legislature thereof may direct, a Number of Electors, equal to the whole Number of Senators and Representatives to which the State may be entitled in the Congress: but no Senator or Representative, or Person holding an Office of Trust or Profit under the United States, shall be appointed an Elector.

The Electors shall meet in their respective States, and vote by Ballot for two Persons, of whom one at least shall not be an Inhabitant of the same State with themselves. And they shall make a List of all the Persons voted for, and of the Number of Votes for each; which List they shall sign and certify, and transmit sealed to the Seat of the Government of the United States, directed to the President of the Senate. The President of the Senate shall, in the Presence of the Senate and House of Representatives, open all the Certificates, and the Votes shall then be counted. The Person having the greatest Number of Votes shall be the President, if such Number be a Majority of the whole Number of Electors appointed; and if there be more than one who have such Majority, and have an equal Number of Votes, then the House of Representatives shall immediately chuse by Ballot one of them for President; and if no person have a Majority, then from the five highest on the List the said House shall in like Manner chuse the President. But in chusing the President, the Votes shall be taken by States, the Representation from each State having one Vote; A quorum for this Purpose shall consist of a Member or Members from two thirds of the States, and a Majority of all the States shall be necessary to a Choice. In every Case, after the Choice of the President, the Person having the greatest Number of Votes of the Electors shall be the Vice President. But if there should remain two or more who have equal Votes, the Senate shall chuse from them by Ballot the Vice President.

The Congress may determine the Time of chusing the Electors, and the Day on which they shall give their Votes; which Day shall be the same throughout the United States.

No Person except a natural born Citizen, or a Citizen of the United States, at the time of the Adoption of this Constitution, shall be eligible to the Office of President; neither shall any Person be eligible to that Office who shall not have attained to the

Age of thirty five Years, and been fourteen Years a Resident within the United States.

In Case of the Removal of the President from Office, or of his Death, Resignation, or Inability to discharge the Powers and Duties of the said Office, the Same shall devolve on the Vice President, and the Congress may by Law provide for the Case of Removal, Death, Resignation or Inability, both of the President and Vice President, declaring what Officer shall then act as President, and such Officer shall act accordingly, until the Disability be removed, or a President shall be elected.

The President shall, at stated Times, receive for his Services, a Compensation, which shall neither be encreased nor diminished during the Period for which he shall have been elected, and he shall not receive within that Period any other Emolument from the United States, or any of them.

Before he enter on the Execution of his Office, he shall take the following Oath or Affirmation: — "I do solemnly swear (or affirm) that I will faithfully execute the Office of President of the United States, and will to the best of my Ability, preserve, protect and defend the Constitution of the United States."

Sec. 2. The President shall be Commander in Chief of the Army and Navy of the United States, and of the Militia of the several States, when called into the actual Service of the United States; he may require the Opinion, in writing, of the principal Officer in each of the executive Departments, upon any Subject relating to the Duties of their respective Offices, and he shall have Power to grant Reprieves and Pardons for Offences against the United States, except in Cases of Impeachment.

He shall have Power, by and with the Advice and Consent of the Senate, to make Treaties, provided two thirds of the Senators present concur; and he shall nominate, and by and with the Advice and Consent of the Senate, shall appoint Ambassadors, other public Ministers and Consuls, Judges of the supreme Court, and all other Officers of the United States, whose Appointments are not herein otherwise provided for, and which shall be established by Law: but the Congress may by Law vest the Appointment of such inferior Officers, as they think proper, in the President alone, in the Courts of Law, or in the Heads of Departments.

The President shall have Power to fill up all Vacancies that may happen during the Recess of the Senate, by granting Commissions which shall expire at the End of their next Session.

Sec. 3. He shall from time to time give to the Congress Information of the State of the Union, and recommend to their Consideration such Measures as he shall judge necessary and expedient; he may, on extraordinary Occasions, convene both Houses, or either of them, and in Case of Disagreement between them, with Respect to the Time of Adjournment, he may adjourn them to such Time as he shall think proper; he shall receive Ambassadors and other public Ministers; he shall take Care that the Laws be faithfully executed, and shall Commission all the Officers of the United States.

Sec. 4. The President, Vice President and all civil Officers of the United States, shall be removed from Office on Impeachment for, and Conviction of, Treason, Bribery, or other high Crimes and Misdemeanors.

ART. III

Sec. 1. The judicial Power of the United States, shall be vested in one supreme Court, and in such inferior Courts as the Congress may from time to time ordain and establish. The Judges, both of the supreme and inferior Courts, shall hold their Offices during good Behaviour, and shall, at stated Times, receive for their Services, a Compensation, which shall not be diminished during their Continuance in Office.

Sec. 2. The judicial Power shall extend to all Cases, in Law and Equity, arising under this Constitution, the Laws of the United States, and Treaties made, or which shall be made, under their Authority; — to all Cases affecting Ambassadors, other public Ministers and Consuls; — to all Cases of admiralty and maritime Jurisdiction; — to Controversies to which the United States shall be a Party; — to Controversies between two or more States; — between a State and Citizens of another State; — between Citizens of different States, — between Citizens of the same State claiming Lands under Grants of different States, and between a State, or the Citizens thereof, and foreign States, Citizens or Subjects.

In all Cases affecting Ambassadors, other public Ministers and Consuls, and those in which a State shall be Party, the supreme Court shall have original Jurisdiction. In all the other cases before mentioned, the supreme Court shall have appellate Jurisdiction, both as to Law and Fact, with such Exceptions, and under such Regulations as the Congress shall make.

The Trial of all Crimes, except in Cases of Impeachment, shall be by Jury; and such Trial shall be held in the State where the said Crimes shall have been committed; but when not committed within any State, the Trial shall be at such Place or Places as the Congress may by Law have directed.

Sec. 3. Treason against the United States, shall consist only in levying War against them, or in adhering to their Enemies, giving them Aid and Comfort. No Person shall be convicted of Treason unless on the Testimony of two Witnesses to the same overt Act, or on Confession in open Court.

The Congress shall have Power to declare the Punishment of Treason, but no Attainder of Treason shall work Corruption of Blood, or Forfeiture except during the Life of the Person attainted.

ART. IV

Sec. 1. Full Faith and Credit shall be given in each State to the Public Acts, Records, and judicial Proceedings of every other State. And the Congress may by general Laws prescribe the Manner in which such Acts, Records and Proceedings shall be proved, and the Effect thereof.

Sec. 2. The Citizens of each State shall be entitled to all Privileges and Immunities of Citizens in the Several States.

A Person charged in any State with Treason, Felony, or other Crime, who shall flee from Justice, and be found in another State, shall on Demand of the executive Authority of the State from which he fled, be delivered up, to be removed to the State having Jurisdiction of the Crime.

No Person held to Service or Labour in one State, under the Laws thereof, escaping into another, shall, in Consequence of any Law or Regulation therein, be discharged from such Service or Labour, but shall be delivered up on Claim of the Party to whom such Service or Labour may be due.

Sec. 3. New States may be admitted by the Congress into this Union; but no new States shall be formed or erected within the Jurisdiction of any other State; nor any State be formed by the Junction of two or more States, or Parts of States, without the Consent of the Legislatures of the States concerned as well as of the Congress.

The Congress shall have Power to dispose of and make all needful Rules and Regulations respecting the Territory or other Property belonging to the United States; and nothing in this Constitution shall be so construed as to Prejudice any Claims of the United States, or of any particular State.

Sec. 4. The United States shall guarantee to every State in this Union a Republican Form of Government, and shall protect each of them against Invasion; and on Application of the Legislature, or of the Executive (when the Legislature cannot be convened) against domestic Violence.

Art. V

The Congress, whenever two thirds of both Houses shall deem it necessary, shall propose Amendments to this Constitution, or, on the Application of the Legislatures of two thirds of the several States, shall call a Convention for proposing Amendments, which, in either Case, shall be valid to all Intents and Purposes, as Part of this Constitution, when ratified by the Legislatures of three fourths of the several States, or by Conventions in three fourths thereof, as the one or the other Mode of Ratification may be proposed by the Congress; Provided that no Amendment which may be made prior to the Year One thousand eight hundred and eight shall in any Manner affect the first and fourth Clauses in the Ninth Section of the first Article; and that no State, without its Consent, shall be deprived of it's equal Suffrage in the Senate.

Art. VI

All Debts contracted and Engagements entered into, before the Adoption of this Constitution, shall be as valid against the United States under this Constitution, as under the Confederation.

This Constitution, and the Laws of the United States which shall be made in Pursuance thereof; and all Treaties made, or which shall be made, under the Authority of the United States, shall be the supreme Law of the Land; and the Judges in every State shall be bound thereby, any Thing in the Constitution or Laws of any State to the Contrary notwithstanding.

The Senators and Representatives before mentioned, and the

Members of the several State Legislatures, and all executive and judicial Officers, both of the United States and of the several States, shall be bound by Oath or Affirmation, to support this Constitution; but no religious Test shall ever be required as a Qualification to any Office or public Trust under the United States.

Art. VII

The Ratification of the Conventions of nine States, shall be sufficient for the Establishment of this Constitution between the States so ratifying the Same.

Done in Convention by the Unanimous Consent of the States present the Seventeenth Day of September in the Year of our Lord one thousand seven hundred and Eighty seven and of the Independance of the United States of America the Twelfth. In witness whereof We have hereunto subscribed our Names,

G° WASHINGTON — Presid[t]

and deputy from Virginia

Delaware
RICHARD BASSETT
GUNNING BEDFORD JUN
JACO: BROOM
JOHN DICKINSON
GEO: READ

Maryland
DAN[L] CARROLL
DAN OF S[T] THO[S] JENIFER
JAMES M[C]HENRY

Virginia
JOHN BLAIR
JAMES MADISON JR.

North Carolina
W[M] BLOUNT
RICH[D] DOBBS SPAIGHT
HU WILLIAMSON

South Carolina
PIERCE BUTLER
CHARLES COTESWORTH
   PINCKNEY
CHARLES PINCKNEY
J. RUTLEDGE

Georgia
ABR BALDWIN
WILLIAM FEW

New Hampshire
NICHOLAS GILMAN
JOHN LANGDON

Massachusetts
NATHANIEL GORHAM
RUFUS KING

Connecticut
W[M] SAM[L] JOHNSON
ROGER SHERMAN

New York
ALEXANDER HAMILTON

New Jersey
DAVID BREARLEY
JONA: DAYTON
WIL: LIVINGSTON
W[M] PATERSON

Pennsylvania
GEO. CLYMER
THO[S] FITZSIMONS
B FRANKLIN
JARED INGERSOLL
THOMAS MIFFLIN
GOUV MORRIS
ROB[T] MORRIS
JAMES WILSON

The Bill of Rights 1791

An intense struggle took place in the states over ratification of the Constitution. Opponents of a strong central government, calling themselves Antifederalists, fought bitterly against the change. When they charged that the Constitution lacked any guarantee of basic human liberties, supporters offered to add a Bill of Rights. In several states this promise was crucial in winning approval for the Constitution, which went into effect in 1789.

In the first Congress, James Madison, the chief author of the Constitution, insisted that a bill of rights be the first order of business. The states submitted over two hundred separate amendments which Madison condensed into twelve. Congress presented these to the states for their approval in September, 1789; the states accepted all but two, and in December, 1791, the first ten amendments became effective. This bill of rights helped win the confidence of opponents of the Constitution in the 1790's and has served ever since as a vital guarantee of fundamental civil liberties.

(During the course of the next 180 years, another sixteen amendments were added to the Constitution, bringing the total to twenty-six. One of the most significant of these — the Fourteenth, which deals with the rights guaranteed to all citizens — is discussed on page 137. The other fifteen Articles appear beginning on page 265.)

R.A.D.

ART. I

Congress shall make no law respecting an establishment of religion, or prohibiting the free exercise thereof; or abridging the freedom of speech, or of the press; or the right of the people peaceably to assemble, and to petition the government for a redress of grievances.

ART. II

A well regulated Militia, being necessary to the Security of a free State, the right of the people to keep and bear Arms, shall not be infringed.

ART. III

No soldier shall, in time of peace be quartered in any house, without the consent of the Owner, nor in time of war, but in a manner to be prescribed by law.

ART. IV

The right of the people to be secure in their persons, houses, papers, and effects, against unreasonable searches and seizures, shall not be violated, and no Warrants shall issue, but upon probable cause, supported by Oath or affirmation, and particularly describing the place to be searched, and the persons or things to be seized.

ART. V

No person shall be held to answer for a capital, or otherwise infamous crime, unless on a presentment or indictment of a Grand Jury, except in cases arising in the land or naval forces, or in the Militia, when in actual service in time of War or public danger; nor shall any person be subject for the same offence to be twice put in jeopardy of life or limb; nor shall be compelled in any criminal case to be a witness against himself, nor be deprived of life, liberty, or property, without due process of law; nor shall private property be taken for public use, without just compensation.

ART. VI

In all criminal prosecutions, the accused shall enjoy the right to a speedy and public trial, by an impartial jury of the State and district wherein the crime shall have been committed, which district shall have been previously ascertained by law, and to be informed of the nature and cause of the accusation; to be confronted with the witnesses against him; to have compulsory process for obtaining witnesses in his favor, and to have the Assistance of Counsel for his defence.

Art. VII

In Suits at common law, where the value in controversy shall exceed twenty dollars, the right of trial by jury shall be preserved, and no fact tried by a jury, shall be otherwise re-examined in any Court of the United States, than according to the rules of the common law.

Art. VIII

Excessive bail shall not be required, nor excessive fines imposed, nor cruel and unusual punishments inflicted.

Art. IX

The enumeration in the Constitution, of certain rights, shall not be construed to deny or disparage others retained by the people.

Art. X

The powers not delegated to the United States by the Constitution, nor prohibited by it to the States, are reserved to the States respectively, or to the people.

Alexander Hamilton: Report on Manufactures 1791

George Washington made many vital contributions to his nation, but few surpassed his appointment of Alexander Hamilton as the first Secretary of the Treasury. Only thirty-four, Hamilton possessed a brilliant mind, rare administrative ability, and a blazing determination to make the new government succeed. Faced with critical financial problems, notably the heavy debt left from the Revolution, Hamilton set out to place the country's finances on a solid basis and at the same time win the loyalty of its prosperous citizens. He achieved his goals by funding the national and state debts — calling in the old certificates of indebtedness and replacing them with new notes at full face value and providing a sinking fund to insure the gradual repayment of both principal and interest. Well-to-do merchants and speculators profited from the funding, as well as from the creation of a national bank under private ownership, while the nation benefited from the restoration of its credit and the achievement of financial solvency.

Hamilton was not content merely with meeting the problems of the past. He had a vision of a future American prosperity based on industry rather than on agriculture. In January, 1790, Congress asked him to prepare a report on the state of manufacturing in the country. For nearly two years, Hamilton conducted a thorough investigation, writing to friends and officials across the country and throughout the world to gather the information he needed. An anonymous English hosier sent him samples of machine-made cotton stockings; a merchant in Canton described the growing China trade; small manufacturers in Massachusetts pooled their knowledge and sent it on to Hamilton, expressing their "full confidence that the ultimate object is to befriend the manufacturers of our country, and not to take advantage of them." On the basis of this data, Hamilton wrote a massive report which he submitted to Congress in December, 1791. Although a Congress dominated by agricultural interests pigeonholed the Report on Manufactures, Hamilton had provided a blueprint for American economic development that inspired future generations.   R.A.D.

The expediency of encouraging manufacturers in the United States, which was not long since deemed very questionable, appears at this time to be pretty generally admitted. The embarrassments which have obstructed the progress of our external trade, have led to serious reflections on the necessity of enlarging the sphere of our domestic commerce. The restrictive regulations, which, in foreign markets, abridge the vent of the increasing surplus of our agricultural produce, serve to beget an earnest desire, that a more extensive demand for that surplus may be created at home; and the complete success which has rewarded manufacturing enterprise, in some valuable branches, conspiring with the promising symptoms which attend some less mature essays in others, justify a hope, that the obstacles to the growth of this species of industry are less formidable than they were apprehended to be; and that it is not difficult to find, in its further extension, a full indemnification for any external disadvantages, which are or may be experienced, as well as an accession of resources, favorable to national independence and safety. . . .

It may be observed, and the idea is of no inconsiderable weight, that however true it might be that a State, which, possessing large tracts of vacant and fertile territory, was at the same time secluded from foreign commerce, would find its interest and the interest of agriculture in diverting a part of its population from tillage to manufactures, yet it will not follow that the same is true of a State which, having such vacant and fertile territory, has at the same time ample opportunity of procuring from abroad, on good terms, all the fabrics of which it stands in need for the supply of its inhabitants. The power of doing this at least secures the great advantage of a division of labor, leaving the farmer free to pursue, exclusively, the culture of his land, and enabling him to procure with its products the manufactured supplies requisite either to his wants or to his enjoyments. And though it should be true that, in settled countries, the diversification of industry is conducive to an increase in the productive powers of labor, and to an augmentation of revenue and capital, yet it is scarcely conceivable that there can be anything of so solid and permanent advantage to an uncultivated and unpeopled country as to convert its wastes into cultivated and inhabited districts. If the revenue, in the meantime, should be less, the capital, in the event, must be greater.

To these observations the following appears to be a satisfactory answer:

1st. If the system of perfect liberty to industry and commerce were the prevailing system of nations, the arguments which dissuade a country, in the predicament of the United States, from the zealous pursuit of manufactures would doubtless have great force. It will not be affirmed that they might not be permitted, with few exceptions, to serve as a rule of national conduct. In such a state of things, each country would have the full benefit of its peculiar advantages to compensate for its deficiencies or disadvantages. If one nation were in a condition to supply manufactured articles on better terms than another, that other might find an abundant indemnification in a superior capacity to furnish the produce of the soil. And a free exchange, mutually beneficial, of the commodities which each was able to supply on the best terms, might be carried on between them, supporting in full vigor the industry of each. And though the circumstances which have been mentioned, and others which will be unfolded hereafter, render it probable that nations, merely agricultural, would not enjoy the same degree of opulence in proportion to their numbers as those which united manufactures with agriculture, yet the progressive improvement of the lands of the former might in the end atone for an inferior degree of opulence in the meantime; and in a case in which opposite considerations are pretty equally balanced, the option ought, perhaps, always to be in favor of leaving industry to its own direction.

But the system which has been mentioned is far from characterizing the general policy of nations. The prevalent one has been regulated by an opposite spirit. The consequence of it is that the United States are, to a certain extent, in the situation of a country precluded from foreign commerce. They can, indeed, without difficulty, obtain from abroad the manufactured supplies of which they are in want; but they experience numerous and very injurious impediments to the emission and vent of their own commodities. Nor is this the case in reference to a single foreign nation only. The regulations of several countries, with which we have the most extensive intercourse, throw serious obstructions in the way of the principal staples of the United States.

In such a position of things, the United States cannot exchange with Europe on equal terms; and the want of reciprocity would render them the victim of a system which would induce them to confine their views to agriculture and refrain from manufactures.

A constant and increasing necessity, on their part, for the commodities of Europe, and only a partial and occasional demand for their own, in return, could not but expose them to a state of impoverishment, compared with the opulence to which their political and natural advantages authorize them to aspire.

Remarks of this kind are not made in the spirit of complaint. It is for the nations, whose regulations are alluded to, to judge for themselves whether by aiming at too much they do not lose more than they gain. It is for the United States to consider by what means they can render themselves least dependent on the combinations, right or wrong, of foreign policy.

It is no small consolation that already the measures which have embarrassed our trade have accelerated internal improvements, which, upon the whole, have bettered our affairs. To diversify and extend these improvements is the surest and safest method of indemnifying ourselves for any inconveniencies which those or similar measures have a tendency to beget. If Europe will not take from us the products of our soil, upon terms consistent with our interest, the natural remedy is to contract, as fast as possible, our wants of her.

2nd. The conversion of their waste into cultivated lands is certainly a point of great moment in the political calculations of the United States. But the degree in which this may possibly be retarded by the encouragement of manufactories does not appear to countervail the powerful inducements to afford that encouragement.

An observation made in another place is of a nature to have great influence upon this question. If it cannot be denied that the interests, even of agriculture, may be advanced more by having such lands of a State as are occupied under a good cultivation, than by having a greater quantity occupied under a much inferior cultivation; and if manufactories, for the reasons assigned, must be admitted to have a tendency to promote a more steady and vigorous cultivation of the lands occupied than would happen without them, it will follow that they are capable of indemnifying a country for a diminution of the progress of new settlements, and may serve to increase both the capital value and the income of its lands, even though they should abridge the number of acres under tillage.

But it does by no means follow that the progress of new settlements would be retarded by the extension of manufactures. The desire of being an independent proprietor of land is founded on such strong principles in the human breast, that, where the opportunity of becoming so is as great as it is in the United States, the proportion will be small of those whose situations would otherwise lead to it, who would be diverted from it toward manufactures. And it is highly probable, as already intimated, that the accessions of foreigners, who, originally drawn over by manufacturing views, would afterward abandon them for agricultural, would be more than an equivalent for those of our own citizens who might happen to be detached from them.

The remaining objections to a particular encouragement of manufactures in the United States now require to be examined.

One of these turns on the proposition that industry, if left to itself, will naturally find its way to the most useful and profitable employment. Whence it is inferred that manufactures, without the aid of government, will grow up as soon and as fast as the natural state of things and the interest of the community may require.

Against the solidity of this hypothesis, in the full latitude of the terms, very cogent reasons may be offered. These have relation to the strong influence of habit and the spirit of imitation; the fear of want of success in untried enterprises; the intrinsic difficulties incident to first essays toward a competition with those who have previously attained to perfection in the business to be attempted; the bounties, premiums, and other artificial encouragements with which foreign nations second the exertions of their own citizens in the branches in which they are to be rivalled.

Experience teaches that men are often so much governed by what they are accustomed to see and practise, that the simplest and most obvious improvements, in the most ordinary occupations, are adopted with hesitation, reluctance, and by slow gradations. The spontaneous transition to new pursuits, in a community long habituated to different ones, may be expected to be attended with proportionately greater difficulty.

When former occupations ceased to yield a profit adequate to the subsistence of their followers, or when there was an absolute deficiency of employment in them owing to the superabundance of hands, changes would ensue; but these changes would be likely to be more tardy than might consist with the interest either of individuals or of the society. In many cases they would not happen, while a bare support could be insured by an adherence to ancient courses, though a resort to a more profitable employment might be practicable. To produce the desirable changes as early as may be expedient may therefore require the incitement and patronage of government.

The apprehension of failing in new attempts is, perhaps, a more serious impediment. There are dispositions apt to be attracted by the mere novelty of an undertaking; but these are not always those best calculated to give it success. To this it is of importance that the confidence of cautious, sagacious capitalists, both citizens and foreigners, should be excited. And to inspire this description of persons with confidence, it is essential that they should be made to see in any project which is new—and for that reason alone, if for no other, precarious—the prospect of such a degree of countenance and support from government, as may be capable of overcoming the obstacles inseparable from first experiments.

The superiority antecedently enjoyed by nations who have preoccupied and perfected a branch of industry, constitutes a more formidable obstacle than either of those which have been mentioned, to the introduction of the same branch into a country in which it did not before exist. To maintain, between the recent establishments of one country and the long-matured establishments of another country, a competition upon equal terms, both as to quality and price, is, in most cases, impracticable. The disparity in the one, or in the other, or in both must necessarily be so considerable as to forbid a successful rivalship, without the extraordinary aid and protection of government.

But the greatest obstacle of all to the successful prosecution of a new branch of industry in a country in which it was before unknown consists, as far as the instances apply, in the bounties, premiums, and other aids which are granted, in a variety of cases, by the nations in which the establishments to be imitated are previously introduced. It is well known (and particular examples, in the course of this report, will be cited) that certain nations grant bounties on the exportation of particular commodities, to enable their own workmen to undersell and supplant all competitors in the countries to which those commodities are sent. Hence the undertakers of a new manufacture have to contend, not only with the natural disadvantages of a new undertaking, but with the gratuities and remunerations which other governments bestow. To be enabled to contend with success it is evident that the interference and aid of their own government are indispensable. . . .

Not only the wealth; but the independence and security of a Country, appear to be materially connected with the prosperity of manufactures. Every nation, with a view to those great objects, ought to endeavour to possess within itself all the essentials of national supply. These comprise the means of *Subsistence habitation clothing* and *defence.*

The possession of these is necessary to the perfection of the body politic, to the safety as well as to the welfare of the society; the want of either, is the want of an important organ of political life and Motion; and in the various crises which await a state, it must severely feel the effects of any such deficiency. The extreme embarrassments of the United States during the late War, from an incapacity of supplying themselves, are still matter of keen recollection: A future war might be expected again to exemplify the mischiefs and dangers of a situation, to which that incapacity is still in too great a degree applicable, unless changed by timely and vigorous exertion. To effect this change as fast as shall be prudent, merits all the attention and all the Zeal of our Public Councils; 'tis the next great work to be accomplished.

Thomas Jefferson: First Inaugural Address 1801

On March 4, 1801, the first real transfer of political power took place in the new nation as Thomas Jefferson succeeded John Adams as President. During the 1790's, opposition to Hamilton's financial policies and controversy over foreign policy had created partisan division between the Federalists, led by Hamilton and Adams, and the Republicans, organized by Madison and Jefferson. Adams defeated Jefferson for the Presidency when Washington stepped down in 1796, but his administration witnessed growing bitterness and dissension as the pro-English Federalists entered into an undeclared naval war with France. Vindictive Federalists in Congress passed the repressive Alien and Sedition Acts, and the Adams administration used them in an effort to silence Republican critics. President Adams finally undercut the Federalist cause by arranging for peace with France over Hamilton's furious objections. In the election of 1800, Jefferson won a narrow but decisive victory, thus ending the Federalist control of the government and ushering in a new era of political harmony.

Jefferson was the first President to take office in the new capital city of Washington—described by a contemporary visitor as "a place with a few bad houses, extensive marshes, hanging on the skirts of a too thinly peopled, weak and barren country." The executive mansion, gleaming with a fresh coat of whitewash, was ready; but at the other end of Pennsylvania Avenue, which was no more than a broad clearing cut through the trees and swamps, the Capitol stood awkwardly unfinished. The north wing was complete, but the rest of the building was still under construction, with the rotunda open to the sky.

Jefferson, who had been staying at a nearby boarding house, walked through the mud to the Senate chamber in the north wing on the fourth of March to take the oath of office. John Adams, in a fit of pique, had left the capital that morning, leaving John Marshall, the Chief Justice, to preside at the inauguration. After taking the oath, Jefferson, who was ill at ease as always before an audience, read his carefully prepared speech. Few in the packed hall could hear his mumbled words, but printed copies were quickly made available. The inaugural address proved immensely popular, reassuring the anxious Federalists and confirming Republican faith in Jefferson's greatness. R.A.D.

Friends and Fellow-Citizens:

Called upon to undertake the duties of the first executive office of our country, I avail myself of the presence of that portion of my fellow-citizens which is here assembled to express my grateful thanks for the favor with which they have been pleased to look toward me, to declare a sincere consciousness that the task is above my talents, and that I approach it with those anxious and awful presentiments which the greatness of the charge and the weakness of my powers so justly inspire. A rising nation, spread over a wide and fruitful land, traversing all the seas with the rich productions of their industry, engaged in commerce with nations who feel power and forget right, advancing rapidly to destinies beyond the reach of mortal eye—when I contemplate these transcendent objects, and see the honor, the happinesss, and the hopes of this beloved country committed to the issue, and the auspices of this day, I shrink from the contemplation, and humble myself before the magnitude of the undertaking. Utterly, indeed, should I despair did not the presence of many whom I here see remind me that in the other high authorities provided by our Constitution I shall find resources of wisdom, of virtue, and of zeal on which to rely under all difficulties. To you, then, gentlemen, who are charged with the sovereign functions of legislation, and to those associated with you, I look with encouragement for that guidance and support which may enable us to steer with safety the vessel in which we are all embarked amidst the conflicting elements of a troubled world.

During the contest of opinion through which we have passed the animation of discussions and of exertions has sometimes worn an aspect which might impose on strangers unused to think freely and to speak and to write what they think; but this being now decided by the voice of the nation, announced according to the rules of the Constitution, all will, of course, arrange themselves under the will of the law, and unite in common efforts for the common good. All, too, will bear in mind this sacred principle, that though the will of the majority is in all cases to prevail, that will to be rightful must be reasonable; that the minority possesses their equal rights, which equal law must protect, and to violate would be oppression. Let us, then, fellow-citizens, unite with one heart and one mind. Let us restore to social intercourse that harmony and affection without which liberty and even life itself are but dreary things. And let us reflect that, having banished from our land that religious intolerance under which mankind so long bled and suffered, we have yet gained little if we countenance a political intolerance as despotic, as wicked, and capable of as bitter and bloody persecutions. During the throes and convulsions of the ancient world, during the agonizing spasms of infuriated man, seeking through blood and slaughter his long-lost liberty, it was not wonderful that the agitation of the billows should reach even this distant and peaceful shore; that this should be more felt and feared by some and less by others, and should divide opinions as to measures of safety. But every difference of opinion is not a difference of principle. We have called by different names brethren of the same principle. We are all Republicans, we are all Federalists. If there be any among us who would wish to dissolve this Union or to change its republican form, let them stand undisturbed as monuments of the safety with which error of opinion may be tolerated where reason is left free to combat it. I know, indeed, that some honest men fear that a republican government can not be strong, that this Government is not strong enough; but would the honest patriot, in the full tide of successful experiment, abandon a government which has so far kept us free and firm on the theoretic and visionary fear that this Government, the world's best hope, may by possibility want energy to preserve itself? I trust not. I believe this, on the contrary, the strongest Government on earth. I believe it the only one where every man, at the call of the law, would fly to the standard of the law, and would meet invasions of the public order as his own personal concern. Sometimes it is said that man can not be trusted with the government of himself. Can he, then, be trusted with the government of others? Or have we found angels in the forms of kings to govern him? Let history answer this question.

Let us, then, with courage and confidence pursue our own Federal and Republican principles, our attachment to union and representative government. Kindly separated by nature and a wide ocean from the exterminating havoc of one quarter of the globe; too high-minded to endure the degradations of the others; possessing a chosen country, with room enough for our descendants to the thousandth and thousandth generation; entertaining a due sense of our equal right to the use of our own faculties, to the acquisitions of our own industry, to honor and confidence from our fellow-citizens, resulting not from birth, but from our actions and their sense of them; enlightened by a benign religion, pro-

fessed, indeed, and practiced in various forms, yet all of them in-
culcating honesty, truth, temperance, gratitude, and the love of
man; acknowledging and adoring an overruling Providence,
which by all its dispensations proves that it delights in the happiness of man here and his greater happiness hereafter—with all
these blessings, what more is necessary to make us a happy and a
prosperous people? Still one thing more, fellow-citizens—a wise
and frugal Government, which shall restrain men from injuring
one another, shall leave them otherwise free to regulate their own
pursuits of industry and improvement, and shall not take from the
mouth of labor the bread it has earned. This is the sum of good
government, and this is necessary to close the circle of our felicities.

About to enter, fellow-citizens, on the exercise of duties which
comprehend everything dear and valuable to you, it is proper you
should understand what I deem the essential principles of our
Government, and consequently those which ought to shape its
Administration. I will compress them within the narrowest com-
pass they will bear, stating the general principle, but not all its
limitations. Equal and exact justice to all men, of whatever state
or persuasion, religious or political; peace, commerce, and honest
friendship with all nations, entangling alliances with none; the support of the State governments in all their rights, as the most competent administrations for our domestic concerns and the surest
bulwarks against antirepublican tendencies; the preservation of the
General Government in its whole constitutional vigor, as the sheet
anchor of our peace at home and safety abroad; a jealous care of
the right of election by the people—a mild and safe corrective of
abuses which are lopped by the sword of revolution where peaceable remedies are unprovided; absolute acquiescence in the decisions of the majority, the vital principle of republics, from which
is no appeal but to force, the vital principle and immediate parent
of despotism; a well-disciplined militia, our best reliance in peace
and for the first moments of war, till regulars may relieve them;
the supremacy of the civil over the military authority; economy in
the public expense, that labor may be lightly burthened; the honest
payment of our debts and sacred preservation of the public faith;
encouragement of agriculture, and of commerce as its handmaid;
the diffusion of information and arraignment of all abuses at the
bar of the public reason; freedom of religion; freedom of the press,
and freedom of person under the protection of the habeas corpus,

and trial by juries impartially selected. These principles form the bright constellation which has gone before us and guided our steps through an age of revolution and reformation. The wisdom of our sages and blood of our heroes have been devoted to their attainment. They should be the creed of our political faith, the text of civic instruction, the touchstone by which to try the services of those we trust; and should we wander from them in moments of error or of alarm, let us hasten to retrace our steps and to regain the road which alone leads to peace, liberty, and safety.

I repair, then, fellow-citizens, to the post you have assigned me. With experience enough in subordinate offices to have seen the difficulties of this the greatest of all, I have learnt to expect that it will rarely fall to the lot of imperfect man to retire from this station with the reputation and the favor which bring him into it. Without pretensions to that high confidence you reposed in our first and greatest revolutionary character, whose preëminent services had entitled him to the first place in his country's love and destined for him the fairest page in the volume of faithful history, I ask so much confidence only as may give firmness and effect to the legal administration of your affairs. I shall often go wrong through defect of judgment. When right, I shall often be thought wrong by those whose positions will not command a view of the whole ground. I ask your indulgence for my own errors, which will never be intentional, and your support against the errors of others, who may condemn what they would not if seen in all its parts. The approbation implied by your suffrage is a great consolation to me for the past, and my future solicitude will be to retain the good opinion of those who have bestowed it in advance, to conciliate that of others by doing them all the good in my power, and to be instrumental to the happiness and freedom of all.

Relying, then, on the patronage of your good will, I advance with obedience to the work, ready to retire from it whenever you become sensible how much better choice it is in your power to make. And may that Infinite Power which rules the destinies of the universe lead our councils to what is best, and give them a favorable issue for your peace and prosperity.

Meriwether Lewis: Letter to Jefferson on the Lewis and Clark Expedition 1806

In April, 1803, a capricious Napoleon Bonaparte suddenly offered to sell to the United States the vast Louisiana territory which he had recently extorted from Spain. Jefferson, who had sent James Monroe to Paris to buy the city of New Orleans and part of Florida, happily assented to the purchase. From his boyhood days in the foothills of the Appalachians, Jefferson had been fascinated by the West. In January, 1803, months before the purchase, he had asked Congress to authorize an exploring expedition across Louisiana to the Pacific. Jefferson's motive was primarily scientific—he yearned to acquire knowledge of the plants, animals, and geography of the unknown interior—but he justified the expedition on commercial grounds, both as an effort to tap the fur trade with the Indians and as an attempt to find a possible water route to the Pacific via the Missouri and Columbia rivers.

Meriwether Lewis, Jefferson's private secretary who was an experienced woodsman, and William Clark, a veteran Indian fighter and younger brother of the Revolutionary War hero George Rogers Clark, headed a group of twenty-five soldiers who left St. Louis in the spring of 1804.

The party spent the first winter among the Mandan Indians in present-day North Dakota, and set off into uncharted territory the following spring. Aided by friendly Shoshone Indians, they found a rugged pass through the Rockies and in November reached the Pacific where Clark carved on a tree, "By land from the U. States in 1804 & 1805." They returned the next year, reaching St. Louis in September, 1806. Lewis immediately sent Jefferson the following letter, which was the first word the President had heard from the expedition since it left the Mandan villages early in 1805.   R.A.D.

Sir,

It is with pleasure that I announce to you the safe arrival of my-self and party at 12 OClk. today at this place with our papers and baggage. In obedience to your orders we have penitrated the Con-tinent of North America to the Pacific Ocean, and sufficiently ex-plored the interior of the country to affirm with confidence that we have discovered the most practicable rout which dose exist across the continent by means of the navigable branches of the Missouri and Columbia Rivers. Such is that by way of the Missouri to the foot of the rapids five miles below the great falls of that river a dis-tance of 2575 miles, thence by land passing the Rocky Mountains to a navigable part of the Kooskooske 340; with the Kooskooske 73 mls. a South Easterly branch of the Columbia 154 miles and the latter river 413 mls. to the Pacific Ocean; making the total distance from the confluence of the Missouri and Mississippi to the dis-charge of the Columbia into the Pacific Ocean 3555 miles. The navigation of the Missouri may be deemed safe and good; it's difficulties arrise from it's falling banks, timber imbeded in the mud of it's channel, it's sand bars and steady rapidity of it's cur-rent, all which may be overcome with a great degree of certainty by taking the necessary precautions. The passage by land of 340 miles from the Missouri to the Kooskooske is the most formidable part of the tract proposed across the Continent; of this distance 200 miles is along a good road, and 140 over tremendious moun-tains which for 60 mls. are covered with eternal snows; however a passage over these mountains is practicable from the latter part of June to the last of September, and the cheep rate at which horses are to be obtained from the Indians of the Rocky Mountains and West of them, reduces the expences of transportation over this portage to a mere trifle. The navigation of the Kooskooske, the South East branch of the Columbia itself is safe and good from the 1st of April to the middle of August, by making three portages on the latter; the first of which in decending is that of 1200 paces at the great falls of the Columbia, 261 mls. from the Ocean, the second of two miles at the long narrows six miles below the falls, and the 3rd also of 2 miles at the great rapids 65 miles still lower down. The tides flow up the Columbia 183 miles, or within seven miles of the great rapids, thus far large sloops might ascend in safety, and vessels of 300 tons burthen could with equal safety reach the entrance of the river Multnomah, a large Southern branch of the Columbia, which taking it's rise on the confines of Mexico with the Callarado and Apostles river, discharges itself into the Columbia 125 miles from it's mouth. From the head of tide water to the foot of the long narrows the Columbia could be most advantageously navigated with large batteauxs, and from thence upwards by perogues. The Missouri possesses sufficient debth of water as far as is specifyed for boats of 15 tons burthen, but those of smaller capacity are to be preferred.

We view this passage across the Continent as affording immence advantages to the fur trade, but fear that the advantages which it offers as a communication for the productions of the Eeast Indies to the United States and thence to Europe will never be found equal on an extensive scale to that by way of the Cape of Good hope; still we believe that many articles not bulky brittle nor of a very perishable nature may be conveyed to the United States by this rout with more facility and at less expence than by that at present practiced.

The Missouri and all it's branches from the Chyenne upwards abound more in beaver and Common Otter, than any other streams on earth, particularly that proportion of them lying within the Rocky Mountains. The furs of all this immence tract of country including such as may be collected on the upper portion of the River St. Peters, Red river and the Assinniboin with the immence country watered by the Columbia, may be conveyed to the mouth of the Columbia by the 1st of August in each year and from thence be shiped to, and arrive in Canton earlier than the furs at present shiped from Montreal annually arrive in London. The British N. West Company of Canada were they permitted by the United States might also convey their furs collected in the Athabaske, on the Saskashawan, and South and West of Lake Winnipic by that rout within the period before mentioned. Thus the productions [of] nine tenths of the most valuable fur country of America could be conveyed by the rout proposed to the East Indies.

In the infancy of the trade across the continent, or during the period that the trading establishments shall be confined to the Missouri and it's branches, the men employed in this trade will be compelled to convey the furs collected in that quarter as low on the Columbia as tide water, in which case they could not return to the falls of the Missouri untill about the 1st of October, which would be so late in the season that there would be considerable danger of the river being obstructed by ice before they could reach this place and consequently that the comodites brought from the East indies would be detained untill the following spring; but this difficulty will at once vanish when establishments are also made on the Columbia, and a sufficient number of men employed at them to convey annually the productions of the East indies to the upper establishment on the Kooskooske, and there exchange them with the men of the Missouri for their furs, in the begining of July. By this means the furs not only of the Missouri but those also of the Columbia may be shiped to the East indies by the season before mentioned, and the comodities of the East indies arrive at St. Louis or the mouth of the Ohio by the last of September in each year.

Although the Columbia dose not as much as the Missouri abound in beaver and Otter, yet it is by no means despicable in this rispect, and would furnish a valuable fur trade distinct from any other consideration in addition to the otter and beaver which it could furnish. There might be collected considerable quantities of the skins of three speceis of bear affording a great variety of colours and of superior delicacy, those also of the tyger cat, several species of fox, martin and several others of an inferior class of furs, besides the valuable Sea Otter of the coast.

If the government will only aid, even in a very limited manner, the enterprize of her Citizens I am fully convinced that we shal shortly derive the benifits of a most lucrative trade from this source, and that in the course of ten or twelve years a tour across the Continent by the rout mentioned will be undertaken by individuals with as little concern as a voyage across the Atlantic is at present.

The British N. West Company of Canada has for several years, carried on a partial trade with the Minnetares Ahwayhaways and Mandans on the Missouri from their establishments on the Assinniboin at the entrance of Mouse river; at present I have good reason for beleiving that they intend shortly to form an establishment near those nations with a view to engroce the fur trade of the Missouri. The known enterprize and resources of this Company, latterly strengthened by an union with their powerfull rival the X. Y. Company renders them formidable in that distant part of the continent to all other traders; and in my opinion if we are to regard the trade of the Missouri as an object of importance to the United States; the strides of this Company towards the Missouri cannot be too vigilantly watched nor too firmly and speedily opposed by our government. The embarrasments under which the nagivation of the Missouri at present labours from the unfriendly dispositions of the Kancez, the several bands of Tetons, Assinniboins and those tribes that resort to the British establishments on the Saskashawan is also a subject which requires the earliest attention of our government. As I shall shortly be with you I have deemed it unnecessary here to detail the several ideas which have presented themselves to my mind on those subjects, more especially when I consider that a thorough knowledge of the geography of the country is absolutely necessary to their being unde[r]stood, and leasure has not yet permited us to make but one general map of the country which I am unwilling to wrisk by the Mail.

As a sketch of the most prominent features of our perigrination since we left the Mandans may not be uninteresting, I shall indeavour to give it to you by way of letter from this place, where I shall necessarily be detained several days in order to settle with and discharge the men who accompanyed me on the voyage as well as to prepare for my rout to the City of Washington.

We left Fort Clatsop where we wintered near the entrance of the Columbia on the 27th of March last, and arrived at the foot of the Rocky mountains on the 10th of May where we were detained untill the 24th of June in consequence of the snow which rendered a passage over the those Mountains impracticable untill that moment; had it not been for this detention I should ere this have joined you at Montichello. In my last communication to you from the Mandans I mentioned my intention of sending back a canoe with a small party from the Rocky Mountains; but on our arrival at the great falls of the Missouri on the 14th of June 1805, in view of that formidable snowey barrier, the discourageing difficulties which we had to encounter in making a portage of eighteen miles of our canoes and baggage around those falls were such that my friend Capt. Clark and myself conceived it inexpedient to reduce the party, lest by doing so we should lessen the ardor of those who remained and thus hazard the fate of the expedition, and therefore declined that measure, thinking it better that the government as well as our friends should for a moment feel some anxiety for our fate than to wrisk so much; experience has since proved the justice of our dicision, for we have more than once owed our lives and the fate of the expedition to our number which consisted of 31 men.

I have brought with me several skins of the Sea Otter, two skins of the native sheep of America, five skins and skelitons complete of the Bighorn or mountain ram, and a skin of the Mule deer beside the skins of several other quadrupeds and birds natives of the countries through which we have passed. I have also preserved a pretty extensive collection of plants, and collected nine other vocabularies.

I have prevailed on the great Cheif of the Mandan nation to accompany me to Washington; he is now with my frind and colligue Capt. Clark at this place, in good health and sperits, and very anxious to proceede.

With rispect to the exertions and services rendered by that esteemable man Capt. William Clark in the course of late voyage I cannot say too much; if sir any credit be due for the success of that arduous enterprize in which we have been mutually engaged, he is equally with myself entitled to your consideration and that of our common country.

The anxiety which I feel in returning once more to the bosom of my friends is a sufficient guarantee that no time will be unnecessarily expended in this quarter.

I have detained the post several hours for the purpose of making you this haisty communication. I hope that while I am pardoned for this detention of the mail, the situation in which I have been compelled to write will sufficiently apologize for having been this laconic.

The rout by which I purpose traveling from hence to Washington is by way of Cahokia, Vincennes, Louisvill Ky., the Crab orchard, Abington, Fincastle, Stanton and Charlottsville. Any letters directed to me at Louisville ten days after the receipt of this will most probably meet me at that place. I am very anxious to learn the state of my friends in Albemarle particularly whether my mother is yet living. I am with every sentiment of esteem Your Obt. and very Humble servent.

MERIWETHER LEWIS CAPT.
1st U.S. Regt. Infty.

N.B. The whole of the party who accompanyed me from the Mandans have returned in good health, which is not, I assure you, to me one of the least pleasing considerations of the Voyage.

M. L.

John Marshall: McCulloch v. Maryland 1819

John Marshall served as Chief Justice for thirty-four years and set many of the nation's basic judicial precedents. Like Jefferson, a product of the Virginia frontier, Marshall nevertheless became a Federalist and developed a powerful concept of nationalism. In one of his earliest decisions, *Marbury v. Madison,* he established the power of judicial review by voiding a law passed by Congress which conflicted with the Constitution. In subsequent cases, much to the dismay of Jefferson and other Republicans, he affirmed the authority of the central government and consistently upheld the sanctity of private contracts. Appointed Chief Justice of the seven-man Supreme Court in 1801, Marshall was able to impress his views upon his colleagues and dominate the Court despite repeated presidential efforts to appoint men who would oppose him.

He delivered one of his most influential decisions in 1819 in the case of *McCulloch v. Maryland.* James W. McCulloch was the cashier of the Baltimore branch of the Second Bank of the United States, chartered in 1816 by Congress to overcome the financial void created after Hamilton's original Bank expired in 1811. The Bank of the United States quickly established eighteen branches, and this led to outcries from state banks which had a difficult time competing with their larger rival.

In early 1818, the Maryland legislature passed a law taxing all "foreign" banks $15,000 a year, an amount intended to drive out the Bank of the United States. When McCulloch, as cashier, refused to pay the tax, Maryland filed suit in a state court and won. The Bank, facing similar taxes in five other states, appealed to the Supreme Court, and in 1819 John Marshall ruled in favor of the Bank for a unanimous Court.

Marshall had to decide two issues—the power of Congress to create a national bank and the right of a state to tax an institution created by the federal government. Marshall disposed of the second point with his famous assertion, "The power to tax involves the power to destroy . . . the power to destroy may defeat and render useless the power to create." He dealt at greater length with the fundamental issue of congressional authority under the Constitution.   R.A.D.

M

arshall, C. J. . . . The first question made in this cause is, has Congress power to incorporate a bank?

It has been truly said, that this can scarcely be considered as an open question, entirely unprejudiced by the former proceedings of the nation respecting it. The principle now contested was introduced at a very early period of our history, has been recognized by many successive legislatures, and has been acted upon by the judicial department, in cases of peculiar delicacy, as a law of undoubted obligation. . . .

In discussing this question, the counsel for the State of Maryland have deemed it of some importance, in the construction of the constitution, to consider that instrument not as emanating from the people, but as the act of sovereign and independent States. The powers of the general government, it has been said, are delegated by the States, who alone are truly sovereign; and must be exercised in subordination to the States, who alone possess supreme dominion.

It would be difficult to sustain this proposition. The convention which framed the constitution was, indeed, elected by the State legislatures. But the instrument, when it came from their hands, was a mere proposal, without obligation, or pretensions to it. It was reported to the then existing Congress of the United States, with a request that it might "be submitted to a convention of Delegates, chosen in each State by the people thereof, under the recommendation of its legislature, for their assent and ratification." This mode of proceeding was adopted; and by the Convention, by Congress, and by the State Legislatures, the instrument was submitted to the people. They acted upon it in the only manner in which they can act safely, effectively, and wisely, on such a subject, by assembling in Convention. It is true, they assembled in their several States—and where else should they have assembled? No political dreamer was ever wild enough to think of breaking down the lines which separate the States, and of compounding the American people into one common mass. Of consequence, when they act, they act in their States. But the measures they adopt do not, on that account, cease to be the measures of the people themselves, or become the measures of the State governments.

From these Conventions the constitution derives its whole authority. The government proceeds directly from the people; is "ordained and established" in the name of the people; and is declared to be ordained, "in order to form a more perfect union, establish justice, insure domestic tranquillity, and secure the blessings of liberty to themselves and to their posterity." The assent of the States, in their sovereign capacity, is implied in calling a Convention, and thus submitting that instrument to the people. But the people were at perfect liberty to accept or reject it; and their act was final. It required not the affirmance, and could not be negatived, by the State governments. The constitution, when thus adopted, was of complete obligation, and bound the State sovereignties. . . .

The government of the Union, then (whatever may be the influence of this fact on the case) is, emphatically and truly a government of the people. In form and in substance it emanates from them. Its powers are granted by them, and are to be exercised directly on them, and for their benefit.

This government is acknowledged by all to be one of enumerated powers. The principle, that it can exercise only the powers granted to it, would seem too apparent to have required to be enforced by all those arguments which its enlightened friends, while it was depending before the people, found it necessary to urge. That principle is now universally admitted. But the question respecting the extent of the powers actually granted, is perpetually arising, and will probably continue to arise, as long as our system shall exist.

In discussing these questions, the conflicting powers of the general and State governments must be brought into view, and the supremacy of their respective laws, when they are in opposition, must be settled.

If any one proposition could command the universal assent of mankind, we might expect it would be this—that the government of the Union, though limited in its powers, is supreme within its sphere of action. This would seem to result necessarily from its nature. It is the government of all; its powers are delegated by all; it represents all, and acts for all. Though any one State may be willing to control its operations, no State is willing to allow others to control them. The nation, on those subjects on which it can act, must necessarily bind its component parts. But this question is not left to mere reason: the people have, in express terms, decided it, by saying, "this constitution, and the laws of the United States, which shall be made in pursuance thereof, shall be the supreme law of the land," and by requiring that the members of the State legislatures, and the officers of the executive and judicial departments of the States, shall take the oath of fidelity to it.

The government of the United States, though limited in its powers, is supreme; and its laws, when made in pursuance of the constitution, form the supreme law of the land, "any thing in the constitution or laws of any State to the contrary notwithstanding." . . .

Although, among the enumerated powers of government, we do not find the word "bank," or "incorporation," we find the great powers to lay and collect taxes; to borrow money; to regulate commerce; to declare and conduct a war; and to raise and support armies and navies. The sword and the purse, all the external relations, and no inconsiderable portion of the industry of the nation, are entrusted to its government. It can never be pretended that these vast powers draw after them others of inferior importance, merely because they are inferior. Such an idea can never be advanced. But it may with great reason be contended, that a government, entrusted with such ample powers, on the due execution of which the happiness and prosperity of the nation so vitally depends, must also be entrusted with ample means for their execution. The power being given, it is the interest of the nation to facilitate its execution. It can never be their interest, and cannot be presumed to have been their intention, to clog and embarrass its execution by withholding the most appropriate means. Throughout this vast republic, from the St. Croix to the Gulf of Mexico, from the Atlantic to the Pacific, revenue is to be collected and expended, armies are to be marched and supported. The exigencies of the nation may require, that the treasure raised in the north should be transported to the south, *that* raised in the east conveyed to the west, or that this order should be reversed. Is that construction of the constitution to be preferred which would render these operations difficult, hazardous, and expensive? Can we adopt that construction (unless the words imperiously require it) which would impute to the framers of that instrument, when granting these powers for the public good, the intention of impeding their exercise by withholding a choice of means? If, indeed, such be the mandate of the constitution, we have only to obey; but that instrument does not profess to enumerate the means by which the powers it confers may be executed; nor does it prohibit the creation of a corporation, if the existence of such a being be essential to the beneficial exercise of those powers. It is, then, the subject of fair inquiry, how far such means may be employed.

It is not denied, that the powers given to the government imply the ordinary means of execution. That, for example, of raising revenue and applying it to national purposes, is admitted to imply the power of conveying money from place to place, as the exigencies of the nation may require, and of employing the usual means of conveyance. But it is denied that the government has its choice of means, or that it may employ the most convenient means; if to employ them it be necessary to erect a corporation. . . .

The government which has a right to do an act, and has imposed on it the duty of performing that act, must, according to the dictates of reason, be allowed to select the means; and those who contend that it may not select any appropriate means, that one particular mode of effecting the object is excepted, take upon themselves the burden of establishing that exception. . . .

But the constitution of the United States has not left the right of Congress to employ the necessary means, for the execution of the powers conferred on the government, to general reasoning. To its enumeration of powers is added that of making "all laws which shall be necessary and proper, for carrying into execution the foregoing powers, and all other powers vested by this constitution, in the government of the United States, or in any department thereof."

The counsel for the State of Maryland have urged various arguments, to prove that this clause, though in terms a grant of power, is not so in effect; but is really restrictive of the general right, which might otherwise be implied, of selecting means of executing the enumerated powers. . . .

But the argument on which most reliance is to be placed, is drawn from the peculiar language of this clause. Congress is not empowered by it to make all laws, which may have relation to the powers conferred on the government, but such only as may be *"necessary and proper"* for carrying them into execution. The word *"necessary"* is considered as controlling the whole sentence, and as limiting the right to pass laws for the execution of the granted powers, to such as are indispensable, and without which the power would be nugatory. That it excludes the choice of means, and leaves to Congress, in each case, that only which is most direct and simple.

Is it true, that this is the sense in which the word "necessary" is always used? Does it always import an absolute physical necessity, so strong, that one thing, to which another may be termed necessary cannot exist without that other? We think it does not. If reference be had to its use, in the common affairs of the world, or in approved authors, we find that it frequently imports no more than that one thing is convenient, or useful, or essential to another. To employ the means necessary to an end, is generally understood as employing any means calculated to produce the end, and not as being confined to those single means, without which the end would be entirely unattainable. Such is the character of human language, that no word conveys to the mind, in all situations one single definite idea; and nothing is more common than to use words in a figurative sense. Almost all compositions contain words, which, taken in their rigorous sense, would convey a meaning different from that which is obviously intended. It is essential to just construction, that many words which import something excessive, should be understood in a more mitigated sense — in that sense which common usage justifies. The word "necessary" is of this description. It has not a fixed character peculiar to itself. It admits of all degrees of comparison; and is often connected with other words, which increase or diminish the impression the mind receives of the urgency it imports. A thing may be necessary, very necessary, absolutely or indispensably necessary. To no mind would the same idea be conveyed, by these several phrases. . . . This word, then, like others, is used in various senses; and, in its construction, the subject, the context, the intention of the person using them, are all to be taken into view.

Let this be done in the case under consideration. The subject is the execution of those great powers on which the welfare of a nation essentially depends. It must have been the intention of those who gave these powers, to insure, as far as human prudence could insure, their beneficial execution. This could not be done by confiding the choice of means to such narrow limits as not to leave it in the power of Congress, to adopt any which might be appropriate, and which were conducive to the end. This provision is made in a constitution intended to endure for ages to come, and, consequently, to be adapted to the various *crises* of human affairs. To have prescribed the means by which government should, in all future time, execute its powers, would have been to change, entirely, the character of the instrument, and give it the properties of a legal code. It would have been an unwise attempt to provide, by immutable rules, for exigencies which, if foreseen at all, must have been seen dimly, and which can be best provided for as they occur. To have declared that the best means shall not be used, but those alone without which the power given would be nugatory, would have been to deprive the legislature of the capacity to avail itself of experience, to exercise its reason, and to accommodate its legislation to circumstances. . . .

The result of the most careful and attentive consideration bestowed upon this clause is, that if it does not enlarge, it cannot be construed to restrain the powers of Congress, or to impair the right of the legislature to exercise its best judgment in the section of measures to carry into execution the constitutional powers of the government. If no other motive for its insertion can be suggested, a sufficient one is found in the desire to legislate on that vast mass of incidental powers which must be involved in the constitution, if that instrument be not a splendid bauble.

We admit, as all must admit, that the powers of the government are limited, and that its limits are not to be transcended. But we think the sound construction of the constitution must allow to the national legislature that discretion, with respect to the means by which the powers it confers are to be carried into execution, which will enable that body to perform the high duties assigned to it, in the manner most beneficial to the people. Let the end be legitimate, let it be within the scope of the constitution, and all means which are appropriate, which are plainly adapted to that end, which are not prohibited, but consist with the letter and spirit of the constitution, are constitutional. . . .

After the most deliberate consideration, it is the unanimous and decided opinion of this court, that the act to incorporate the Bank of the United States is a law made in pursuance of the constitution, and is a part of the supreme law of the land.

Thomas Jefferson: Letter on the Missouri Compromise 1820

The rapid and uneven growth of the United States in the first two decades of the nineteenth century created a serious sectional problem. The northern states began to move ahead in economic development and in population—by 1820 there were 105 Congressmen from the North compared to 81 representing the South, and the gap was widening. In 1819 the expanding westward movement brought on a crisis when settlers in the Missouri Territory asked to be admitted to the Union. Most of these people were from the South and as a matter of course they proposed a constitution that protected the institution of slavery. As yet the northern conscience was not greatly troubled by the morality of slavery, but politicians worried over the fact that the entry of Missouri would unbalance the even division between free and slave states. Accordingly, Representative James Tallmadge of New York offered an amendment to the bill admitting Missouri, which would ban the introduction of any new slaves into the state and provide for the gradual elimination of slavery in Missouri in the future. Southerners were furious, and though the House of Representatives approved the amendment by a straight sectional vote, the Senate rejected it.

In 1820 congressional moderates worked out a formula to cool the sectional passions: the compromise maintained regional balance by admitting both Missouri and Maine, a free state, and stipulating that in the future, slavery would be prohibited in the remainder of the Louisiana Purchase territory north of the line 36°30'.

Thomas Jefferson, living in retirement at Monticello, sadly watched this sectional crisis unfold. In the years since his Presidency, he had busied himself with the management of his estate and with the founding of his beloved University of Virginia. He did not take an active part in politics but still maintained an extensive correspondence, and all through the Missouri debate he commented on its political significance. Unlike many of his contemporaries, Jefferson recognized the fundamental moral issue that lay beneath the sectional squabbling. In a letter to John Holmes, a Massachusetts senator, he expressed his apprehensions, which paralleled those of his old rival, John Adams, who commented in his diary, "I take it for granted that the present question is a mere preamble—a title-page to a great, tragic volume."   R.A.D.

I thank you, dear Sir, for the copy you have been so kind as to send me of the letter to your constituents on the Missouri question. It is a perfect justification to them. I had for a long time ceased to read newspapers, or pay any attention to public affairs, confident they were in good hands, and content to be a passenger in our bark to the shore from which I am not distant. But this momentous question, like a fire bell in the night, awakened and filled me with terror. I considered it at once as the knell of the Union. It is hushed, indeed, for the moment. But this is a reprieve only, not a final sentence. A geographical line, coinciding with a marked principle, moral and political, once conceived and held up to the angry passions of men will never be obliterated; and every new irritation will mark it deeper and deeper. I can say, with conscious truth, that there is not a man on earth who would sacrifice more than I would to relieve us from this heavy reproach, in any *practicable* way. The cession of that kind of property, for so it is misnamed, is a bagatelle which would not cost me a second thought, if, in that way, a general emancipation and *expatriation* could be effected; and gradually, and with due sacrifices, I think it might be. But as it is, we have the wolf by the ears, and we can neither hold him, nor safely let him go. Justice is in one scale and self-preservation in the other. Of one thing I am certain, that as the passage of slaves from one State to another, would not make a slave of a single human being who would not be so without it, so their diffusion over a greater surface would make them individually happier, and proportionally facilitate the accomplishment of their emancipation, by dividing the burthen on a greater number of coadjutors. An abstinence too, from this act of power, would remove the jealousy excited by the undertaking of Congress to regulate the condition of the different descriptions of men composing a State. This certainly is the exclusive right of every State, which nothing in the constitution has taken from them and given to the General Government. Could Congress, for example say, that the non-freemen of Connecticut shall be freemen, or that they shall not emigrate into any other State?

I regret that I am now to die in the belief that the useless sacrifice of themselves by the generation of 1776, to acquire self-government and happiness to their country, is to be thrown away by the unwise and unworthy passions of their sons, and that my only consolation is to be, that I live not to weep over it. If they would but dispassionately weigh the blessings they will throw away, against an abstract principle more likely to be effected by union than by scission, they would pause before they would perpetrate this act of suicide on themselves, and of treason against the hopes of the world. To yourself, as the faithful advocate of the Union, I tender the offering of my high esteem and respect.

Thomas Jefferson

James Monroe: The Monroe Doctrine 1823

The classic statement of American foreign policy in the Western Hemisphere grew out of a series of misapprehensions about European intentions. After the defeat of Napoleon, the nations of Europe, led by Austria's Count Metternich and Czar Alexander I of Russia, formed the Holy Alliance and dedicated themselves to suppressing revolution and liberalism on the Continent. When French forces entered Spain in 1821 to put down a liberal revolt, President James Monroe and many of his cabinet members feared that the Holy Alliance, if successful there, would cross the Atlantic to end the anticolonial revolutions taking place throughout Latin America and then restore the Spanish empire. At the same time, Secretary of State John Quincy Adams, the crabbed but brilliant son of the second President, worried about the possible expansion of Russia down the west coast from its base in Alaska.

Although neither the Holy Alliance nor Czarist Russia actually planned any encroachments on the New World, the United States responded vigorously. In a conversation with the Russian minister in Washington in the summer of 1823, Adams bluntly told him that "the American continents are no longer subject for any new European colonial establishments." Adams' colleagues, who were much more concerned about the threat of the Holy Alliance, were delighted when the powerful British government proposed a joint Anglo-American declaration to warn the continental European powers to stay out of the New World. President Monroe, armed with affirmative letters from ex-Presidents Madison and Jefferson, was ready to accept the British proposal when Adams objected strenuously. Ridiculing the fears of his fellow cabinet members, Adams scoffed at the idea of a foreign invasion of Latin America, shrewdly pointing out that regardless of what the United States did, the English navy would prevent the Holy Alliance from invading the Americas. The American government, Adams declared, should announce its own independent policy to the world rather than "to come in as a cock-boat in the wake of the British man-of-war."

Impressed by Adams' nationalistic argument, Monroe decided to reject joint action with Britain and to declare instead American opposition to the Holy Alliance. He did so in his annual State of the Union message to Congress on December 2, 1823. Although his words had little effect at the time, since English diplomacy had already removed whatever slight chance there had been of an invasion of the New World, Monroe's speech set forth a historic claim to future American dominance of the Western Hemisphere.   R.A.D.

A... t the proposal of the Russian Imperial Government, made through the minister of the Emperor residing here, a full power and instructions have been transmitted to the minister of the United States at St. Petersburg to arrange by amicable negotiation the respective rights and interests of the two nations on the northwest coast of this continent. A similar proposal has been made by His Imperial Majesty to the Government of Great Britain, which has likewise been acceded to. The Government of the United States has been desirous by this friendly proceeding of manifesting the great value which they have invariably attached to the friendship of the Emperor and their solicitude to cultivate the best understanding with his Government. In the discussions to which this interest has given rise and in the arrangements by which they may terminate the occasion has been judged proper for asserting, as a principle in which the rights and interests of the United States are involved, that the American continents, by the free and independent condition which they have assumed and maintain, are henceforth not to be considered as subjects for future colonization by any European powers. . . .

It was stated at the commencement of the last session that a great effort was then making in Spain and Portugal to improve the condition of the people of those countries, and that it appeared to be conducted with extraordinary moderation. It need scarcely be remarked that the result has been so far very different from what was then anticipated. Of events in that quarter of the globe, with which we have so much intercourse and from which we derive our origin, we have always been anxious and interested spectators. The citizens of the United States cherish sentiments the most friendly in favor of the liberty and happiness of their fellow-men on that side of the Atlantic. In the wars of the European powers in matters relating to themselves we have never taken any part, nor does it comport with our policy so to do. It is only when our rights are invaded or seriously menaced that we resent injuries or make preparation for our defense. With the movements in this hemisphere we are of necessity more immediately connected, and by causes which must be obvious to all enlightened and impartial observers. The political system of the allied powers is essentially different in this respect from that of America. This difference proceeds from that which exists in their respective Governments; and to the defense of our own, which has been achieved by the loss of so much blood and treasure, and matured by the wisdom of their most enlightened citizens, and under which we have enjoyed unexampled felicity, this whole nation is devoted. We owe it, therefore, to candor and to the amicable relations existing between the United States and those powers to declare that we should consider any attempt on their part to extend their system to any portion of this hemisphere as dangerous to our peace and safety. With the existing colonies or dependencies of any European power we have not interfered and shall not interfere. But with the Governments who have declared their independence and maintained it, and whose independence we have, on great consideration and on just principles, acknowledged, we could not view any interposition for the purpose of oppressing them, or controlling in any other manner their destiny, by any European power in any other light than as the manifestation of an unfriendly disposition toward the United States. In the war between those new Governments and Spain we declared our neutrality at the time of their recognition, and to this we have adhered, and shall continue to adhere, provided no change shall occur which, in the judgment of the competent authorities of this Government, shall make a corresponding change on the part of the United States indispensable to their security.

The late events in Spain and Portugal shew that Europe is still unsettled. Of this important fact no stronger proof can be adduced than that the allied powers should have thought it proper, on any principle satisfactory to themselves, to have interposed by force in the internal concerns of Spain. To what extent such interposition may be carried, on the same principle, is a question in which all independent powers whose governments differ from theirs are interested, even those most remote, and surely none more so than the United States. Our policy in regard to Europe, which was adopted at an early stage of the wars which have so long agitated that quarter of the globe, nevertheless remains the same, which is, not to interfere in the internal concerns of any of its powers; to consider the government *de facto* as the legitimate government for us; to cultivate friendly relations with it, and to preserve those relations by a frank, firm, and manly policy, meeting in all instances the just claims of every power, submitting to injuries from none. But in regard to those continents circumstances are eminently and conspicuously different. It is impossible that the allied powers should extend their political system to any portion of either continent without endangering our peace and happiness; nor can anyone believe that our southern brethren, if left to themselves, would adopt it of their own accord. It is equally impossible, therefore, that we should behold such interposition in any form with indifference. If we look to the comparative strength and resources of Spain and those new Governments, and their distance from each other, it must be obvious that she can never subdue them. It is still the true policy of the United States to leave the parties to themselves, in the hope that other powers will pursue the same course. . . .

William Lloyd Garrison: The Liberator 1831

Concern over the evil of slavery developed slowly in the United States. Humanitarians focused their attention on the slave trade, which was ended legally in 1808, and on a plan for the gradual return of Negroes to Africa. In 1817 a group of prominent Americans, including Henry Clay and John Marshall, formed the American Colonization Society. Carefully observing the legality of slavery, the new society sought simply to colonize free Negroes and emancipated slaves either in Haiti or in what eventually became the new republic of Liberia. Despite great fanfare, the colonizers' achievements were slight; by 1830 less than fifteen hundred blacks had emigrated, and nearly all of those were freemen.

William Lloyd Garrison first entered the antislavery movement as an advocate of colonization. As an orphaned boy in New England, he had learned the printing trade and in 1829 he joined with Benjamin Lundy, a Quaker reformer, in publishing the *Genius of Universal Emancipation* in Baltimore. Garrison quickly became impatient with Lundy's moderate approach. A stubborn, dogmatic man, he saw slavery as an absolute evil that required an all-out frontal attack if it were to be overcome. After serving a seven-week jail sentence for libel in 1830, Garrison broke with Lundy and returned to New England determined to found his own newspaper. The powerful oratory of a speech he gave in Boston converted two Unitarian ministers, Samuel Sewall and Samuel May, who later commented, "That night my soul was baptized in his spirit, and ever since I have been a disciple and fellow laborer of William Lloyd Garrison."

On January 1, 1831, the twenty-five-year-old Garrison and his partner Isaac Knapp began publishing the *Liberator* in Boston. Living ascetically on water and stale bread from a neighboring bakery, and using borrowed type, week after week Garrison issued a strident call for the immediate end of slavery and transformed a slumbering antislavery movement into the abolitionist crusade. R.A.D.

To the Public.

In the month of August, I issued proposals for publishing *"The Liberator"* in Washington City; but the enterprise, though hailed in different sections of the country, was palsied by public indifference. Since that time, the removal of the *Genius of Universal Emancipation* to the Seat of Government has rendered less imperious the establishment of a similar periodical in that quarter.

During my recent tour for the purpose of exciting the minds of the people by a series of discourses on the subject of slavery, every place that I visited gave fresh evidence of the fact, that a greater revolution in public sentiment was to be effected in the free states— *and particularly in New England*—than at the south. I found contempt more bitter, opposition more active, detraction more relentless, prejudice more stubborn, and apathy more frozen, than among slave owners themselves. Of course, there were individual exceptions to the contrary. This state of things afflicted, but did not dishearten me. I determined, at every hazard, to lift up the standard of emancipation in the eyes of the nation, *within sight of Bunker Hill and in the birth place of liberty.* That standard is now unfurled; and long may it float, unhurt by the spoliations of time or the missiles of a desperate foe—yea, till every chain be broken, and every bondman set free! Let Southern oppressors tremble— let their secret abettors tremble—let their Northern apologists tremble—let all the enemies of the persecuted blacks tremble.

I deem the publication of my original Prospectus unnecessary, as it has obtained a wide circulation. The principles therein inculcated will be steadily pursued in this paper, excepting that I shall not array myself as the political partisan of any man. In defending the great cause of human rights, I wish to derive the assistance of all religions and of all parties.

Assenting to the "self evident truth" maintained in the American Declaration of Independence, "that all men are created equal, and endowed by their Creator with certain inalienable rights—among which are life, liberty and the pursuit of happiness," I shall strenuously contend for the immediate enfranchisement of our slave population. In Park-Street Church, on the Fourth of July, 1829, in an address on slavery, I unreflectingly assented to the popular but pernicious doctrine of *gradual* abolition. I seize this opportunity to make a full and unequivocal recantation, and thus publicly to ask pardon of my God, of my country, and of my brethren the poor slaves, for having uttered a sentiment so full of timidity, injustice and absurdity. A similar recantation, from my pen, was published in the *Genius of Universal Emancipation* at Baltimore, in September, 1829. My conscience is now satisfied.

I am aware, that many object to the severity of my language; but is there not cause for severity? I *will be* as harsh as truth, and as uncompromising as justice. On this subject, I do not wish to think, or speak, or write, with moderation. No! No! Tell a man whose house is on fire, to give a moderate alarm; tell him to moderately rescue his wife from the hands of the ravisher; tell the mother to gradually extricate her babe from the fire into which it has fallen; —but urge me not to use moderation in a cause like the present. I am in earnest—I will not equivocate—I will not excuse—I will not retreat a single inch—*AND I WILL BE HEARD*. The apathy of the people is enough to make every statue leap from its pedestal, and to hasten the resurrection of the dead.

It is pretended, that I am retarding the cause of emancipation by the coarseness of my invective, and the precipitancy of my measures. *The charge is not true.* On this question my influence,—humble as it is,—is felt at this moment to a considerable extent, and shall be felt in coming years—not perniciously, but beneficially —not as a curse, but as a blessing; and posterity will bear testimony that I was right. I desire to thank God, that he enables me to disregard "the fear of man which bringeth a snare," and to speak his truth in its simplicity and power. . . .

EXPANSION AND CONFLICT

The Granger Collection

In 1793, two years after Alexander Hamilton had proclaimed the benefits of a manufacturing economy, Samuel Slater founded the first U.S. cotton mill (above) in Pawtucket, Rhode Island, beginning the development of New England's textile industry.

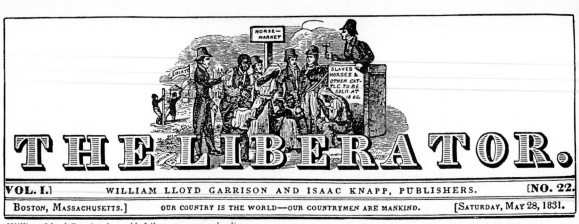

THE LIBERATOR.

VOL. I.]   WILLIAM LLOYD GARRISON AND ISAAC KNAPP, PUBLISHERS.   **[NO. 22.**

BOSTON, MASSACHUSETTS.]   OUR COUNTRY IS THE WORLD—OUR COUNTRYMEN ARE MANKIND.   [SATURDAY, MAY 28, 1831.

William Lloyd Garrison's weekly Liberator *was a leading organ of the anti-slavery movement in the United States.*

The question of whether slavery should be allowed in newly admitted states was hotly debated in the pre-Civil War period. Here, Henry Clay addresses the senate on the Compromise of 1850, which admitted California to the Union as a non-slave state. His opponent, John C. Calhoun (left of the chair), listens.

Escaped Southern slaves toward refuge in the Nort

The Granger Collection

Thomas Hovenden's The Last Moments of John Brown *shows the abolitionist martyr on his way to the gallows.*

Abraham Lincoln opposes the extension of slavery in one of his debates with Stephen A. Douglas during the Illinois senatorial campaign of 1858.

The Bettmann Archive

The Granger Collection

After the opening (1787) of the Northwest Territory, the acquisition (1803) of Louisiana, and the annexation of the Southwest as a result of the Mexican War (1846–48), Americans came to regard it as their "manifest destiny" to spread across the continent. This Currier and Ives lithograph portrays the westward movement of pioneers by wagon train.

The Granger Collection

A few weeks after Lincoln's inauguration, Confederate forces attacked Union-held Fort Sumter in the Charleston, South Carolina, harbor, and the Civil War began.

Lincoln, visiting the Army of the Potomac in October 1862, posed for the camera with General George B. McClellan (center, facing the President) and his staff. After unsuccessfully trying to persuade McClellan to adopt a more aggressive strategy, Lincoln removed him from command.

The Granger Collection

The Union victory at Gettysburg, Pennsylvania, in July 1863 marked a turning point in the Civil War, coinciding with General Grant's capture of the Confederate fortress of Vicksburg.

Union troops under General William T. Sherman attack a position defended by Confederates under General Joseph E. Johnston at Kenesaw Mountain, Georgia, on June 27, 1864. Although the attack failed, Johnston was forced to retreat, and Sherman continued his relentless advance toward Atlanta.

The Granger Collection

Executive Mansion,

Washington,   , 186

Four score and seven years ago our fathers brought forth, upon this continent, a new nation, conceived in liberty, and dedicated to the proposition that "all men are created equal"

Now we are engaged in a great civil war, testing whether that nation, or any nation so conceived, and so dedicated, can long endure. We are met on a great battle field of that war. We have come to dedicate a portion of it, as a final resting place for those who died here, that the nation might live. This we may, in all propriety do. But, in a larger sense, we can not dedicate— we can not consecrate— we can not hallow, this ground— The brave men, living and dead, who struggled here, have hallowed it, far above our poor power to add or detract. The world will little note, nor long remember what we say here; while it can never forget what they did here.

It is rather for us, the living, to stand here,

ted to the great task remaining before us— that, from these honored dead we take increased devotion to that cause for which they here, gave the last full measure of devotion— that we here highly resolve these dead shall not have died in vain; that this nation, shall have a new birth of freedom, and that government of the people by the people for the people, shall not perish from the earth.

This is one of five autographed copies of Lincoln's Gettysburg Address. Although the wording differs in some places from the version that usually appears in print, it is probably the copy that Lincoln used when he delivered the address.

Lincoln is shown speaking at the dedication of the Gettysburg cemetery in a lithogr done long after the event. His brief address became one of the most famous oration American hist

The Granger Collection

Andrew Jackson: Veto of the Bank Bill 1832

Andrew Jackson viewed his electoral victory over John Quincy Adams in 1828 as a great vindication. Four years earlier, Congress had declared the aloof and forbidding Adams the victor in a disputed election despite the fact that Jackson had captured a larger popular vote. In office, Jackson continued to view politics in personal terms, and it was this trait that led him into the bank war.

Nicholas Biddle, a brilliant though arrogant Philadelphian, had become president of the Second Bank of the United States in 1823 and had transformed it into an extremely efficient and powerful financial institution. By controlling the notes issued by local banks, Biddle kept the nation's currency sound; but in the process he made many enemies—among them rival bankers, debtor groups in the South and West, restless promoters who yearned for easy money, and westerners like Jackson who distrusted all banks. Biddle's enormous economic power disturbed the President, who candidly told him, "I do not dislike your Bank any more than all banks. But ever since I read the history of the South Sea Bubble I have been afraid of banks."

Biddle understandably became concerned, and for protection he drew closer to the National Republican Party (the future Whigs) of Henry Clay and Daniel Webster. Since the Bank's charter would expire in 1836, he tried to win political support by extending loans to members of Congress. In 1832 the National Republicans, looking for an issue for Clay to exploit in the forthcoming election, persuaded Biddle to seek recharter four years early. Congress passed the bill for recharter by narrow margins, and Clay flung down the gauntlet, declaring, "Should Jackson veto it, I shall veto him." The President responded just as Clay had calculated. "The Bank is trying to kill me, *but I will kill it*," Jackson told Martin Van Buren as he wrote his veto message. Although Biddle termed the veto "a manifesto of anarchy," saying, "It has all the fury of a chained panther, biting the bars of his cage," Congress sustained Jackson, and in the fall election he won a sweeping victory over Clay.

The veto of the bank bill did irreparable damage to the nation's financial structure, but in the words of Arthur Schlesinger, Jr., the message stands out as "a ringing statement of Jackson's belief in the essential rights of the common man."   R.A.D.

To the Senate:

The bill "to modify and continue" the act entitled "An act to incorporate the subscribers to the Bank of the United States" was presented to me on the 4th July instant. Having considered it with that solemn regard to the principles of the Constitution which the day was calculated to inspire, and come to the conclusion that it ought not to become a law, I herewith return it to the Senate, in which it originated, with my objections.

A bank of the United States is in many respects convenient for the Government and useful to the people. Entertaining this opinion, and deeply impressed with the belief that some of the powers and privileges possessed by the existing bank are unauthorized by the Constitution, subversive of the rights of the States, and dangerous to the liberties of the people, I felt it my duty at an early period of my Administration to call the attention of Congress to the practicability of organizing an institution combining all its advantages and obviating these objections. I sincerely regret that in the act before me I can perceive none of those modifications of the bank charter which are necessary, in my opinion, to make it compatible with justice, with sound policy, or with the Constitution of our country.

The present corporate body, denominated the president, directors, and company of the Bank of the United States, will have existed at the time this act is intended to take effect twenty years. It enjoys an exclusive privilege of banking under the authority of the General Government, a monopoly of its favor and support, and, as a necessary consequence, almost a monopoly of the foreign and domestic exchange. The powers, privileges, and favors bestowed upon it in the original charter, by increasing the value of the stock far above its par value, operated as a gratuity of many millions to the stockholders.

An apology may be found for the failure to guard against this result in the consideration that the effect of the original act of incorporation could not be certainly foreseen at the time of its passage. The act before me proposes another gratuity to the holders of the same stock, and in many cases to the same men, of at least seven millions more. This donation finds no apology in any uncertainty as to the effect of the act. On all hands it is conceded that its passage will increase at least 20 or 30 per cent more the market price of the stock, subject to the payment of the annuity of $200,000 per year secured by the act, thus adding in a moment one-fourth to its par value. It is not our own citizens only who are to receive the bounty of our Government. More than eight millions of the stock of this bank are held by foreigners. By this act the American Republic proposes virtually to make them a present of some millions of dollars. For these gratuities to foreigners and to some of our own opulent citizens the act secures no equivalent whatever. They are the certain gains of the present stockholders under the operation of this act, after making full allowance for the payment of the bonus.

Every monopoly and all exclusive privileges are granted at the expense of the public, which ought to receive a fair equivalent. The many millions which this act proposes to bestow on the stockholders of the existing bank must come directly or indirectly out of the earnings of the American people. It is due to them, therefore, if their Government sell monopolies and exclusive privileges, that they should at least exact for them as much as they are worth in open market. The value of the monopoly in this case may be correctly ascertained. The twenty-eight millions of stock would probably be at an advance of 50 per cent, and command in market at least $42,000,000, subject to the payment of the present bonus. The present value of the monopoly, therefore, is $17,000,000, and this the act proposes to sell for three millions, payable in fifteen annual installments of $200,000 each.

It is not conceivable how the present stockholders can have any claim to the special favor of the Government. The present corporation has enjoyed its monopoly during the period stipulated in the original contract. If we must have such a corporation, why should not the Government sell out the whole stock and thus secure to the people the full market value of the privileges granted? Why should not Congress create and sell twenty-eight millions of stock, incorporating the purchasers with all the powers and privileges secured in this act and putting the premium upon the sales into the Treasury?

But this act does not permit competition in the purchase of this monopoly. It seems to be predicated on the erroneous idea that the present stockholders have a prescriptive right not only to the favor but to the bounty of Government. It appears that more than a fourth part of the stock is held by foreigners and the residue is held by a few hundred of our own citizens, chiefly of the richest class. For their benefit does this act exclude the whole American people from competition in the purchase of this monopoly and dispose of it for many millions less than it is worth. This seems the less excusable because some of our citizens not now stockholders petitioned that the door of competition might be opened, and offered to take a charter on terms much more favorable to the Government and country.

But this proposition, although made by men whose aggregate wealth is believed to be equal to all the private stock in the existing bank, has been set aside, and the bounty of our Government is proposed to be again bestowed on the few who have been fortunate enough to secure the stock and at this moment wield the power of the existing institution. I can not perceive the justice or policy of this course. If our Government must sell monopolies, it would seem to be its duty to take nothing less than their full value, and if gratuities must be made once in fifteen or twenty years let them not be bestowed on the subjects of a foreign government nor upon a designated and favored class of men in our own country. It is but justice and good policy, as far as the nature of the case will admit, to confine our favors to our own fellow-citizens, and let each in his turn enjoy an opportunity to profit by our bounty. In the bearings of the act before me upon these points I find ample reasons why it should not become a law. . . .

The bank is professedly established as an agent of the executive branch of the Government, and its constitutionality is maintained on that ground. Neither upon the propriety of present action nor upon the provisions of this act was the Executive consulted. It has had no opportunity to say that it neither needs nor wants an agent clothed with such powers and favored by such exemptions. There is nothing in its legitimate functions which makes it necessary or proper. Whatever interest or influence, whether public or private, has given birth to this act, it can not be found either in the wishes or necessities of the executive department, by which present action is deemed premature, and the powers conferred upon its agent not only unnecessary, but dangerous to the Government and country.

It is to be regretted that the rich and powerful too often bend the acts of government to their selfish purposes. Distinctions in society will always exist under every just government. Equality of talents, of education, or of wealth can not be produced by human institutions. In the full enjoyment of the gifts of Heaven and the fruits of superior industry, economy, and virtue, every man is equally entitled to protection by law; but when the laws undertake to add to these natural and just advantages artificial distinctions, to grant titles, gratuities, and exclusive privileges, to make the rich richer and the potent more powerful, the humble members of society—the farmers, mechanics, and laborers—who have neither the time nor the means of securing like favors to themselves, have a right to complain of the injustice of their Government. There are no necessary evils in government. Its evils exist only in its abuses. If it would confine itself to equal protection, and, as Heaven does its rains, shower its favors alike on the high and the low, the rich and the poor, it would be an unqualified blessing. In the act before me there seems to be a wide and unnecessary departure from these just principles.

Nor is our Government to be maintained or our Union preserved by invasions of the rights and powers of the several States. In thus attempting to make our General Government strong we make it weak. Its true strength consists in leaving individuals and States as much as possible to themselves—in making itself felt, not in its power, but in its beneficence; not in its control, but in its protection; not in binding the States more closely to the center, but leaving each to move unobstructed in its proper orbit.

Experience should teach us wisdom. Most of the difficulties our Government now encounters and most of the dangers which impend over our Union have sprung from an abandonment of the legitimate objects of Government by our national legislation, and the adoption of such principles as are embodied in this act. Many of our rich men have not been content with equal protection and equal benefits, but have besought us to make them richer by act of Congress. By attempting to gratify their desires we have in the results of our legislation arrayed section against section, interest against interest, and man against man, in a fearful commotion which threatens to shake the foundations of our Union. It is time to pause in our career to review our principles, and if possible revive that devoted patriotism and spirit of compromise which distinguished the sages of the Revolution and the fathers of our Union. If we can not at once, in justice to interests vested under improvident legislation, make our Government what it ought to be, we can at least take a stand against all new grants of monopolies and exclusive privileges, against any prostitution of our

Government to the advancement of the few at the expense of the many, and in favor of compromise and gradual reform in our code of laws and system of political economy.

I have now done my duty to my country. If sustained by my fellow-citizens, I shall be grateful and happy; if not, I shall find in the motives which impel me ample grounds for contentment and peace. In the difficulties which surround us and the dangers which threaten our institutions there is cause for neither dismay nor alarm. For relief and deliverance let us firmly rely on that kind Providence which I am sure watches with peculiar care over the destinies of our Republic, and on the intelligence and wisdom of our countrymen. Through *His* abundant goodness and *their* patriotic devotion our liberty and Union will be preserved.

Horace Mann: Report on Education for 1845

The growing democratization of American life in the Jacksonian era proceeded unevenly, with the greatest lag in the area of public education. There were five hundred thousand adult white illiterates in the United States in 1840; a decade later the number had increased to one million. Except in New England, there was a strong prejudice against free public education. The poor viewed free schools as a form of charity, while the wealthy vehemently objected to paying taxes to educate the masses. In the Middle States, only one child in seven went to a public school; in the West, the ratio was only slightly better; and in the South, public education was virtually unknown in the ante-bellum years. Even in New England, the Puritan school system inherited from the colonial period had deteriorated.

Horace Mann led the movement to bring America's schools into line with other branches of national development. A graduate of Brown University, Mann enjoyed a career as a successful lawyer and state legislator until 1837, when, at considerable financial sacrifice, he accepted the position of secretary of the newly-created Massachusetts Board of Education. In eleven years Mann transformed the state's school system into a model for the nation to follow. Using his legislative experience to advantage, he secured much larger appropriations for education, greatly increased salaries for teachers, and helped establish the first normal school at Lexington in 1839. After a trip to Europe in 1843, he introduced advanced German educational techniques that placed a new emphasis on learning rather than discipline, which helped make the classroom a more exciting and less terrifying place for students. Above all, Mann realized the relationship between public schools and democracy, and in his annual reports he set forth his emerging philosophy with an eloquence that won him national attention.   R.A.D.

The great, the all-important, the only important question still remains: By what spirit are our schools animated? Do they cultivate the higher faculties in the nature of childhood,—its conscience, its benevolence, a reverence for whatever is true and sacred? or are they only developing, upon a grander scale, the lower instincts and selfish tendencies of the race,—the desires which prompt men to seek, and the powers which enable them to secure, sensual ends,—wealth, luxury, preferment,—irrespective of the well-being of others? Knowing, as we do, that the foundations of national greatness can be laid only in the industry, the integrity, and the spiritual elevation of the people, are we equally sure that our schools are forming the character of the rising generation upon the everlasting principles of duty and humanity? or, on the other hand, are they only stimulating the powers which lead to a base pride of intellect, which prompt to the ostentation instead of the reality of virtue, and which give augury that life is to be spent only in selfish competitions between those who should be brethren? Above all others, must the children of a republic be fitted for society as well as for themselves. As each citizen is to participate in the power of governing others, it is an essential preliminary that he should be imbued with a feeling for the wants, and a sense of the rights, of those whom he is to govern; because the power of governing others, if guided by no higher motive than our own gratification, is the distinctive attribute of oppression; an attribute whose nature and whose wickedness are the same, whether exercised by one who calls himself a republican, or by one born an irresponsible despot. In a government like ours, each individual must think of the welfare of the State, as well as of the welfare of his own family, and, therefore, of the children of others as well as his own. It becomes, then, a momentous question, whether the children in our schools are educated in reference to themselves and their private interests only, or with a regard to the great social duties and prerogatives that await them in after-life. Are they so educated, that, when they grow up, they will make better philanthropists and Christians, or only grander savages? For, however loftily the intellect of man may have been gifted, however skillfully it may have been trained, if it be not guided by a sense of justice, a love of mankind, and a devotion to duty, its possessor is only a more splendid, as he is a more dangerous, barbarian.

John L. O'Sullivan: Manifest Destiny 1845

The unceasing flow of settlers to the frontier became a dominant theme of nineteenth-century American development. Westward expansion went on in good times and bad, slowing slightly during the depression years following the panic of 1837, but booming again in the early 1840's. By then, some ten thousand Americans had transformed Texas from a Mexican province into an independent republic which sought admission to the Union as a slave state. A smaller vanguard of frontiersmen had taken the long, rugged journey to Oregon, a territory jointly claimed by the United States and England, and to California, which was nominally under Mexican control but which was in a state of near-anarchy. The exaggerated tales the pioneers sent back to their friends and relatives in the East touched off a feverish desire to add these lands to the American domain and thus fulfill the continental vision of men like Thomas Jefferson and John Quincy Adams.

The Democrats, now led by the relatively obscure and colorless James K. Polk of Tennessee, shrewdly seized on the expansionist fervor in the election of 1844. Promising to secure Texas for the South and Oregon for the North, Polk offered a balanced program that caught his Whig opponent, Henry Clay, off guard. Clay desperately tried to catch up with the rising westward tide, but his innate caution led him to temper his campaign speeches to retain the support of easterners who opposed expansion. When Polk won an extremely narrow victory, outgoing President John Tyler chose to interpret it as a mandate for expansion and managed to secure congressional approval for the annexation of Texas just two days before his term ended. Polk then concentrated his efforts on winning a favorable settlement from the British in Oregon and on laying plans for the acquisition of California, which culminated in the Mexican War in 1846.

The foremost expansionist spokesman was an easterner, John L. O'Sullivan. Born in Ireland, O'Sullivan had migrated to America and settled down in New York City, where he founded the *United States Magazine and Democratic Review* as a vehicle for the Democratic Party. Like Thomas Paine, this talented newcomer proved able to express more eloquently than native-born Americans the popular yearnings of his time. In an article published in his journal in the summer of 1845, O'Sullivan coined the phrase "manifest destiny," which later generations came to accept as the perfect description of the feelings of national pride and restless adventure that pulsed through America on the eve of the War with Mexico.   R.A.D.

It is time now for opposition to the Annexation of Texas to cease, all further agitation of the waters of bitterness and strife, at least in connexion with this question,—even though it may perhaps be required of us as a necessary condition of the freedom of our institutions, that we must live on for ever in a state of unpausing struggle and excitement upon some subject of party division or other. But, in regard to Texas, enough has now been given to Party. It is time for the common duty of Patriotism to the Country to succeed;—or if this claim will not be recognized, it is at least time for common sense to acquiesce with decent grace in the inevitable and the irrevocable.

Texas is now ours. Already, before these words are written, her Convention has undoubtedly ratified the acceptance, by her Congress, of our proffered invitation into the Union; and made the requisite changes in her already republican form of constitution to adopt it to its future federal relations. Her star and her stripe may already be said to have taken their place in the glorious blazon of our common nationality; and the sweep of our eagle's wing already includes within its circuit the wide extent of her fair and fertile land. She is no longer to us a mere geographical space—a certain combination of coast, plain, mountain, valley, forest and stream. She is no longer to us a mere country on the map. She comes within the dear and sacred designation of Our Country; no longer a "*pays,*" she is a part of "*la patrie;*" and that which is at once a sentiment and a virtue, Patriotism, already begins to thrill for her too within the national heart. . . .

Why, were other reasoning wanting, in favor of now elevating this question of the reception of Texas into the Union, out of the lower region of our past party dissensions, up to its proper level of a high and broad nationality, it surely is to be found, found abundantly, in the manner in which other nations have undertaken to intrude themselves into it, between us and the proper parties to the case, in a spirit of hostile interference against us, for the avowed object of thwarting our policy and hampering our power, limiting our greatness and checking the fulfilment of our manifest destiny to overspread the continent allotted by Providence for the free development of our yearly multiplying millions. . . .

It is wholly untrue, and unjust to ourselves, the pretence that the Annexation has been a measure of spoliation, unrightful and unrighteous—of military conquest under forms of peace and law—

of territorial aggrandizement at the expense of justice, and justice due by a double sanctity to the weak. This view of the question is wholly unfounded, and has been before so amply refuted in these pages, as well as in a thousand other modes, that we shall not again dwell upon it. The independence of Texas was complete and absolute. It was an independence, not only in fact but of right. No obligation of duty towards Mexico tended in the least degree to restrain our right to effect the desired recovery of the fair province once our own—whatever motives of policy might have prompted a more deferential consideration of her feelings and her pride, as involved in the question. If Texas became peopled with an American population, it was by no contrivance of our government, but on the express invitation of that of Mexico herself; accompanied with such guaranties of State independence, and the maintenance of a federal system analogous to our own, as constituted a compact fully justifying the strongest measures of redress on the part of those afterwards deceived in this guaranty, and sought to be enslaved under the yoke imposed by its violation. She was released, rightfully and absolutely released, from all Mexican allegiance, or duty of cohesion to the Mexican political body, by the acts and fault of Mexico herself, and Mexico alone. There never was a clearer case. It was not revolution; it was resistance to revolution; and resistance under such circumstances as left independence the necessary resulting state, caused by the abandonment of those with whom her former federal association had existed. What then can be more preposterous than all this clamor by Mexico and the Mexican interest, against Annexation, as a violation of any rights of hers, any duties of ours? . . .

Nor is there any just foundation of the charge that Annexation is a great pro-slavery measure—calculated to increase and perpetuate that institution. Slavery had nothing to do with it. . . . The country which was the subject of Annexation in this case, from its geographical position and relations, happens to be—or rather the portion of it now actually settled, happens to be—a slave country. But a similar process might have taken place in proximity to a different section of our Union; and indeed there is a great deal of Annexation yet to take place, within the life of the present generation, along the whole line of our northern border. Texas has been absorbed into the Union in the inevitable fulfillment of the general law which is rolling our population westward; the connexion of which with that ratio of growth in population which is destined within a hundred years to swell our numbers to the enormous population of *two hundred and fifty millions* (if not more), is too evident to leave us in doubt of the manifest design of Providence in regard to the occupation of this continent. It was disintegrated from Mexico in the natural course of events, by a process perfectly legitimate on its own part, blameless on ours; and in which all the censures due to wrong, perfidy and folly, rest on Mexico alone. And possessed as it was by a population which was in truth but a colonial detachment from our own, and which was still bound by myriad ties of the very heartstrings to its old relations, domestic and political, their incorporation into the Union was not only inevitable, but the most natural, right and proper thing in the world—and it is only astonishing that there should be any among ourselves to say it nay. . . .

California will, probably, next fall away from the loose adhesion which, in such a country as Mexico, holds a remote province in a slight equivocal kind of dependence on the metropolis. Imbecile and distracted, Mexico never can exert any real governmental authority over such a country. The impotence of the one and the distance of the other, must make the relation one of virtual independence; unless, by stunting the province of all natural growth, and forbidding that immigration which can alone develope its capabilities and fulfill the purposes of its creation, tyranny may retain a military dominion which is no government in the legitimate sense of the term. In the case of California this is now impossible. The Anglo-Saxon foot is already on its borders. Already the advance guard of the irresistible army of Anglo-Saxon emigration has begun to pour down upon it, armed with the plough and the rifle, and marking its trail with schools and colleges, courts and representative halls, mills and meeting-houses. A population will soon be in actual occupation of California, over which it will be idle for Mexico to dream of dominion. They will necessarily become independent. All this without agency of our government, without responsibility of our people—in the natural flow of events, the spontaneous working of principles, and the adaptation of the tendencies and wants of the human race to the elemental circumstances in the midst of which they find themselves placed. And they will have a right to independence—to self-government—to the possession of the homes conquered from the wilderness by their own labors and dangers, sufferings and sacrifices—a better and a truer right than the artificial title of sovereignty in Mexico a thousand miles distant, inheriting from Spain a title good only against those who have none better. Their right to independence will be the natural right of self-government belonging to any community strong enough to maintain it—distinct in position, origin and character, and free from any mutual obligations of membership of a common political body, binding it to others by the duty of loyalty and compact of public faith. This will be their title to independence; and by this title, there can be no doubt that the population now fast streaming down upon California will both assert and maintain that independence. Whether they will then attach themselves to our Union or not, is not to be predicted with any certainty. Unless the projected rail-road across the continent to the Pacific be carried into effect, perhaps they may not; though even in that case, the day is not distant when the Empires of the Atlantic and Pacific would again flow together into one, as soon as their inland border should approach each other. But that great work, colossal as appears the plan on its first suggestion, cannot remain long unbuilt. Its necessity for this very purpose of binding and holding together in its iron clasp our fast settling Pacific region with that of the Mississippi valley—the natural facility of the route—the ease with which any amount of labor for the construction can be drawn in from the overcrowded populations of Europe, to be paid in the lands made valuable by the progress of the work itself—and its immense utility to the commerce of the world with the whole eastern coast of Asia, alone almost sufficient for the support of such a road—these considerations give assurance that the day cannot be distant which shall witness the conveyance of the representatives from Oregon and California to Washington within less time than a few years ago was devoted to a similar journey by those from Ohio; while the magnetic telegraph will enable the editors of the "San Francisco Union," the "Astoria Evening Post," or the "Nootka Morning News" to set up in type the first half of the President's Inaugural, before the echoes of the latter half shall have died away beneath the lofty porch of the Capitol, as spoken from his lips.

Away, then, with all idle French talk of *balances of power* on the American Continent. There is no growth in Spanish America! Whatever progress of population there may be in the British Canadas, is only for their own early severance of their present colonial relation to the little island three thousand miles across the Atlantic; soon to be followed by Annexation, and destined to swell the still accumulating momentum of our progress. And whatsoever may hold the balance, though they should cast into the opposite scale all the bayonets and cannon, not only of France and England, but of Europe entire, how would it kick the beam against the simple solid weight of the two hundred and fifty or three hundred millions — and American millions — destined to gather beneath the flutter of the stripes and stars, in the fast hastening year of the Lord 1945?

Seneca Falls Declaration of Sentiments and Resolutions 1848

A wave of humanitarian reform swept across mid-nineteenth century America. Zealous men and women created a new prison system, secured humane treatment for the insane, attacked the national habit of overindulgence in alcohol, and formed a vigorous peace movement. The abolition of slavery gradually became their greatest concern, but in the course of this struggle the male leaders refused to grant an equal voice to women and thereby touched off a vigorous feminist crusade.

In 1840 delegates from all over the world came to London to attend a world antislavery convention. The American group included nine prominent women, among them Lucretia Mott, a Philadelphia Quaker active in many reforms, and Elizabeth Cady Stanton, a young girl from upstate New York who later led the temperance movement. Despite the protests of William Lloyd Garrison, the convention refused to permit women to attend the sessions, and Mrs. Mott and Mrs. Stanton returned to the United States determined to end the prevailing discrimination against women. Though a few individual women had gained an education and entered the professions, American society by and large regarded the female sex as inferior, denying women the right to vote, to own property, or to challenge male supremacy in politics or business. Lucretia Mott and Elizabeth Stanton became too involved in other reforms to advance the new cause in the early 1840's, but in 1848 they joined with other feminists and issued a call for a women's rights convention in Seneca Falls, New York, Mrs. Stanton's home town.

On July 19 over a hundred men and women attended the meeting (presided over, in an ironic display of male chauvinism, by James Mott, Lucretia's husband) and adopted a manifesto modeled after the Declaration of Independence. The delegates approved the resolutions unanimously except for one which called for the right of women to vote; Frederick Douglass, the Negro abolitionist, helped Mrs. Stanton win a narrow victory for what was then considered an extreme demand. Though contemporaries ridiculed it, the Declaration of Sentiments and Resolutions succeeded in giving the women's rights movement a solid base for its future growth in the United States. R.A.D.

DECLARATION OF SENTIMENTS

When, in the course of human events, it becomes necessary for one portion of the family of man to assume among the people of the earth a position different from that which they have hitherto occupied, but one to which the laws of nature and of nature's God entitle them, a decent respect to the opinions of mankind requires that they should declare the causes that impel them to such a course.

We hold these truths to be self-evident: that all men and women are created equal; that they are endowed by their Creator with certain inalienable rights; that among these are life, liberty, and the pursuit of happiness; that to secure these rights governments are instituted, deriving their just powers from the consent of the governed. Whenever any form of government becomes destructive of these ends, it is the right of those who suffer from it to refuse allegiance to it, and to insist upon the institution of a new government, laying its foundation on such principles, and organizing its powers in such form, as to them shall seem most likely to effect their safety and happiness. Prudence, indeed, will dictate that governments long established should not be changed for light and transient causes; and accordingly all experience hath shown that mankind are more disposed to suffer while evils are sufferable, than to right themselves by abolishing the forms to which they are accustomed. But when a long train of abuses and usurpations, pursuing invariably the same object, evinces a design to reduce them under absolute despotism, it is their duty to throw off such government, and to provide new guards for their future security. Such has been the patient sufferance of the women under this government, and such is now the necessity which constrains them to demand the equal station to which they are entitled.

The history of mankind is a history of repeated injuries and usurpations on the part of man toward woman, having in direct object the establishment of an absolute tyranny over her. To prove this, let facts be submitted to a candid world.

He has never permitted her to exercise her inalienable right to the elective franchise.

He has compelled her to submit to laws, in the formation of which she had no voice.

He has withheld from her rights which are given to the most ignorant and degraded men — both natives and foreigners.

Having deprived her of this first right of a citizen, the elective franchise, thereby leaving her without representation in the halls of legislation, he has oppressed her on all sides.

He has made her, if married, in the eye of the law, civilly dead.

He has taken from her all right in property, even to the wages she earns.

He has made her, morally, an irresponsible being, as she can commit many crimes with impunity, provided they be done in the presence of her husband. In the covenant of marriage, she is compelled to promise obedience to her husband, he becoming, to all intents and purposes, her master—the law giving him power to deprive her of her liberty, and to administer chastisement.

He has so framed the laws of divorce, as to what shall be the proper causes, and in case of separation, to whom the guardianship of the children shall be given, as to be wholly regardless of the happiness of women—the law, in all cases, going upon a false supposition of the supremacy of man, and giving all power into his hands.

After depriving her of all rights as a married woman, if single, and the owner of property, he has taxed her to support a government which recognizes her only when her property can be made profitable to it.

He has monopolized nearly all the profitable employments, and from those she is permitted to follow, she receives but a scanty remuneration. He closes against her all the avenues to wealth and distinction which he considers most honorable to himself. As a teacher of theology, medicine, or law, she is not known.

He has denied her the facilities for obtaining a thorough education, all colleges being closed against her.

He allows her in Church, as well as State, but a subordinate position, claiming Apostolic authority for her exclusion from the ministry, and, with some exceptions, from any public participation in the affairs of the Church.

He has created a false public sentiment by giving to the world a different code of morals for men and women, by which moral delinquencies which exclude women from society, are not only tolerated, but deemed of little account in man.

He has usurped the prerogative of Jehovah himself, claiming it as his right to assign for her a sphere of action, when that belongs to her conscience and to her God.

He has endeavored, in every way that he could, to destroy her

113

confidence in her own powers, to lessen her self-respect and to make her willing to lead a dependent and abject life.

Now, in view of this entire disfranchisement of one-half the people in this country, their social and religious degradation—in view of the unjust laws above mentioned, and because women do feel themselves aggrieved, oppressed, and fraudulently deprived of their most sacred rights, we insist that they have immediate admission to all the rights and privileges which belong to them as citizens of the United States.

In entering upon the great work before us, we anticipate no small amount of misconception, misrepresentation, and ridicule; but we shall use every instrumentality within our power to effect our object. We shall employ agents, circulate tracts, petition the State and National legislatures, and endeavor to enlist the pulpit and the press in our behalf. We hope this Convention will be followed by a series of Conventions embracing every part of the country.

RESOLUTIONS

Whereas, The great precept of nature is conceded to be, that "man shall pursue his own true and substantial happiness." Blackstone in his Commentaries remarks, that this law of Nature being coeval with mankind, and dictated by God himself, is of course superior in obligation to any other. It is binding over all the globe, in all countries and at all times; no human laws are of any validity if contrary to this, and such of them as are valid, derive all their force, and all their validity, and all their authority, mediately and immediately, from this original; therefore,

Resolved, That all laws which prevent woman from occupying such a station in society as her conscience shall dictate, or which place her in a position inferior to that of man, are contrary to the great precept of nature, and therefore of no force or authority.

Resolved, That woman is man's equal—was intended to be so by the Creator, and the highest good of the race demands that she should be recognized as such.

Resolved, That the women of this country ought to be enlightened in regard to the laws under which they live, that they may no longer publish their degradation by declaring themselves satisfied with their present position, nor their ignorance, by asserting that they have all the rights they want.

Resolved, That inasmuch as man, while claiming for himself intellectual superiority, does accord to woman moral superiority, it is pre-eminently his duty to encourage her to speak and teach, as she has an opportunity, in all religious assemblies.

Resolved, That the same amount of virtue, delicacy, and refinement of behavior that is required of woman in the social state, should also be required of man, and the same transgressions should be visited with equal severity on both man and woman.

Resolved, That the objection of indelicacy and impropriety, which is so often brought against woman when she addresses a public audience, comes with a very ill-grace from those who encourage, by their attendance, her appearance on the stage, in the concert, or in feats of the circus.

Resolved, That woman has too long rested satisfied in the circumscribed limits which corrupt customs and a perverted application of the Scriptures have marked out for her, and that it is time she should move in the enlarged sphere which her great Creator has assigned her.

Resolved, That it is the duty of the women of this country to secure to themselves their sacred right to the elective franchise.

Resolved, That the equality of human rights results necessarily from the fact of the identity of the race in capabilities and responsibilities.

Resolved, That the speedy success of our cause depends upon the zealous and untiring efforts of both men and women, for the overthrow of the monopoly of the pulpit, and for the securing to women an equal participation with men in the various trades, professions, and commerce.

Resolved, therefore, That, being invested by the Creator with the same capabilities, and the same consciousness of responsibility for their exercise, it is demonstrably the right and duty of woman, equally with man, to promote every righteous cause by every righteous means; and especially in regard to the great subjects of morals and religion, it is self-evidently her right to participate with her brother in teaching them, both in private and in public, by writing and by speaking, by any instrumentalities proper to be used, and in any assemblies proper to be held; and this being a self-evident truth growing out of the divinely implanted principles of human nature, any custom or authority adverse to it, whether modern or wearing the hoary sanction of antiquity, is to be regarded as a self-evident falsehood, and at war with mankind.

John C. Calhoun: Speech on the Compromise of 1850

The Mexican War renewed the controversy over the expansion of slavery. As early as August, 1846, Representative David Wilmot of Pennsylvania presented a resolution in Congress to ban slavery from all territory won from Mexico. Southerners blocked the Wilmot Proviso in the Senate, but the issue continued to fester as the United States acquired California and the intervening New Mexico territory in the Treaty of Guadalupe Hidalgo. Politicians tried to procrastinate, dodging the issue in the election of 1848, but the discovery of gold in the American River near Sutter's Mill and the tumultuous rush of people to California made a decision imperative. In November, 1849, California, with a population of over one hundred thousand, adopted a constitution banning slavery and prepared a formal request for admission into the Union as a free state. When Congress convened the next month, Senator Henry Clay, now in his seventies and resigned to failure in his relentless quest for the Presidency, rose above partisan politics to offer a compromise to heal the sectional breach. He proposed that California be admitted as a free state, that the rest of the Southwest be organized as a territory without mention of slavery, and, as a concession to the South, that Congress enact a stringent fugitive slave law to insure the return of runaway Negroes.

Moderates rallied behind Clay's proposals, but ardent southerners saw in them only one more concession to northern dominance. A few, including Jefferson Davis of Mississippi, spoke out against the compromise, but most southerners waited to hear the verdict of their great champion, John C. Calhoun of South Carolina. Ill and feeble, Calhoun had been unable to attend the Senate session when Clay spoke, but he was determined to give the South's reply. In late February, 1850, he began dictating his speech and his associates quickly spread the word that on Monday, March 4, Calhoun would appear before the Senate. Every senator except one was in the chamber when Calhoun entered, leaning on the arm of a colleague, and they were shocked at his emaciated appearance. Too weak to speak himself, he asked Senator James M. Mason of Virginia to read the address. As Mason began, Calhoun sat grimly like a ghost from the past, his mane of long gray hair flowing over a black cloak. Only the eyes seemed alive, as intense and defiant as his uncompromising words.

Three-and-a-half weeks later, Calhoun was dead. His objections had slowed, but did not halt, the adoption of the compromise of 1850. In the summer Congress approved Clay's proposals one by one, thereby achieving a tenuous sectional peace. But Calhoun's brilliant last speech had revealed the depth of the split between North and South. R.A.D.

I have, Senators, believed from the first that the agitation of the subject of slavery would, if not prevented by some timely and effective measure, end in disunion. Entertaining this opinion, I have, on all proper occasions, endeavored to call the attention of each of the two great parties which divide the country to adopt some measure to prevent so great a disaster, but without success. The agitation has been permitted to proceed, with almost no attempt to resist it, until it has reached a period when it can no longer be disguised or denied that the Union is in danger. You have thus had forced upon you the greatest and the gravest question that can ever come under your consideration: How can the Union be preserved?

To give a satisfactory answer to this mighty question, it is indispensable to have an accurate and thorough knowledge of the nature and the character of the cause by which the Union is endangered. Without such knowledge it is impossible to pronounce, with any certainty, by what measure it can be saved; just as it would be impossible for a physician to pronounce, in the case of some dangerous disease, with any certainty by what remedy the patient could be saved, without familiar knowledge of the nature and character of the cause of the disease. The first question, then, presented for consideration, in the investigation I propose to make, in order to obtain such knowledge, is: What is it that has endangered the Union?

To this question there can be but one answer: that the immediate cause is the almost universal discontent which pervades all the States composing the southern section of the Union. This widely-extended discontent is not of recent origin. It commenced with the agitation of the slavery question, and has been increasing ever since. The next question, going one step further back, is: What has caused this widely-diffused and almost universal discontent?

It is a great mistake to suppose, as is by some, that it originated with demagogues, who excited the discontent with the intention of aiding their personal advancement, or with the disappointed ambition of certain politicians, who resorted to it as the means of retrieving their fortunes. On the contrary, all the great political influences of the section were arrayed against excitement, and exerted to the utmost to keep the people quiet. The great mass of the people of the South were divided, as in the other section, into Whigs and Democrats. The leaders and the presses of both parties

in the South were very solicitous to prevent excitement and to preserve quiet; because it was seen that the effects of the former
would necessarily tend to weaken, if not destroy, the political
ties which united them with their respective parties in the other
section. Those who know the strength of party ties will readily
appreciate the immense force which this cause exerted against
agitation and in favor of preserving quiet. But, as great as it was,
it was not sufficiently so to prevent the wide-spread discontent
which now pervades the section. No; some cause, far deeper and
more powerful than the one supposed, must exist, to account for
discontent so wide and deep. The question, then, recurs: What is
the cause of this discontent? It will be found in the belief of the
people of the southern States, as prevalent as the discontent itself, that they cannot remain, as things now are, consistently with
honor and safety, in the Union. The next question to be considered is: What has caused this belief?

One of the causes is, undoubtedly, to be traced to the long-con-
tinued agitation of the slave question on the part of the North,
and the many aggressions which they have made on the rights
of the South during the time. I will not enumerate them at present,
as it will be done hereafter, in its proper place.

There is another, lying back of it, with which this is intimately
connected, that may be regarded as the great and primary cause.
That is to be found in the fact that the equilibrium between the
two sections in the Government, as it stood when the constitution
was ratified and the Government put in action, has been destroyed.
At that time there was nearly a perfect equilibrium between the
two, which afforded ample means to each to protect itself against
the aggression of the other; but, as it now stands, one section has
the exclusive power of controlling the Government, which leaves
the other without any adequate means of protecting itself against
its encroachment and oppression. . . .

That the [Federal] Government claims, and practically maintains,
the right to decide in the last resort as to the extent of its powers,
will scarcely be denied by any one conversant with the political
history of the country. That it also claims the right to resort to
force to maintain whatever power she claims, against all opposition, is equally certain. Indeed it is apparent, from what we daily
hear, that this has become the prevailing and fixed opinion of a
great majority of the community. Now, I ask, what limitation can

possibly be placed upon the powers of a Government claiming and exercising such rights? And, if none can be, how can the separate governments of the States maintain and protect the powers reserved to them by the Constitution, or the people of the several States maintain those which are reserved to them, and among others, the sovereign powers by which they ordained and established, not only their separate State constitutions and governments, but also the Constitution and Government of the United States? But, if they have no constitutional means of maintaining them against the right claimed by this Government, it necessarily follows that they hold them at its pleasure and discretion, and that all the powers of the system are in reality concentrated in it. It also follows that the character of the Government has been changed, in consequence, from a Federal Republic, as it originally came from the hands of its framers, and that it has been changed into a great national consolidated democracy. It has indeed, at present, all the characteristics of the latter, and not one of the former, although it still retains its outward form.

The result of the whole of these causes combined is, that the North has acquired a decided ascendancy over every department of this Government, and through it a control over all the powers of the system. A single section, governed by the will of the numerical majority, has now, in fact, the control of the Government and the entire powers of the system. What was once a constitutional Federal Republic is now converted, in reality, into one as absolute as that of the Autocrat of Russia, and as despotic in its tendency as any absolute Government that ever existed.

As, then, the North has the absolute control over the Government, it is manifest that on all questions between it and the South, where there is a diversity of interests, the interests of the latter will be sacrificed to the former, however oppressive the effects may be, as the South possesses no means by which it can resist through the action of the Government. But if there was no question of vital importance to the South, in reference to which there was a diversity of views between the two sections, this state of things might be endured without the hazard of destruction to the South. But such is not the fact. There is a question of vital importance to the southern section, in reference to which the views and feelings of the two sections are as opposite and hostile as they can possibly be.

I refer to the relation between the two races in the southern section, which constitutes a vital portion of her social organization. Every portion of the North entertains views and feelings more or less hostile to it. Those most opposed and hostile regard it as a sin, and consider themselves under the most sacred obligation to use every effort to destroy it. Indeed to the extent that they conceive they have power, they regard themselves as implicated in the sin, and responsible for suppressing it by the use of all and every means. Those less opposed and hostile, regard it as a crime — an offence against humanity, as they call it; and although not so fanatical, feel themselves bound to use all efforts to effect the same object; while those who are least opposed and hostile, regard it as a blot and a stain on the character of what they call the nation, and feel themselves accordingly bound to give it no countenance or support. On the contrary, the southern section, regards the relation as one which cannot be destroyed without subjecting the two races to the greatest calamity, and the section to poverty, desolation, and wretchedness; and accordingly they feel bound by every consideration of interest and safety, to defend it.

This hostile feeling on the part of the North towards the social organization of the South long lay dormant, but it only required some cause to act on those who felt most intensely that they were responsible for its continuance, to call it into action. The increasing power of this Government, and of the control of the northern section over all its departments, furnished the cause. It was this which made an impression on the minds of many that there was little or no restraint to prevent the Government from doing whatever it might choose to do. This was sufficient of itself to put the most fanatical portion of the North in action for the purpose of destroying the existing relation between the two races in the South. . . .

It is a great mistake to suppose that disunion can be effected by a single blow. The cords which bind these States together in one common Union are far too numerous and powerful for that. Disunion must be the work of time. It is only through a long process, and successively, that the cords can be snapped, until the whole fabric falls asunder. Already the agitation of the slavery question has snapped some of the most important, and has greatly weakened all the others, as I shall proceed to show.

The cords that bind the States together are not only many, but various in character. Some are spiritual or ecclesiastical; some political; others social. Some appertain to the benefit conferred by the Union, and others to the feeling of duty and obligation.

The strongest of those of a spiritual and ecclesiastical nature consisted in the unity of the great religious denominations, all of which originally embraced the whole Union. All these denominations, with the exception, perhaps, of the Catholics, were organized very much upon the principle of our political institutions; beginning with smaller meetings corresponding with the political divisions of the country, their organization terminated in one great central assemblage, corresponding very much with the character of Congress. At these meetings the principal clergymen and lay members of the respective denominations from all parts of the Union met to transact business relating to their common concerns. It was not confined to what appertained to the doctrines and discipline of the respective denominations, but extended to plans for disseminating the Bible, establishing missionaries, distributing tracts, and of establishing presses for the publication of tracts, newspapers, and periodicals, with a view of diffusing religious information, and for the support of the doctrines and creeds of the denomination. All this combined, contributed greatly to strengthen the bonds of the Union. The strong ties which held each denomination together formed a strong cord to hold the whole Union together; but, as powerful as they were, they have not been able to resist the explosive effect of slavery agitation. . . .

The strongest cord of a political character consists of the many and strong ties that have held together the two great parties, which have, with some modifications, existed from the beginning of the Government. They both extended to every portion of the Union, and strongly contributed to hold all its parts together. But this powerful cord has fared no better than the spiritual. It resisted for a long time the explosive tendency of the agitation, but has finally snapped under its force—if not entirely, in a great measure. Nor is there one of the remaining cords which have not been greatly weakened. To this extent the Union has already been destroyed by agitation, in the only way it can be, by snapping asunder and weakening the cords which bind it together.

If the agitation goes on, the same force, acting with increased intensity, as has been shown, will finally snap every cord, when nothing will be left to hold the States together except force. But surely that can, with no propriety of language, be called a union, when the only means by which the weaker is held connected with the stronger portion is force. It may, indeed, keep them connected; but the connection will partake much more of the character of subjugation, on the part of the weaker to the stronger, than the union of free, independent, and sovereign States, in one confederation, as they stood in the early stages of the Government, and which only is worthy of the sacred name of union.

. . . I return to the question with which I commenced, How can the Union be saved? There is but one way by which it can with any certainty; and that is, by a full and final settlement, on the principle of justice, of all the questions at issue between the two sections. The South asks for justice, simple justice, and less she ought not to take. She has no compromise to offer but the Constitution, and no concession or surrender to make. She has already surrendered so much that she has little left to surrender. Such a settlement would go to the root of the evil, and remove all cause of discontent, by satisfying the South she could remain honorably and safely in the Union, and thereby restore the harmony and fraternal feelings between the sections which existed anterior to the Missouri agitation. Nothing else can, with any certainty, finally and forever settle the questions at issue, terminate agitation, and save the Union.

But can this be done? Yes, easily; not by the weaker party, for it can of itself do nothing—not even protect itself—but by the stronger. The North has only to will it to accomplish it—to do justice by conceding to the South an equal right in the acquired territory, and to do her duty by causing the stipulations relative to fugitive slaves to be faithfully fulfilled—to cease the agitation of the slave question, and to provide for the insertion of a provision in the Constitution, by an amendment, which will restore to the South in substance the power she possessed of protecting herself, before the equilibrium between the sections was destroyed by the action of this Government. There will be no difficulty in devising such a provision—one that will protect the South, and which at the same time will improve and strengthen the Government, instead of impairing and weakening it.

But will the North agree to do this? It is for her to answer this question. But, I will say, she cannot refuse, if she has half the love of the Union which she professes to have, or without justly exposing herself to the charge that her love of power and aggrandizement is far greater than her love of the Union. At all events, the responsibility of saving the Union rests on the North, and not the South. The South cannot save it by any act of hers, and the North may save it without any sacrifice whatever, unless to do justice, and to perform her duties under the Constitution should be regarded by her as a sacrifice.

It is time, Senators, that there should be an open and manly avowal on all sides, as to what is intended to be done. If the question is not now settled, it is uncertain whether it ever can hereafter be; and we, as the representatives of the States of this Union, regarded as governments, should come to a distinct understanding as to our respective views, in order to ascertain whether the great questions at issue can be settled or not. If you, who represent the stronger portion, cannot agree to settle them on the broad principle of justice and duty, say so, and let the States we both represent agree to separate and part in peace. If you are unwilling we should part in peace, tell us so, and we shall know what to do, when you reduce the question to submission or resistance. If you remain silent, you will compel us to infer by your acts what you intend. In that case, California will become the test question. If you admit her, under all the difficulties that oppose her admission, you compel us to infer that you intend to exclude us from the whole of the acquired territories, with the intention of destroying irretrievably the equilibrium between the two sections. We would be blind not to perceive, in that case, that your real objects are power and aggrandizement, and infatuated not to act accordingly.

I have now, Senators, done my duty in expressing my opinions fully, freely, and candidly, on this solemn occasion. In doing so, I have been governed by the motives which have governed me in all the stages of the agitation of the slavery question since its commencement. I have exerted myself, during the whole period, to arrest it, with the intention of saving the Union, if it could be done; and, if it could not, to save the section where it has pleased Providence to cast my lot, and which I sincerely believe has justice and the Constitution on its side. Having faithfully done my duty to the best of my ability, both to the Union and my section, throughout this agitation. I shall have the consolation, let what will come, that I am free from all responsibility.

John Brown: Last Speech in Court 1859

Tension between the North and the South was approaching the breaking point in 1859. Five years earlier, the Kansas-Nebraska Act had re-opened the issue of the expansion of slavery; and even though Kansas eventually became a free state, the bitter contest there between northern and southern settlers greatly intensified sectional feelings. In this delicate situation, John Brown, who earlier had killed five pro-slavery men in a raid at Pottawatomie Creek in Kansas, attacked the federal arsenal at Harpers Ferry, Virginia, in a futile effort to launch a slave rebellion.

Within two days Virginia militia and federal troops commanded by Colonel Robert E. Lee decimated the small band of raiders and took the wounded Brown prisoner. A week later he went on trial for murder and treason in a Virginia court. He was quickly found guilty and sentenced to hang, thus providing abolitionists with a martyr who was far more dangerous to the South in death than he had ever been while alive.

John Brown was a fanatic. Born in Connecticut, he was the son of a roving father and a mother who died insane. A restless, unstable man himself, Brown led a nomadic life, marrying twice and fathering twenty children, engaging in a series of business ventures in five states that all ended disastrously. In the 1850's, he became caught up in the abolitionist movement and was driven by a compulsion to free the slaves personally. In 1858 he conducted a raid from Kansas into Missouri, captured eleven slaves, and took them to Canada for freedom. He conceived of the attack on Harpers Ferry as the signal for a massive slave uprising in which Negroes would flock to his banner, and he would march down the Appalachians into the heart of the South to wipe out slavery by the sword.

At the end of the trial when the judge was about to pass sentence, he asked the prisoner if he had anything to say. Rising from the cot where he had lain throughout the trial, Brown spoke slowly and deliberately for five minutes. It was his final chance to appeal to the world and he made the most of it. In the North his words transformed the horror at his deeds into a new respect for his cause and led Ralph Waldo Emerson to call him a "new saint" who "will make the gallows glorious like the cross."   R.A.D.

I have, may it please the Court, a few words to say.

In the first place, I deny everything but what I have all along admitted,—the design on my part to free the slaves. I intended certainly to have made a clean thing of that matter, as I did last winter, when I went into Missouri and there took slaves without the snapping of a gun on either side, moved them through the country, and finally left them in Canada. I designed to have done the same thing again, on a larger scale. That was all I intended. I never did intend murder, or treason, or the destruction of property, or to excite or incite slaves to rebellion, or to make insurrection.

I have another objection; and that is, it is unjust that I should suffer such a penalty. Had I interfered in the manner which I admit, and which I admit has been fairly proved (for I admire the truthfulness and candor of the greater portion of the witnesses who have testified in this case),—had I so interfered in behalf of the rich, the powerful, the intelligent, the so-called great, or in behalf of any of their friends,—either father, mother, brother, sister, wife, or children, or any of that class,—and suffered and sacrificed what I have in this interference, it would have been all right; and every man in this court would have deemed it an act worthy of reward rather than punishment.

This court acknowledges, as I suppose, the validity of the law of God. I see a book kissed here which I suppose to be the Bible, or at least the New Testament. That teaches me that all things whatsoever I would that men should do to me, I should do even so to them. It teaches me, further, to "remember them that are in bonds, as bound with them." I endeavored to act up to that instruction. I say, I am yet too young to understand that God is any respecter of persons. I believe that to have interfered as I have done—as I have always freely admitted I have done—in behalf of His despised poor, was not wrong, but right. Now, if it is deemed necessary that I should forfeit my life for the furtherance of the ends of justice, and mingle my blood further with the blood of my children and with the blood of millions in this slave country whose rights are disregarded by wicked, cruel, and unjust enactments,—I submit; so let it be done!

Let me say one word further.

I feel entirely satisfied with the treatment I have received on my trial. Considering all the circumstances, it has been more generous than I expected. But I feel no consciousness of guilt. I have stated from the first what was my intention, and what was not. I never had any design against the life of any person, nor any disposition to commit treason, or excite slaves to rebel, or make any general insurrection. I never encouraged any man to do so, but always discouraged any idea of that kind.

Let me say, also, a word in regard to the statements made by some of those connected with me. I hear it has been stated by some of them that I have induced them to join me. But the contrary is true. I do not say this to injure them, but as regretting their weakness. There is not one of them but joined me of his own accord, and the greater part of them at their own expense. A number of them I never saw, and never had a word of conversation with, till the day they came to me; and that was for the purpose I have stated.

Now I have done.

Abraham Lincoln: First Inaugural Address 1861

The Republican victory in the election of 1860 touched off a series of events which culminated in civil war the following April. Although Abraham Lincoln received only about 40 per cent of the popular vote, he swept the North and the West and thus won a large margin in the electoral college. The deep South, convinced that the Republicans meant to abolish slavery, made good its threat to secede from the Union; and President James Buchanan, a weak man in an impossible situation, made no effort to halt the exodus of southern states during the final four months of his term. Lincoln received contradictory advice on how to handle the secession crisis. A group of militants within his party, led by Senator Charles Sumner of Massachusetts and Salmon P. Chase, incoming Secretary of the Treasury, demanded that the President-elect offer no concessions to the South; while William Seward, Lincoln's chief rival for the Republican nomination in 1860 and his choice as Secretary of State, pleaded for a conciliatory policy. While Lincoln refused to disclose his intentions publicly, he made it clear that he would not compromise on the issue of slavery in the territories. Hoping to prevent Virginia and the border states from joining the newly formed Confederacy, he kept searching for a way to preserve the Union short of war.

In mid-February the President-elect left his home in Springfield for the long train trip to Washington. In speeches along the way, Lincoln continually stressed his desire to keep the nation intact, but gave no hint of how he planned to proceed once in office. Rumors of a plot against his life forced him to enter the nation's capital in disguise during the early hours of the morning. He went to Willard's Hotel where he waited nine more days to take the oath of office while the sectional crisis intensified.

On March 4 outgoing President Buchanan rode with Lincoln in an open carriage to the steps of the Capitol for the inauguration ceremony. Twenty-five thousand people were on hand, along with a large military detachment, complete with sharpshooters hidden on the roofs of nearby buildings. Lincoln had written his speech a month before in Springfield, but he had made a number of changes, many at Seward's request, in an effort to appeal to the South. Wearing steel spectacles, Lincoln read from his manuscript in a loud, shrill voice and then took the oath from Chief Justice Roger Taney. Although his words failed to conciliate the South, he did succeed in putting forth the case for the Union with simple eloquence.

R.A.D.

In compliance with a custom as old as the Government itself, I appear before you to address you briefly, and to take in your presence the oath prescribed by the Constitution of the United States to be taken by the President "before he enters on the execution of his office." . . .

Apprehension seems to exist among the people of the Southern States that by the accession of a Republican administration their property and their peace and personal security are to be endangered. There has never been any reasonable cause for such apprehension. Indeed, the most ample evidence to the contrary has all the while existed and been open to their inspection. It is found in nearly all the published speeches of him who now addresses you. I do but quote from one of those speeches when I declare that—

I have no purpose, directly or indirectly, to interfere with the institution of slavery in the States where it exists. I believe I have no lawful right to do so, and I have no inclination to do so. . . .

I now reiterate these sentiments, and in doing so I only press upon the public attention the most conclusive evidence of which the case is susceptible that the property, peace, and security of no section are to be in any wise endangered by the now incoming administration. I add, too, that all the protection which, consistently with the Constitution and the laws, can be given will be cheerfully given to all the States when lawfully demanded, for whatever cause —as cheerfully to one section as to another. . . .

I take the official oath to-day with no mental reservations and with no purpose to construe the Constitution or laws by any hypercritical rules; and while I do not choose now to specify particular acts of Congress as proper to be enforced, I do suggest that it will be much safer for all, both in official and private stations, to conform to and abide by all those acts which stand unrepealed than to violate any of them trusting to find impunity in having them held to be unconstitutional. . . .

A disruption of the Federal Union, heretofore only menaced, is now formidably attempted.

I hold that in contemplation of universal law and of the Constitution the Union of these States is perpetual. Perpetuity is implied, if not expressed, in the fundamental law of all national governments. It is safe to assert that no government proper ever had a provision in its organic law for its own termination. Continue to execute all the express provisions of our National Constitution, and the Union will endure forever, it being impossible to destroy it except by some action not provided for in the instrument itself.

Again: If the United States be not a government proper, but an association of States in the nature of contract merely, can it, as a contract, be peaceably unmade by less than all the parties who made it? One party to a contract may violate it—break it, so to speak—but does it not require all to lawfully rescind it?

Descending from these general principles, we find the proposition that in legal contemplation the Union is perpetual confirmed by the history of the Union itself. The Union is much older than the Constitution. It was formed, in fact, by the Articles of Association in 1774. It was matured and continued by the Declaration of Independence in 1776. It was further matured, and the faith of all the then thirteen States expressly plighted and engaged that it should be perpetual, by the Articles of Confederation in 1778. And finally, in 1787, one of the declared objects for ordaining and establishing the Constitution was *"to form a more perfect Union."*

But if destruction of the Union by one or by a part only of the States be lawfully possible, the Union is *less* perfect than before the Constitution, having lost the vital element of perpetuity.

It follows from these views that no State upon its own mere motion can lawfully get out of the Union; that *resolves* and *ordinances* to that effect are legally void, and that acts of violence within any State or States against the authority of the United States are insurrectionary or revolutionary, according to circumstances.

I therefore consider that in view of the Constitution and the laws the Union is unbroken, and to the extent of my ability, I shall take care, as the Constitution itself expressly enjoins upon me, that the laws of the Union be faithfully executed in all the States. Doing this I deem to be only a simple duty on my part, and I shall perform it so far as practicable unless my rightful masters, the American people, shall withhold the requisite means or in some authoritative manner direct the contrary. I trust this will not be regarded as a menace, but only as the declared purpose of the Union that it *will* constitutionally defend and maintain itself.

In doing this there needs to be no bloodshed or violence, and there shall be none unless it be forced upon the national authority. The power confided to me will be used to hold, occupy, and possess the property and places belonging to the Government and to collect the duties and imposts; but beyond what may be necessary for these objects, there will be no invasion, no using of force against or among the people anywhere. Where hostility to the United States in any interior locality shall be so great and universal as to prevent competent resident citizens from holding the Federal offices, there will be no attempt to force obnoxious strangers among the people for that object. While the strict legal right may exist in the Government to enforce the exercise of these offices, the attempt to do so would be so irritating and so nearly impracticable withal that I deem it better to forego for the time the uses of such offices.

The mails, unless repelled, will continue to be furnished in all parts of the Union. So far as possible the people everywhere shall have that sense of perfect security which is most favorable to calm thought and reflection. The course here indicated will be followed unless current events and experience shall show a modification or change to be proper, and in every case and exigency my best discretion will be exercised, according to circumstances actually existing and with a view and a hope of a peaceful solution of the national troubles and the restoration of fraternal sympathies and affections.

That there are persons in one section or another who seek to destroy the Union at all events and are glad of any pretext to do it I will neither affirm nor deny; but if there be such, I need address no word to them. To those, however, who really love the Union may I not speak?

Before entering upon so grave a matter as the destruction of our national fabric, with all its benefits, its memories, and its hopes, would it not be wise to ascertain precisely why we do it? Will you hazard so desperate a step while there is any possibility that any portion of the ills you fly from have no real existence? Will you, while the certain ills you fly to are greater than all the real ones you fly from, will you risk the commission of so fearful a mistake?

All profess to be content in the Union if all constitutional rights can be maintained. Is it true, then, that any right plainly written in the Constitution has been denied? I think not. Happily, the human mind is so constituted that no party can reach to the audacity of doing this. Think, if you can, of a single instance in which a plainly written provision of the Constitution has ever been denied. If by the mere force of numbers a majority should deprive a minority of any clearly written constitutional right, it might in a moral point of view justify revolution; certainly would if such right were a vital one. But such is not our case. All the vital rights of minorities and of individuals are so plainly assured to them by affirmations and negations, guaranties and prohibitions, in the Constitution that controversies never arise concerning them. But no organic law can ever be framed with a provision specifically applicable to every question which may occur in practical administration. No foresight can anticipate nor any document of reasonable length contain express provisions for all possible questions. Shall fugitives from labor be surrendered by national or by State authority? The Constitution does not expressly say. *May* Congress prohibit slavery in the Territories? The Constitution does not expressly say. *Must* Congress protect slavery in the Territories? The Constitution does not expressly say.

From questions of this class spring all our constitutional controversies, and we divide upon them into majorities and minorities. If the minority will not acquiesce, the majority must, or the Government must cease. There is no other alternative, for continuing the Government is acquiescence on one side or the other.

If a minority in such case will secede rather than acquiesce, they make a precedent which in turn will divide and ruin them, for a minority of their own will secede from them whenever a majority refuses to be controlled by such minority. For instance, why may not any portion of a new confederacy a year or two hence arbitrarily secede again, precisely as portions of the present Union now claim to secede from it? All who cherish disunion sentiments are now being educated to the exact temper of doing this.

Is there such perfect identity of interests among the States to compose a new Union as to produce harmony only and prevent renewed secession?

Plainly the central idea of secession is the essence of anarchy. A majority held in restraint by constitutional checks and limitations, and always changing easily with deliberate changes of popular opinions and sentiments, is the only true sovereign of a free people. Whoever rejects it does of necessity fly to anarchy or to despotism. Unanimity is impossible. The rule of a minority, as a permanent arrangement, is wholly inadmissable; so that, rejecting the majority principle, anarchy or despotism in some form is all that is left.

I do not forget the position assumed by some that constitutional questions are to be decided by the Supreme Court, nor do I deny that such decisions must be binding in any case upon the parties to a suit as to the object of that suit, while they are also entitled to very high respect and consideration in all parallel cases by all other departments of the Government. And while it is obviously possible that such decision may be erroneous in any given case, still the evil effect following it, being limited to that particular case, with the chance that it may be overruled and never become a precedent for other cases, can better be borne than could the evils of a different practice. At the same time, the candid citizen must confess that if the policy of the Government upon vital questions affecting the whole people is to be irrevocably fixed by decisions of the Supreme Court, the instant they are made in ordinary litigation between parties in personal actions the people will have ceased to be their own rulers, having to that extent practically resigned the Government into the hands of that eminent tribunal. Nor is there in this view any assault upon the court or the judges. It is a duty from which they may not shrink to decide cases properly brought before them, and it is no fault of theirs if others seek to turn their decisions to political purposes.

One section of our country believes slavery is *right* and ought to be extended, while the other believes it is *wrong* and ought not to be extended. This is the only substantial dispute. The fugitive-slave clause of the Constitution and the law for the suppression of the foreign slave trade are each as well enforced, perhaps, as any law can ever be in a community where the moral sense of the people imperfectly supports the law itself. The great body of the people abide by the dry legal obligation in both cases, and a few break over in each. This, I think, can not be perfectly cured, and it would be worse in both cases *after* the separation of the sections than before. The foreign slave trade, now imperfectly suppressed, would be ultimately revived without restriction in one section, while fugitive slaves, now only partially surrendered, would not be surrendered at all by the other.

Physically speaking, we can not separate. We can not remove our respective sections from each other nor build an impassable wall between them. A husband and wife may be divorced and go out of the presence and beyond the reach of each other, but the different parts of our country can not do this. They can not but remain face to face, and intercourse, either amicable or hostile, must continue between them. Is it possible, then, to make that intercourse more advantageous or more satisfactory *after* separation than *before?* Can aliens make treaties easier than friends can make laws? Can treaties be more faithfully enforced between aliens than laws can among friends? Suppose you go to war, you can not fight always; and when, after much loss on both sides and no gain on either, you cease fighting, the identical old questions, as to terms of intercourse, are again upon you.

This country, with its institutions, belongs to the people who inhabit it. Whenever they shall grow weary of the existing Government, they can exercise their *constitutional* right of amending it or their *revolutionary* right to dismember or overthrow it. I can not be ignorant of the fact that many worthy and patriotic citizens are desirous of having the National Constitution amended. While I make no recommendation of amendments, I fully recognize the rightful authority of the people over the whole subject, to be exercised in either of the modes prescribed in the instrument itself; and I should, under existing circumstances, favor rather than oppose a fair opportunity being afforded the people to act upon it. I will venture to add that to me the convention mode seems preferable, in that it allows amendments to originate with the people themselves, instead of only permitting them to take or reject propositions orginated by others, not especially chosen for the purpose, and which might not be precisely such as they would wish to either accept or refuse. I understand a proposed amendment to the Constitution — which amendment, however, I have not seen — has passed Congress, to the effect that the Federal Government shall never interfere with the domestic institutions of the States, including that of persons held to service. To avoid misconstruction of what I have said, I depart from my purpose not to speak of particular amendments so far as to say that, holding such a provision to now be implied constitutional law, I have no objection to its being made express and irrevocable. . . .

Why should there not be a patient confidence in the ultimate justice of the people? Is there any better or equal hope in the world? In our present differences, is either party without faith of being in the right? If the Almighty Ruler of Nations, with His eternal truth and justice, be on your side of the North, or on yours of the South, that truth and that justice will surely prevail by the judgment of this great tribunal of the American people.

By the frame of the Government under which we live this same people have wisely given their public servants but little power for mischief, and have with equal wisdom provided for the return of that little to their own hands at very short intervals. While the people retain their virtue and vigilance no Administration by any extreme of wickedness or folly can very seriously injure the Government in the short space of four years.

My countrymen, one and all, think calmly and *well* upon this whole subject. Nothing valuable can be lost by taking time. If there be an object to *hurry* any of you in hot haste to a step which you would never take *deliberately,* that object will be frustrated by taking time; but no good object can be frustrated by it. Such of you as are now dissatisfied still have the old Constitution unimpaired, and, on the sensitive point, the laws of your own framing under it; while the new Administration will have no immediate power, if it would, to change either. If it were admitted that you who are dissatisfied hold the right side in the dispute, there still is no single good reason for precipitate action. Intelligence, patriotism, Christianity, and a firm reliance on Him who has never yet forsaken this favored land are still competent to adjust in the best way all our present difficulty.

In *your* hands, my dissatisfied fellow-countrymen, and not in *mine,* is the momentous issue of civil war. The Government will not assail *you. You* can have no conflict without being yourselves the aggressors. *You* have no oath registered in heaven to destroy the Government, while I shall have the most solemn one to "preserve, protect, and defend it."

I am loath to close. We are not enemies, but friends. We must not be enemies. Though passion may have strained, it must not break, our bonds of affection. The mystic chords of memory, stretching from every battlefield and patriot grave to every living heart and hearthstone all over this broad land, will yet swell the chorus of the Union when again touched, as surely they will be, by the better angels of our nature.

Abraham Lincoln: The Gettysburg Address 1863

"I claim not to have controlled events," Abraham Lincoln admitted, "but confess plainly that events have controlled me." The firing on Fort Sumter, the steady stream of northern defeats while Lincoln searched for a winning general, the radical pressure which finally drove a reluctant President to issue the Emancipation Proclamation —all confirm Lincoln's assertion. But characteristically he was too modest in his analysis. His political skill kept the various factions of his own party working together; his shrewd intelligence enabled him, despite his lack of military experience, to perform ably as commander in chief; and his determination to preserve the Union gave the northern cause a dignity and meaning it desperately needed.

Lincoln's greatness is best revealed in his most famous wartime speech. Shortly after the crucial battle at Gettysburg, Pennsylvania, a group of northern governors created a commission to establish a national cemetery at the battlefield. The trustees planned an impressive dedication ceremony and they asked Edward Everett, the foremost orator of the time, to give the principal address. They invited the President, members of his cabinet, and congressmen to attend; and out of courtesy they asked Lincoln to make a few remarks. To the surprise of his associates, Lincoln accepted the invitation and prepared two drafts of a brief talk before he took the train to Gettysburg on November 18, 1863. The next morning he made some minor changes in his speech, and then after lunch he joined some fifteen thousand to listen for more than two hours as Everett delivered his elaborate and eloquent formal address from memory. After a brief pause, Lincoln spoke from his single folded page, adding one phrase extemporaneously, and then sat down before many in the audience were aware he had begun. The scattered applause came belatedly, a photographer took the President's picture, and the event was over. Yet in less than 300 words Lincoln had given the nation a perfect statement of what the war was all about.　　　R.A.D.

Four score and seven years ago our fathers brought forth on this continent, a new nation, conceived in Liberty, and dedicated to the proposition that all men are created equal.

Now we are engaged in a great civil war, testing whether that nation, or any nation so conceived and so dedicated, can long endure. We are met on a great battle-field of that war. We have come to dedicate a portion of that field, as a final resting place for those who here gave their lives that that nation might live. It is altogether fitting and proper that we should do this.

But, in a larger sense, we can not dedicate—we can not consecrate—we can not hallow—this ground. The brave men, living and dead, who struggled here, have consecrated it, far above our poor power to add or detract. The world will little note, nor long remember what we say here, but it can never forget what they did here. It is for us the living, rather, to be dedicated here to the unfinished work which they who fought here have thus far so nobly advanced. It is rather for us to be here dedicated to the great task remaining before us—that from these honored dead we take increased devotion to that cause for which they gave the last full measure of devotion—that we here highly resolve that these dead shall not have died in vain—that this nation, under God, shall have a new birth of freedom—and that government of the people, by the people, for the people, shall not perish from the earth.

The Fourteenth Amendment 1868

Lincoln's tragic assassination elevated Andrew Johnson to the Presidency and complicated the already difficult problem of reconstruction. Radical Republicans in Congress, bent on imposing their will on the defeated South, had already clashed with Lincoln's moderate policies. At first they saw in Johnson an ally, since he had made a number of statements critical of the southern aristocracy. But Johnson, a prewar Democrat from Tennessee who had stayed loyal to the Union, championed the small farmers of the South, and he soon broke with the Radicals. An intemperate, stubborn man, Johnson was a maverick who lacked the capacity to lead the nation. His penchant for quarreling with Congress and his callous attitude toward the newly freed Negroes soon drove many of the moderate Republicans, who held the balance of power in Congress, into the Radical ranks.

When Congress convened in the fall of 1865, it quickly established a Joint Committee on Reconstruction to oppose the President's plan to readmit the southern states into the Union on lenient terms. Many Radicals were enraged by the Black Codes, laws enacted in the southern states to limit drastically the personal and economic freedom of Negroes. Congress passed a Civil Rights Act to give federal protection to the freedmen, and although a majority of two-thirds overrode Johnson's veto, many Radicals felt that only a constitutional amendment would guarantee Negro rights in the South. Moderates and Radicals worked out a compromise amendment which passed both Houses easily in 1866, but the opposition of the southern states blocked ratification. Two years later, after Congress reimposed military rule over the South and made ratification a condition for the readmission of the southern states, the Fourteenth Amendment became effective.

The first section contained sweeping constitutional guarantees designed to protect the freedmen from coercive state action; the other sections dealt with immediate problems of reconstruction. In later years, the Supreme Court interpreted the word "person" so as to exempt corporations from state regulation; still later, the Court used the "due process" clause to protect the civil liberties of both black and white Americans on innumerable occasions.

R.A.D.

Sec. 1. All persons born or naturalized in the United States, and subject to the jurisdiction thereof, are citizens of the United States and of the State wherein they reside. No State shall make or enforce any law which shall abridge the privileges or immunities of citizens of the United States; nor shall any State deprive any person of life, liberty, or property, without due process of law; nor deny to any person within its jurisdiction the equal protection of the laws.

Sec. 2. Representatives shall be apportioned among the several States according to their respective numbers, counting the whole number of persons in each State, excluding Indians not taxed. But when the right to vote at any election for the choice of electors for President and Vice President of the United States, Representatives in Congress, the Executive and Judicial officers of a State, or the members of the Legislature thereof, is denied to any of the male inhabitants of such State, being twenty-one years of age, and citizens of the United States, or in any way abridged, except for participation in rebellion, or other crime, the basis of representation therein shall be reduced in the proportion which the number of such male citizens shall bear to the whole number of male citizens twenty-one years of age in such State.

Sec. 3. No person shall be a Senator or Representative in Congress, or elector of President and Vice President, or hold any office, civil or military, under the United States, or under any State, who, having previously taken an oath, as a member of Congress, or as an officer of the United States, or as a member of any State legislature, or as an executive or judicial officer of any State, to support the Constitution of the United States, shall have engaged in insurrection or rebellion against the same, or given aid or comfort to the enemies thereof. But Congress may by a vote of two-thirds of each House, remove such disability.

Sec. 4. The validity of the public debt of the United States, authorized by law, including debts incurred for payment of pensions and bounties for services in suppressing insurrection or rebellion, shall not be questioned. But neither the United States nor any State shall assume or pay any debt or obligation incurred in aid of insurrection or rebellion against the United States, or any claim for the loss or emancipation of any slave; but all such debts, obligations and claims shall be held illegal and void.

Sec. 5. The Congress shall have power to enforce, by appropriate legislation, the provisions of this article.

Preamble to the Constitution of the Knights of Labor 1878

In the years after the Civil War, industry grew rapidly in the United States, especially in the Northeast and Midwest. For workingmen, it was a time of bewildering change. They trooped into the factories to man the new machines which moved at an ever-faster pace to turn out a vast array of identical products. The human relationship between owner and worker disappeared as impersonal corporations employed tens of thousands of workers. Craftsmen, their skills no longer in demand, were forced to compete with an increasing number of immigrants for the monotonous jobs on the assembly lines.

Workers began to seek refuge through organization. The National Labor Union, a loose grouping of existing craft unions, flourished briefly after the war and then collapsed. In 1869 Uriah S. Stephens, a Philadelphia tailor, joined with eight coworkers to found the Noble and Holy Order of the Knights of Labor. A former Baptist minister and inveterate joiner, Stephens broke with previous union practice in the United States by stressing the theme of the brotherhood of all workers. Instead of limiting the Knights to skilled workers, Stephens opened the door to everyone, workers and owners, men and women, whites and blacks. (Only doctors, lawyers, bankers, and liquor dealers were excluded!) Playing down such traditional concepts as strikes and economic bargaining, Stephens hoped to fuse all labor together into a single secret association, on the model of a fraternal lodge, which could better life for all.

The Knights grew slowly in the 1870's, but a series of violent and unsuccessful railway strikes in 1877 demonstrated the need for a national labor movement. On January 1, 1878, the Knights held their first general assembly in Reading, Pennsylvania, and adopted a constitution, complete with a preamble which expressed the aspirations of American labor in the new industrial era. In the next few years, the Knights expanded at a fantastic rate—from less than ten thousand members in 1878 to over seven hundred thousand by 1886. Then the Haymarket riot in Chicago and the subsequent public reaction against organized labor destroyed the Knights and permitted the more conservative American Federation of Labor to take its place at the head of the trade union movement. R.A.D.

The recent alarming development and aggression of aggregated wealth, which, unless checked, will invariably lead to the pauperization and hopeless degradation of the toiling masses, render it imperative, if we desire to enjoy the blessings of life, that a check should be placed upon its power and upon unjust accumulation, and a system adopted which will secure to the laborer the fruits of his toil; and as this much-desired object can only be accomplished by the thorough unification of labor, and the united efforts of those who obey the divine injunction that "In the sweat of thy brow shalt thou eat bread," we have formed the [Knights] with a view of securing the organization and direction, by co-operative effort, of the power of the industrial classes; and we submit to the world the object sought to be accomplished by our organization, calling upon all who believe in securing "the greatest good to the greatest number" to aid and assist us:—

I. To bring within the folds of organization every department of productive industry, making knowledge a standpoint for action, and industrial and moral worth, not wealth, the true standard of individual and national greatness.

II. To secure to the toilers a proper share of the wealth that they create; more of the leisure that rightfully belongs to them; more societary advantages; more of the benefits, privileges, and emoluments of the world; in a word, all those rights and privileges necessary to make them capable of enjoying, appreciating, defending, and perpetuating the blessings of good government.

III. To arrive at the true condition of the producing masses in their educational, moral, and financial condition, by demanding from the various governments the establishment of bureaus of Labor Statistics.

IV. The establishment of co-operative institutions, productive and distributive.

V. The reserving of the public lands—the heritage of the people—for the actual settler;—not another acre for railroads or speculators.

VI. The abrogation of all laws that do not bear equally upon capital and labor, the removal of unjust technicalities, delays, and discriminations in the administration of justice, and the adopting of measures providing for the health and safety of those engaged in mining, manufacturing, or building pursuits.

VII. The enactment of laws to compel chartered corporations to pay their employes weekly, in full, for labor performed during the preceding week, in the lawful money of the country.

VIII. The enactment of laws giving mechanics and laborers a first lien on their work for their full wages.

IX. The abolishment of the contract system on national, State, and municipal work.

X. The substitution of arbitration for strikes, whenever and wherever employers and employes are willing to meet on equitable grounds.

XI. The prohibition of the employment of children in workshops, mines, and factories before attaining their fourteenth year.

XII. To abolish the system of letting out by contract the labor of convicts in our prisons and reformatory institutions.

XIII. To secure for both sexes equal pay for equal work.

XIV. The reduction of the hours of labor to eight per day, so that the laborers may have more time for social enjoyment and intellectual improvement, and be enabled to reap the advantages conferred by the laborsaving machinery which their brains have created.

XV. To prevail upon governments to establish a purely national circulating medium, based upon the faith and resources of the nation, and issued directly to the people, without the intervention of any system of banking corporations, which money shall be a legal tender in payment of all debts, public or private.

John W. Powell: Report on the Arid Region of the West 1878

In their relentless push westward, American pioneers had learned to adapt to the challenge posed by the forest and prairies of the Middle West. In the years after the Civil War, however, they faced a far more difficult environment — the vast treeless plains that stretched westward from the hundredth meridian to the foothills of the Rockies. With unshakable confidence, the frontier farmers moved out into what early explorers had called the Great American Desert and a cycle of unusually wet years in the 1870's gave them a false sense of security. In a decade, the population of the plains doubled as men filed for the 160 acres offered them under the Homestead Act of 1862. Few realized that the dry plains were unsuited to the traditional family farm — only huge ranches or small, irrigated plots could normally support agriculture in this region.

John Wesley Powell was the first man to try to make the nation's land policy conform to the realities of the West. The son of an abolitionist Methodist preacher, Powell had grown up on a small farm in the Midwest. As a schoolteacher in Illinois, he began a career as an explorer and naturalist; he then went off to the Civil War, rising to the rank of major and losing an arm at Shiloh. He became a professor of natural history, and in 1869, despite his physical handicap, he led a party down the hitherto unexplored Colorado River and became the first white man to traverse the Grand Canyon. In the 1870's Powell conducted a geological and topographical survey of the Colorado plateau which convinced him that the standard policy of dividing the land into 160-acre tracts would not work in a region where rainfall fell below twenty inches a year. When President Rutherford B. Hayes appointed Carl Schurz, the German-born writer and reformer, as Secretary of the Interior, Powell hurriedly prepared a long report on the arid lands of the West and presented it to Schurz on April 1, 1878. Although Congress failed to act on Powell's recommendations, which included plans for 80-acre plots for irrigated farms and 2,560-acre ranches restricted to grazing, his revolutionary ideas have influenced all subsequent thinking on the West.   R.A.D.

T he eastern portion of the United States is supplied with abundant rainfall for agricultural purposes, receiving the necessary amount from the evaporation of the Atlantic Ocean and the Gulf of Mexico; but westward the amount of aqueous precipitation diminishes in a general way until at last a region is reached where the climate is so arid that agriculture is not successful without irrigation. This Arid Region begins about midway in the Great Plains and extends across the Rocky Mountains to the Pacific Ocean. . . .

The limit of successful agriculture without irrigation has been set at 20 inches, that the extent of the Arid Region should by no means be exaggerated; but at 20 inches agriculture will not be uniformly successful from season to season. Many droughts will occur; many seasons in a long series will be fruitless; and it may be doubted whether, on the whole, agriculture will prove remunerative. On this point it is impossible to speak with certainty. A larger experience than the history of agriculture in the western portion of the United States affords is necessary to a final determination of the question. . . .

Within the Arid Region only a small portion of the country is irrigable. These irrigable tracts are lowlands lying along the streams. On the mountains and high plateaus forests are found at elevations so great that frequent summer frosts forbid the cultivation of the soil. Here are the natural timber lands of the Arid Region—an upper region set apart by nature for the growth of timber necessary to the mining, manufacturing, and agricultural industries of the country. Between the low irrigable lands and the elevated forest lands there are valleys, mesas, hills, and mountain slopes bearing grasses of greater or less value for pasturage purposes.

Then, in discussing the lands of the Arid Region, three great classes are recognized—the irrigable lands below, the forest lands above, and the pasturage lands between. . . .

If the irrigable lands are to be sold, it should be in quantities to suit purchasers, and but one condition should be imposed, namely, that the lands should be actually irrigated before the title is transferred to the purchaser. This method would provide for the redemption of these lands by irrigation through the employment of capital. If these lands are to be reserved for actual settlers, in small quantities, to provide homes for poor men, on the principle involved in the homestead laws, a general law should be enacted under which a number of persons would be able to organize and settle on irrigable districts, and establish their own rules and regulations for the use of the water and subdivision of the lands, but in obedience to the general provisions of the law. . . .

If divisional surveys were extended over the pasturage lands, favorable sites at springs and along small streams would be rapidly taken under the homestead and preëmption privileges for the nuclei of pasturage farms.

Unentered lands contiguous to such pasturage farms could be controlled to a greater or less extent by those holding the water, and in this manner the pasturage of the country would be rendered practicable. But the great body of land would remain in the possession of the Government; the farmers owning the favorable spots could not obtain possession of the adjacent lands by homestead or preëmption methods, and if such adjacent lands were offered for sale, they could not afford to pay the Government price.

Certain important facts relating to the pasturage farms may be advantageously restated.

The farm unit should not be less than 2,560 acres; the pasturage farms need small bodies of irrigable land; the division of these lands should be controlled by topographic features to give water fronts; residences of the pasturage lands should be grouped; the pasturage farms cannot be fenced—they must be occupied in common.

The homestead and preëmption methods are inadequate to meet these conditions. A general law should be enacted to provide for the organization of pasturage districts, in which the residents should have the right to make their own regulations for the division of the lands, the use of the water for irrigation and for watering stock, and for the pasturage of the lands in common or in severalty. But each division or pasturage farm of the district should be owned by an individual; that is, these lands could be settled and improved by the "colony" plan better than by any other. It should not be understood that the colony system applies only to such persons as migrate from the east in a body; any number of persons already in this region could thus organize. In fact very large bodies of these lands would be taken by people who are already in the country and who have herds with which they roam about seeking water and grass, and making no permanent residences and no valuable improvements. Such a plan would give immediate relief to all these people.

This district or colony system is not untried in this country. It is essentially the basis of all the mining district organizations of the west. Under it the local rules and regulations for the division of mining lands, the use of water, timber, etc., are managed better than they could possibly be under specific statutes of the United States. The association of a number of people prevents single individuals from having undue control of natural privileges, and secures an equitable division of mineral lands; and all this is secured in obedience to statutes of the United States providing general regulations.

Customs are forming and regulations are being made by common consent among the people in some districts already; but these provide no means for the acquirement of titles to land, no incentive is given to the improvement of the country, and no legal security to pasturage rights.

If, then, the irrigable lands can be taken in quantities to suit purchasers, and the colony system provided for poor men who wish to coöperate in this industry; if the timber lands are opened to timber enterprises, and the pasturage lands offered to settlement under a colony plan like that indicated above, a land system would be provided for the Arid Region adapted to the wants of all persons desiring to become actual settlers therein. Thousands of men who now own herds and live a semi-nomadic life; thousands of persons who now roam from mountain range to mountain range prospecting for gold, silver, and other minerals; thousands of men who repair to that country and return disappointed from the fact that they are practically debarred from the public lands; and thousands of persons in the eastern states without employment, or discontented with the rewards of labor, would speedily find homes in the great Rocky Mountain Region.

The Sherman Anti-Trust Act 1890

The explosive growth of industry in the last third of the nineteenth century led to chaotic conditions as competing businessmen sought to exploit new economic opportunities. Inevitably, shrewder and more far-sighted entrepreneurs began to bring order out of confusion by merging the many small competitors into large corporations. John D. Rockefeller set the pattern in the oil industry. Beginning as a small refiner in Cleveland in the 1860's, he had achieved a genuine monopoly of the petroleum industry in less than a decade, controlling over 90 per cent of all refineries in the country. In 1879 he completed his empire with the formation of the Standard Oil Trust. Rockefeller and his associates surrendered their stock in the many small companies they controlled in return for trust certificates, thereby enabling the nine trustees, acting as Rockefeller's agents, to operate the scattered Standard Oil holdings as if they were one company. The result was much greater efficiency and huge profits for Rockefeller, who now became the richest man in America. Other industrialists quickly adopted the trust device, so that by 1890 there were a dozen huge combinations dominating major sectors of the American economy.

The consolidation movement, despite its real benefits in order and productivity, soon brought forth protests from businessmen who had been squeezed out by the new corporations and from social reformers who renewed the old Jacksonian war cry against monopoly. As conservative a figure as former President Rutherford Hayes asked rhetorically in 1887, "Shall the will of monopolies take the place of the government of the people?" James Weaver, a spokesman for farmers, viewed the trusts in a sinister light: "Like the cat, they walk in quest of prey with velvet feet, and like the assassin, they lie in wait and spring upon you without warning." This rising tide of social protest spilled over into politics in 1888 when both major parties adopted platforms promising to curb the power of trusts. Accordingly, in December, 1889, Senator John Sherman of Ohio, brother of the Civil War general and a leading Republican politician, introduced an antitrust bill which became the basis for congressional action. Radically altered in committee, Sherman's bill moved through the legislative process with astonishing ease, passing the House unanimously and the Senate with only one dissenting vote. Although the sweeping language of the bill made it easy for conservative judges to hamper its enforcement, the Sherman Anti-Trust Act signified the determination of the American people to limit the power of corporations in national life. R.A.D.

An ACT To protect trade and commerce against unlawful restraints and monopolies. . . .

Be it enacted

SEC. 1. Every contract, combination in the form of trust or otherwise, or conspiracy, in restraint of trade or commerce among the several States, or with foreign nations, is hereby declared to be illegal. Every person who shall make any such contract or engage in any such combination or conspiracy, shall be deemed guilty of a misdemeanor, and, on conviction thereof, shall be punished by fine not exceeding five thousand dollars, or by imprisonment not exceeding one year, or by both said punishments, in the discretion of the court.

SEC. 2. Every person who shall monopolize, or attempt to monopolize, or combine or conspire with any other person or persons, to monopolize any part of the trade or commerce among the several States, or with foreign nations, shall be deemed guilty of a misdemeanor, and, on conviction thereof, shall be punished by fine not exceeding five thousand dollars, or by imprisonment not exceeding one year, or by both said punishments, in the discretion of the court.

SEC. 3. Every contract, combination in form of trust or otherwise, or conspiracy, in restraint of trade or commerce in any Territory of the United States or of the District of Columbia, or in restraint of trade or commerce between any such Territory and another, or between any such Territory or Territories and any State or States or the District of Columbia, or with foreign nations, or between the District of Columbia and any State or States or foreign nations, is hereby declared illegal. Every person who shall make any such contract or engage in any such combination or conspiracy, shall be deemed guilty of a misdemeanor, and, on conviction thereof, shall be punished by fine not exceeding five thousand dollars, or by imprisonment not exceeding one year, or by both said punishments, in the discretion of the court.

SEC. 4. The several circuit courts of the United States are hereby invested with jurisdiction to prevent and restrain violations of this act; and it shall be the duty of the several district attorneys of the United States, in their respective districts, under the direction of the Attorney-General, to institute proceedings in equity to prevent and restrain such violations. Such proceedings may be by way of petition setting forth the case and praying that such violation shall be enjoined or otherwise prohibited. When the parties complained of shall have been duly notified of such petition the courts shall proceed, as soon as may be, to the hearing and determination of the case; and pending such petition and before final decrees, the court may at any time make such temporary restraining order or prohibition as shall be deemed just in the premises.

SEC. 5. Whenever it shall appear to the court before which any proceeding under Section Four of this act may be pending, that the ends of justice require that other parties should be brought before the court, the court may cause them to be summoned, whether they reside in the district in which the court is held or not; and subpœnas to that end may be served in any district by the marshal thereof.

SEC. 6. Any property owned under any contract or by any combination, or pursuant to any conspiracy (and being the subject thereof) mentioned in Section One of this act, and being in the course of transportation from one State to another, or to a foreign country, shall be forfeited to the United States, and may be seized and condemned by like proceedings as those provided by law for the forfeiture, seizure, and condemnation of property imported into the United States contrary to law.

SEC. 7. Any person who shall be injured in his business or property by any other person or corporation by reason of anything forbidden or declared to be unlawful by this act, may sue therefor in any circuit court of the United States in the district in which the defendant resides or is found, without respect to the amount in controversy, and shall recover threefold the damages by him sustained, and the costs of suit, including a reasonable attorney's fee.

SEC. 8. That the word "person," or "persons," wherever used in this act shall be deemed to include corporations and associations existing under or authorized by the laws of either the United States, the laws of any of the Territories, the laws of any State, or the laws of any foreign country.

Platform of the Populist Party 1892

The American farmer was a casualty of the Industrial Revolution. Although farm output grew rapidly in the years after the Civil War, the farmers' share of the national income fell steadily. The expansion of agriculture into new lands, especially on the Great Plains, and the increasing mechanization of farming led to overproduction of market crops such as wheat and cotton, and a corresponding decline in their prices. Ten-cent cotton and sixty-cent wheat forced desperate farmers to seek means of raising prices artificially: in the 1870's, they joined the Greenback Movement to expand the currency; by 1890 they thought they saw a panacea in the Populists' cry for the unlimited coinage of silver.

The People's Party originated in Kansas in the congressional elections of 1890. Agrarian spokesmen such as Mary Ellen Lease—a fiery Irishwoman who became known as "Mary Yellin'" and "Patrick Henry in Petticoats"—and "Sockless Jerry" Simpson, a shrewd Kansan who capitalized on the farmers' dislike of city slickers, stirred up a political tornado. ". . . it was a religious revival, a crusade, a pentecost of politics in which a tongue of flame sat upon every man, and each spake as the spirit gave him utterance," commented one awed observer. The Populists won control of the Kansas legislature, elected a United States senator, and sent "Sockless Jerry" to Congress, where there were nearly fifty members representing various forms of agrarian radicalism.

In early 1892, farm leaders gathered in St. Louis to found a national party under the leadership of Ignatius Donnelly, a dynamic Minnesota reformer who wrote apocalyptic novels, dabbled in real estate, and once confessed, "For my part, I rather like walking on volcanoes." In July the Populists reassembled in Omaha to nominate James Weaver as their presidential candidate and to adopt a platform, complete with a lurid preamble written by Donnelly, which offered a sweeping package of reforms. Although the Populists showed considerable strength in local elections, they fared badly on a national level, carrying only four sparsely populated western states in the presidential election and losing ground in Congress. Four years later, William Jennings Bryan, a Democrat, stole their cry of free silver, and the People's Party gradually died out. But the Populist agitation won national attention for the farmers' plight and led to eventual adoption of many of the measures first advocated in the Omaha platform of 1892. R.A.D.

Assembled upon the 116th anniversary of the Declaration of Independence, the People's Party of America, in their first national convention, invoking upon their action the blessing of Almighty God, put forth in the name and on behalf of the people of this country, the following preamble and declaration of principles:

PREAMBLE

The conditions which surround us best justify our co-operation; we meet in the midst of a nation brought to the verge of moral, political, and material ruin. Corruption dominates the ballot-box, the Legislatures, the Congress, and touches even the ermine of the bench. The people are demoralized; most of the States have been compelled to isolate the voters at the polling places to prevent universal intimidation and bribery. The newspapers are largely subsidized or muzzled, public opinion silenced, business prostrated, homes covered with mortgages, labor improverished, and the land concentrating in the hands of capitalists. The urban workmen are denied the right to organize for self-protection, imported pauperized labor beats down their wages, a hireling standing army, unrecognized by our laws, is established to shoot them down, and they are rapidly degenerating into European conditions. The fruits of the toil of millions are boldly stolen to build up colossal fortunes for a few, unprecedented in the history of mankind; and the possessors of these, in turn, despise the Republic and endanger liberty. From the same prolific womb of governmental injustice we breed the two great classes—tramps and millionaires.

The national power to create money is appropriated to enrich bond-holders; a vast public debt payable in legal-tender currency has been funded into gold-bearing bonds, thereby adding millions to the burdens of the people.

Silver, which has been accepted as coin since the dawn of history, has been demonetized to add to the purchasing power of gold by decreasing the value of all forms of property as well as human labor, and the supply of currency is purposely abridged to fatten usurers, bankrupt enterprise, and enslave industry. A vast conspiracy against mankind has been organized on two continents, and it is rapidly taking possession of the world. If not met and overthrown at once it forebodes terrible social convulsions, the destruction of civilization, or the establishment of an absolute despotism.

We have witnessed for more than a quarter of a century the struggles of the two great political parties for power and plunder, while grievous wrongs have been inflicted upon the suffering people. We charge that the controlling influences dominating both these parties have permitted the existing dreadful conditions to develop without serious effort to prevent or restrain them. Neither do they now promise us any substantial reform. They have agreed together to ignore, in the coming campaign, every issue but one. They propose to drown the outcries of a plundered people with the uproar of a sham battle over the tariff, so that capitalists, corporations, national banks, rings, trusts, watered stock, the demonetization of silver and the oppressions of the usurers may all be lost sight of. They propose to sacrifice our homes, lives, and children on the altar of mammon; to destroy the multitude in order to secure corruption funds from the millionaires.

Assembled on the anniversary of the birthday of the nation, and filled with the spirit of the grand general and chief who established our independence, we seek to restore the government of the Republic to the hands of the "plain people," with which class it originated. We assert our purposes to be identical with the purposes of the National Constitution; to form a more perfect union and establish justice, insure domestic tranquillity, provide for the common defence, promote the general welfare, and secure the blessings of liberty for ourselves and our posterity.

We declare that this Republic can only endure as a free government while built upon the love of the people for each other and for the nation; that it cannot be pinned together by bayonets; that the Civil War is over, and that every passion and resentment which grew out of it must die with it, and that we must be in fact, as we are in name, one united brotherhood of free men.

Our country finds itself confronted by conditions for which there is no precedent in the history of the world; our annual agricultural productions amount to billions of dollars in value, which must, within a few weeks or months, be exchanged for billions of dollars' worth of commodities consumed in their production; the existing currency supply is wholly inadequate to make this exchange; the results are falling prices, the formation of combines and rings, the impoverishment of the producing class. We pledge ourselves that if given power we will labor to correct these evils by wise and reasonable legislation, in accordance with the terms of our platform.

We believe that the power of government—in other words, of the people—should be expanded (as in the case of the postal service) as rapidly and as far as the good sense of an intelligent people and the teachings of experience shall justify, to the end that oppression, injustice, and poverty shall eventually cease in the land.

While our sympathies as a party of reform are naturally upon the side of every proposition which will tend to make men intelligent, virtuous, and temperate, we nevertheless regard these questions, important as they are, as secondary to the great issues now pressing for solution, and upon which not only our individual prosperity but the very existence of free institutions depend; and we ask all men to first help us to determine whether we are to have a republic to administer before we differ as to the conditions upon which it is to be administered, believing that the forces of reform this day organized will never cease to move forward until every wrong is righted and equal rights and equal privileges securely established for all the men and women of this country.

PLATFORM

We declare, therefore—

First.—That the union of the labor forces of the United States this day consummated shall be permanent and perpetual; may its spirit enter into all hearts for the salvation of the Republic and the uplifting of mankind.

Second.—Wealth belongs to him who creates it, and every dollar taken from industry without an equivalent is robbery. "If any will not work, neither shall he eat." The interests of rural and civil labor are the same; their enemies are identical.

Third.—We believe that the time has come when the railroad corporations will either own the people or the people must own the railroads; and should the government enter upon the work of owning and managing all railroads, we should favor an amendment to the constitution by which all persons engaged in the government service shall be placed under a civil-service regulation of the most rigid character, so as to prevent the increase of the power of the national administration by the use of such additional government employes.

FINANCE.—We demand a national currency, safe, sound, and flexible issued by the general government only, a full legal tender for all debts, public and private, and that without the use of banking corporations; a just, equitable, and efficient means of distribution direct to the people, at a tax not to exceed 2 per cent, per annum, to be provided as set forth in the sub-treasury plan of the Farmers' Alliance, or a better system; also by payments in discharge of its obligations for public improvements.

1. We demand free and unlimited coinage of silver and gold at the present legal ratio of 16 to 1.
2. We demand that the amount of circulating medium be speedily increased to not less than $50 per capita.
3. We demand a graduated income tax.
4. We believe that the money of the country should be kept as much as possible in the hands of the people, and hence we demand that all State and national revenues shall be limited to the necessary expenses of the government, economically and honestly administered.
5. We demand that postal savings banks be established by the government for the safe deposit of the earnings of the people and to facilitate exchange.

TRANSPORTATION. — Transportation being a means of exchange and a public necessity, the government should own and operate the railroads in the interest of the people. The telegraph and telephone, like the post-office system, being a necessity for the transmission of news, should be owned and operated by the government in the interest of the people.

LAND. — The land, including all the natural sources of wealth, is the heritage of the people, and should not be monopolized for speculative purposes, and alien ownership of land should be prohibited. All land now held by railroads and other corporations in excess of their actual needs, and all lands now owned by aliens should be reclaimed by the government and held for actual settlers only.

EXPRESSION OF SENTIMENTS

Your Committee on Platform and Resolutions beg leave unanimously to report the following:

Whereas, Other questions have been presented for our consideration, we hereby submit the following, not as a part of the Platform of the People's Party, but as resolutions expressive of the sentiment of this Convention.

1. RESOLVED, That we demand a free ballot and a fair count in all

elections, and pledge ourselves to secure it to every legal voter without Federal intervention, through the adoption by the States of the unperverted Australian or secret ballot system.

2. RESOLVED, That the revenue derived from a graduated income tax should be applied to the reduction of the burden of taxation now levied upon the domestic industries of this country.

3. RESOLVED, That we pledge our support to fair and liberal pensions to ex-Union soldiers and sailors.

4. RESOLVED, That we condemn the fallacy of protecting American labor under the present system, which opens our ports to the pauper and criminal classes of the world and crowds out our wage-earners; and we denounce the present ineffective laws against contract labor, and demand the further restriction of undesirable emigration.

5. RESOLVED, That we cordially sympathize with the efforts of organized workingmen to shorten the hours of labor, and demand a rigid enforcement of the existing eight-hour law on Government work, and ask that a penalty clause be added to the said law.

6. RESOLVED, That we regard the maintenance of a large standing army of mercenaries, known as the Pinkerton system, as a menace to our liberties, and we demand its abolition; and we condemn the recent invasion of the Territory of Wyoming by the hired assassins of plutocracy, assisted by Federal officers.

7. RESOLVED, That we commend to the favorable consideration of the people and the reform press the legislative system known as the initiative and referendum.

8. RESOLVED, That we favor a constitutional provision limiting the office of President and Vice-President to one term, and providing for the election of Senators of the United States by a direct vote of the people.

9. RESOLVED, That we oppose any subsidy or national aid to any private corporation for any purpose.

10. RESOLVED, That this convention sympathizes with the Knights of Labor and their righteous contest with the tyrannical combine of clothing manufacturers of Rochester, and declare it to be a duty of all who hate tyranny and oppression to refuse to purchase the goods made by the said manufacturers, or to patronize any merchants who sell such goods.

William McKinley: Message Calling for Intervention in Cuba 1898

Americans rediscovered the world in the 1890's. Since the era of the Napoleonic Wars, the United States had turned inward, concentrating on westward expansion, the deepening sectional crisis, and economic development. Then, gradually, the nation became interested in expansion overseas. In 1867 William Seward arranged for the purchase of Alaska; a decade later, an American naval officer acquired a lonely outpost at Pago Pago in the Samoas. Americans in Hawaii overthrew the native monarch in Honolulu in 1893; and though President Grover Cleveland at first blocked a treaty of annexation, five years later Hawaii became American territory. These tentative outward moves reached a climax in 1898 when the United States went to war with Spain over Cuba and thereby ended its traditonal policy of isolation.

The Cuban rebellion began in 1895 as guerrillas tried to oust the Spanish from the island. Spain retaliated with repressive measures that outraged the American conscience, especially when William Randolph Hearst and Joseph Pulitzer, who were engaged in a cutthroat newspaper war in New York City, exploited the Cuban tragedy in their "yellow" journals. William McKinley, a shrewd but cautious Ohio Republican, tried to cool passions in the United States while applying increasing pressure on Spain to give Cuba independence, but an explosion which destroyed the battleship *Maine* in Havana harbor in mid-February, 1898, undermined McKinley's patient diplomacy; American honor as well as humanitarian concern was now involved.

The President made a final effort at peace, asking Spain to seek an armistice with the rebels and to allow the United States to act as mediator in Cuba. The Spanish, too weak to resist but too proud to surrender, took refuge in procrastination. McKinley prepared a message to Congress in early April calling for intervention in Cuba, but he waited several days to permit American citizens to be evacuated from the island. In the interim, Spain agreed to an armistice, but ignored McKinley's demand for American mediation. Accordingly, the President delivered his message to Congress on April 11. After a week of hectic debate, Congress voted for intervention and what John Hay later termed "The Splendid Little War" was under way. Within four months the United States had defeated Spain decisively, occupied Cuba, Puerto Rico, Guam, and the Philippines, and assumed a new role of world power which it would never again relinquish.

R.A.D.

To the Congress of the United States:

Obedient to that precept of the Constitution which commands the President to give from time to time to the Congress information of the state of the Union and to recommend to their consideration such measures as he shall judge necessary and expedient, it becomes my duty to now address your body with regard to the grave crisis that has arisen in the relations of the United States to Spain by reason of the warfare that for more than three years has raged in the neighboring island of Cuba. . . .

The present revolution is but the successor of other similar insurrections which have occurred in Cuba against the dominion of Spain, extending over a period of nearly half a century, each of which during its progress has subjected the United States to great effort and expense in enforcing its neutrality laws, caused enormous losses to American trade and commerce, caused irritation, annoyance, and disturbance among our citizens, and, by the exercise of cruel, barbarous, and uncivilized practices of warfare, shocked the sensibilities and offended the human sympathies of our people. . . .

Our trade has suffered, the capital invested by our citizens in Cuba has been largely lost, and the temper and forbearance of our people have been so sorely tried as to beget a perilous unrest among our own citizens, which has inevitably found its expression from time to time in the National Legislature, so that issues wholly external to our own body politic engross attention and stand in the way of that close devotion to domestic advancement that becomes a self-contained commonwealth whose primal maxim has been the avoidance of all foreign entanglements. All this must needs awaken, and has, indeed, aroused, the utmost concern on the part of this Government, as well during my predecessor's term as in my own. . . .

The forcible intervention of the United States as a neutral to stop the war, according to the large dictates of humanity and following many historical precedents where neighboring states have interfered to check the hopeless sacrifices of life by internecine conflicts beyond their borders, is justifiable on rational grounds. It involves, however, hostile constraint upon both the parties to the contest, as well to enforce a truce as to guide the eventual settlement.

The grounds for such intervention may be briefly summarized

as follows:

First. In the cause of humanity and to put an end to the barbarities, bloodshed, starvation, and horrible miseries now existing there, and which the parties to the conflict are either unable or unwilling to stop or mitigate. It is no answer to say this is all in another country, belonging to another nation, and is therefore none of our business. It is specially our duty, for it is right at our door.

Second. We owe it to our citizens in Cuba to afford them that protection and indemnity for life and property which no government there can or will afford, and to that end to terminate the conditions that deprive them of legal protection.

Third. The right to intervene may be justified by the very serious injury to the commerce, trade, and business of our people and by the wanton destruction of property and devastation of the island.

Fourth, and which is of the utmost importance. The present condition of affairs in Cuba is a constant menace to our peace and entails upon this Government an enormous expense. With such a conflict waged for years in an island so near us and with which our people have such trade and business relations; when the lives and liberty of our citizens are in constant danger and their property destroyed and themselves ruined; where our trading vessels are liable to seizure and are seized at our very door by war ships of a foreign nation; the expeditions of filibustering that we are powerless to prevent altogether, and the irritating questions and entanglements thus arising—all these and others that I need not mention, with the resulting strained relations, are a constant menace to our peace and compel us to keep on a semi-war footing with a nation with which we are at peace.

These elements of danger and disorder already pointed out have been strikingly illustrated by a tragic event which has deeply and justly moved the American people. I have already transmitted to Congress the report of the naval court of inquiry on the destruction of the battle ship *Maine* in the harbor of Havana during the night of the 15th of February. The destruction of that noble vessel has filled the national heart with inexpressible horror. Two hundred and fifty-eight brave sailors and marines and two officers of our Navy, reposing in the fancied security of a friendly harbor, have been hurled to death, grief and want brought to their homes and sorrow to the nation.

The naval court of inquiry, which, it is needless to say, commands the unqualified confidence of the Government, was unanimous in its conclusion that the destruction of the *Maine* was caused by an exterior explosion—that of a submarine mine. It did not assume to place the responsibility. That remains to be fixed.

In any event, the destruction of the *Maine,* by whatever exterior cause, is a patent and impressive proof of a state of things in Cuba that is intolerable. That condition is thus shown to be such that the Spanish Government can not assure safety and security to a vessel of the American Navy in the harbor of Havana on a mission of peace, and rightfully there. . . .

The long trial has proved that the object for which Spain has waged the war can not be attained. The fire of insurrection may flame or may smolder with varying seasons, but it has not been and it is plain that it can not be extinguished by present methods. The only hope of relief and repose from a condition which can no longer be endured is the enforced pacification of Cuba. In the name of humanity, in the name of civilization, in behalf of endangered American interests which give us the right and the duty to speak and to act, the war in Cuba must stop.

In view of these facts and of these considerations I ask the Congress to authorize and empower the President to take measures to secure a full and final termination of hostilities between the Government of Spain and the people of Cuba, and to secure in the island the establishment of a stable government, capable of maintaining order and observing its international obligations, insuring peace and tranquillity and the security of its citizens as well as our own, and to use the military and naval forces of the United States as may be necessary for these purposes.

And in the interest of humanity and to aid in preserving the lives of the starving people of the island I recommend that the distribution of food and supplies be continued and that an appropriation be made out of the public Treasury to supplement the charity of our citizens.

The issue is now with the Congress. It is a solemn responsibility. I have exhausted every effort to relieve the intolerable condition of affairs which is at our doors. Prepared to execute every obligation imposed upon me by the Constitution and the law, I await your action.

Yesterday, and since the preparation of the foregoing message, official information was received by me that the latest decree of the Queen Regent of Spain directs General Blanco, in order to prepare and facilitate peace, to proclaim a suspension of hostilities, the duration and details of which have not yet been communicated to me.

This fact, with every other pertinent consideration, will, I am sure, have your just and careful attention in the solemn deliberations upon which you are about to enter. If this measure attains a successful result, then our aspirations as a Christian, peace-loving people will be realized. If it fails, it will be only another justification for our contemplated action.

Theodore Roosevelt: Corollary to the Monroe Doctrine 1904

The assassin's bullet that killed William McKinley in September, 1901, opened up a new era in American life by elevating Theodore Roosevelt to the Presidency. A bold and colorful leader, Teddy Roosevelt was an exuberant nationalist who used the powers of his office to promote reform at home and to extend American influence abroad. Despite his jingoist rhetoric, he pursued cautious, balance-of-power policies in Europe and Asia; but in Latin America he lived up to his reputation by transforming the Caribbean into an American lake.

A canal across the Isthmus of Panama dominated Roosevelt's strategic thinking. In 1903 he abetted a revolution against Colombia and authorized premature recognition of the new government in order to secure U.S. rights in perpetuity to a ten-mile-wide canal zone. As construction of the canal got under way, Roosevelt displayed an obsessive concern over potential threats to the waterway, which he viewed as a life line for a two-ocean American Navy. He permitted U.S. troops to be withdrawn from Cuba, but only after the Cubans agreed to the Platt Amendment, which gave the United States a naval base at Guantánamo Bay and permitted future American intervention on the island in case of political turmoil. In 1902 an Anglo-German blockade of Venezuela over a debt dispute alarmed Roosevelt.

Many Central American and Caribbean republics were heavily in debt to foreign banks, and he feared that default on payments would give the European nations an excuse to intervene in areas close to the future canal.

In 1904 such a situation seemed to be developing in the Dominican Republic. The bankrupt government was unable to meet its foreign obligations and several European countries, led by Germany, expressed concern. Under pressure from Roosevelt, the Dominican government allowed a private American company to attempt to straighten out the country's chaotic finances. In explaining his policy to a friend, Roosevelt commented, "I want to do nothing but what a policeman has to do in Santo Domingo. . . . I have about the same desire to annex it as a gorged boa constrictor might have to swallow a porcupine wrong-end-to." When the European powers protested America's action, Roosevelt dealt at length with the problem in his annual message to Congress, expounding a principle which soon became known as the Roosevelt Corollary to the Monroe Doctrine. In 1905 Roosevelt invoked the Corollary when he forced Dominican authorities to turn control of their finances over to the United States, a step which led eventually to the liquidation of both the debt and the threat of foreign intervention close to the Panama Canal.   R.A.D.

THE EMERGING GIANT

The Granger Collection

The Great Plains—the area that John W. Powell called the Arid Region of the West—
were settled in the years between the Civil War and the beginning of the twentieth
century. This poster, displayed at the Chicago World's Fair of 1893, advertises the
attractions of life in South Dakota.

The Granger Collection

The completion of the transcontinental railroad in 1869 was an important step in the development of the Plains region. The image of the railroad as a bearer of civilization is conveyed in this Currier and Ives print.

An 1877 lithograph shows the interior of one of the West's richest silver mines, the Comstock Lode at Virginia City, Nevada. Silver mining interests helped stimulate the demand for free coinage of silver that was taken up by the Populists in the 1890s.

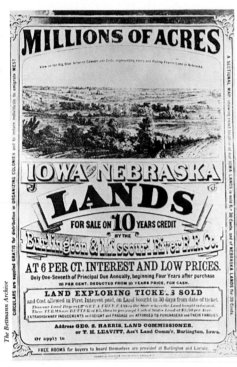

The Bettmann Archive

The railroads helped spur migration to Nebraska and Iowa in the 1870s by offering cheap land to newcomers.

A family of homesteaders poses in front of its Nebraska sod house in the 1880s.

S. D. Butcher Collection/Nebraska State Historical Soc

Believing with the Populists that the gold standard favored the rich at the expense of the poor, Democratic presidential candidate William Jennings Bryan warned its defenders: "You shall not press down upon the brow of labor this crown of thorns, you shall not crucify mankind upon a cross of gold!" An 1896 cartoon ridicules his blend of politics and religion.

The Granger Collection

The Granger Collection

Millions of immigrants provided labor for America's growing industries in the late 19th century. In this 1887 engraving, steerage passengers on a vessel entering New York Harbor gaze at the newly completed Statue of Liberty.

Culver

The American labor movement gathered strength in the decades after the founding (1869) of the Knights of Labor. Here, young working women march in a New York May Day parade in the early 1900s.

The campaign for women's rights had become a major force in American life by 1888, when Elizabeth Cady Stanton (seated, third from right) and feminist leaders from around the world gathered in Washington to mark the fortieth anniversary of the Seneca Falls Declaration.

The Library of Congress

Responding to President McKinley's message calling for intervention in Cuba, Congress declared war on Spain in April 1898. A few days later, an American squadron under Admiral George Dewey attacked and destroyed a Spanish fleet in Manila Bay.

Joseph Keppler's cartoon "The Bosses of the Senate" (1889) satirizes the political influence of business monopolies just before the passage of the Sherman Anti-Trust Act.

The Granger Collection

Theodore Roosevelt is pictured here in the uniform of the Rough Riders, a volunteer unit he led in Cuba during the Spanish-American War. In his Corollary to the Monroe Doctrine, Roosevelt vigorously asserted the right of the United States to intervene in Latin America.

PUNCH, OR THE LONDON CHARIVARI.—September 25, 1901.

"THE ROUGH RIDER."

WITH MR. PUNCH'S BEST WISHES TO PRESIDENT ROOSEVELT.

The Library of Congress

Woodrow Wilson stands on the deck of the George Washington, *sailing to Europe for the Paris Peace Conference in December 1918.*

I... t is not true that the United States feels any land hunger or entertains any projects as regards the other nations of the Western Hemisphere save such as are for their welfare. All that this country desires is to see the neighboring countries stable, orderly, and prosperous. Any country whose people conduct themselves well can count upon our hearty friendship. If a nation shows that it knows how to act with reasonable efficiency and decency in social and political matters, if it keeps order and pays its obligations, it need fear no interference from the United States. Chronic wrongdoing, or an impotence which results in a general loosening of the ties of civilized society, may in America, as elsewhere, ultimately require intervention by some civilized nation, and in the Western Hemisphere the adherence of the United States to the Monroe Doctrine may force the United States, however reluctantly, in flagrant cases of such wrongdoing or impotence, to the exercise of an international police power. If every country washed by the Caribbean Sea would show the progress in stable and just civilization which with the aid of the Platt amendment Cuba has shown since our troops left the island, and which so many of the republics in both Americas are constantly and brilliantly showing, all question of interference by this Nation with their affairs would be at an end. Our interests and those of our southern neighbors are in reality identical. They have great natural riches, and if within their borders the reign of law and justice obtains, prosperity is sure to come to them. While they thus obey the primary laws of civilized society they may rest assured that they will be treated by us in a spirit of cordial and helpful sympathy. We would interfere with them only in the last resort, and then only if it became evident that their inability or unwillingness to do justice at home and abroad had violated the rights of the United States or had invited foreign aggression to the detriment of the entire body of American nations. It is a mere truism to say that every nation, whether in America or anywhere else, which desires to maintain its freedom, its independence, must ultimately realize that the right of such independence can not be separated from the responsibility of making good use of it. . . .

Declaration of the Conservation Conference 1908

In the first decade of the twentieth century, Americans suddenly became concerned about their country's dwindling supply of natural resources. The rapid economic growth since the Civil War had led to a frantic exploitation of land, forests, and mineral deposits. Although there were still five hundred million acres of public land available for settlement, the choice farming and grazing land was all in private hands. Four-fifths of the nation's forests had been cut down; the best dam sites for water power and flood control had passed out of government ownership; the rich supplies of minerals, such as the Mesabi iron range and the Pennsylvania oil fields, were approaching exhaustion.

Theodore Roosevelt, an ardent lover of the out-of-doors, launched a vigorous campaign to make the public aware of the need for conservation. Building on the efforts of his predecessors, the President set aside nearly one hundred fifty million acres of forest land, making them national forest preserves, and secured congressional approval of the Newlands Act to provide for federal dams and reclamation projects. Working closely with Gifford Pinchot, the chief of the Bureau of Forests, Roosevelt lent his vivid personality to the conservationist cause. In 1907 he issued a public call for a governor's conference on natural resources. Under Pinchot's adroit management, governors from thirty-four states assembled in Washington in mid-May, 1908, to meet with members of Congress, Supreme Court justices, leading scientists, and such prominent private citizens as William Jennings Bryan and Andrew Carnegie. For three days the conferees discussed all aspects of the conservation problem and then adopted a declaration expressing their concern. The conference provided the spark needed to arouse public opinion; it led to the creation of conservation commissions in thirty-six states and to a useful inventory of the nation's natural resources. Even so hostile a critic of Roosevelt as Senator Robert La Follette could find no fault in TR's conservation effort; he praised the President "for staying territorial waste" and saving the things "on which alone a peaceful, progressive and happy race life can be founded."

R.A.D.

We the Governors of the States and Territories of the United States of America, in Conference assembled, do hereby declare the conviction that the great prosperity of our country rests upon the abundant resources of the land chosen by our forefathers for their homes and where they laid the foundation of this great Nation.

We look upon these resources as a heritage to be made use of in establishing and promoting the comfort, prosperity, and happiness of the American People, but not to be wasted, deteriorated, or needlessly destroyed.

We agree that our country's future is involved in this; that the great natural resources supply the material basis on which our civilization must continue to depend, and on which the perpetuity of the Nation itself rests.

We agree, in the light of facts brought to our knowledge and from information received from sources which we can not doubt, that this material basis is threatened with exhaustion. Even as each succeeding generation from the birth of the Nation has performed its part in promoting the progress and development of the Republic, so do we in this generation recognize it as a high duty to perform our part; and this duty in large degree lies in the adoption of measures for the conservation of the natural wealth of the country.

We declare our firm conviction that this conservation of our natural resources is a subject of transcendent importance, which should engage unremittingly the attention of the Nation, the States, and the People in earnest cooperation. These natural resources include the land on which we live and which yields our food; the living waters which fertilize the soil, supply power, and form great avenues of commerce; the forests which yield the materials for our homes, prevent erosion of the soil, and conserve the navigation and other uses of our streams; and the minerals which form the basis of our industrial life, and supply us with heat, light, and power.

We agree that the land should be so used that erosion and soil-wash shall cease; that there should be reclamation of arid and semi-arid regions by means of irrigation, and of swamp and over-flowed regions by means of drainage; that the waters should be so conserved and used as to promote navigation, to enable the arid regions to be reclaimed by irrigation, and to develop power in the interests of the People; that the forests which regulate our rivers, support our industries, and promote the fertility and productiveness of the soil should be preserved and perpetuated; that the minerals found so abundantly beneath the surface should be so used as to prolong their utility; that the beauty, healthfulness, and habitability of our country should be preserved and increased; that the sources of national wealth exist for the benefit of the People, and that monopoly thereof should not be tolerated.

We commend the wise forethought of the President in sounding the note of warning as to the waste and exhaustion of the natural resources of the country, and signify our high appreciation of his action in calling this Conference to consider the same and to seek remedies therefor through cooperation of the Nation and the States.

We agree that this cooperation should find expression in suitable action by the Congress within the limits of and coextensive with the national jurisdiction of the subject, and, complementary thereto, by the legislatures of the several States within the limits of and coextensive with their jurisdiction.

We declare the conviction that in the use of the natural resources our independent States are interdependent and bound together by ties of mutual benefits, responsibilities and duties.

We agree in the wisdom of future conferences between the President, Members of Congress, and the Governors of States on the conservation of our natural resources with a view of continued cooperation and action on the lines suggested; and to this end we advise that from time to time, as in his judgment may seem wise, the President call the Governors of the States and Members of Congress and others into conference.

We agree that further action is advisable to ascertain the present condition of our natural resources and to promote the conservation of the same; and to that end we recommend the appointment by each State of a Commission on the Conservation of Natural Resources, to cooperate with each other and with any similar commission of the Federal Government.

We urge the continuation and extension of forest policies adapted to secure the husbanding and renewal of our diminishing timber supply, the prevention of soil erosion, the protection of headwaters, and the maintenance of the purity and navigability of our streams. We recognize that the private ownership of forest lands entails responsibilities in the interests of all the People, and we favor the enactment of laws looking to the protection and replacement of privately owned forests.

We recognize in our waters a most valuable asset of the People of the United States, and we recommend the enactment of laws looking to the conservation of water resources for irrigation, water supply, power, and navigation, to the end that navigable and source streams may be brought under complete control and fully utilized for every purpose. We especially urge on the Federal Congress the immediate adoption of a wise, active, and thorough waterway policy, providing for the prompt improvement of our streams and the conservation of their watersheds required for the uses of commerce and the protection of the interests of our People.

We recommend the enactment of laws looking to the prevention of waste in the mining and extraction of coal, oil, gas, and other minerals with a view to their wise conservation for the use of the People, and to the protection of human life in the mines.

Let us conserve the foundations of our prosperity.

Respectfully submitted,

[Signatures]

Woodrow Wilson: First Inaugural Address 1913

The election of 1912 was one of the most exciting and significant of the twentieth century. Theodore Roosevelt, who had stepped down voluntarily from the Presidency four years earlier, tried to wrest the Republican nomination from William Howard Taft; when he failed, Teddy bolted the G.O.P. and ran for the Presidency on a third-party, "Bull Moose" ticket. Taft knew he had little chance to win, but stayed in the race to spite Roosevelt. The Democrats, who had been out of power since 1896, nearly muffed the opportunity handed them by the Republican split; it took forty-six ballots for their nominating convention to reject the mediocre Champ Clark and come forward with a bold new leader in Woodrow Wilson. A former professor of government and president of Princeton University, Wilson had entered politics late in life, winning the governorship of New Jersey in 1910. He had been a conservative, but once in office he saw the need for change, and by 1912 Wilson was an ardent advocate of progressive reform.

During the campaign Wilson used the phrase "The New Freedom" to describe his program for America. Disturbed by Roosevelt's emphasis on federal control and regulation of the economy, Wilson preached a more Jeffersonian version of reform and called for legislation to restore the free competition of an earlier day. His eloquence, together with the division within Republican ranks, enabled him to win a decisive victory in the electoral college, though he received only 42 per cent of the popular vote.

Exhausted from the strenuous campaign, Wilson went to Bermuda to recuperate and plan for the first Democratic administration in sixteen years. After returning to the States, he gave speeches across the nation in an effort to consolidate public support for the New Freedom. Worrying over conservative opposition, Wilson warned the businessman not to start a financial panic to undermine his administration. "If he does," Wilson declared, "I promise him, not for myself but for my countrymen, a gibbet as high as Haman."

On March 4, 1913, a bright, clear day in Washington, Wilson brushed aside his anxieties and delivered an eloquent and moving address which expressed his vision of the future.

R.A.D.

There has been a change of government. It began two years ago, when the House of Representatives became Democratic by a decisive majority. It has now been completed. The Senate about to assemble will also be Democratic. The offices of President and Vice-President have been put into the hands of Democrats. What does the change mean? That is the question that is uppermost in our minds to-day. That is the question I am going to try to answer, in order, if I may, to interpret the occasion.

It means much more than the mere success of a party. The success of a party means little except when the Nation is using that party for a large and definite purpose. No one can mistake the purpose for which the Nation now seeks to use the Democratic Party. It seeks to use it to interpret a change in its own plans and point of view. Some old things with which we had grown familiar, and which had begun to creep into the very habit of our thought and of our lives, have altered their aspect as we have latterly looked critically upon them, with fresh, awakened eyes; have dropped their disguises and shown themselves alien and sinister. Some new things, as we look frankly upon them, willing to comprehend their real character, have come to assume the aspect of things long believed in and familiar, stuff of our own convictions. We have been refreshed by a new insight into our own life.

We see that in many things that life is very great. It is incomparably great in its material aspects, in its body of wealth, in the diversity and sweep of its energy, in the industries which have been conceived and built up by the genius of individual men and the limitless enterprise of groups of men. It is great, also, very great, in its moral force. Nowhere else in the world have noble men and women exhibited in more striking forms the beauty and the energy of sympathy and helpfulness and counsel in their efforts to rectify wrong, alleviate suffering, and set the weak in the way of strength and hope. We have built up, moreover, a great system of government, which has stood through a long age in many respects a model for those who seek to set liberty upon foundations that will endure against fortuitous change, against storm and accident. Our life contains every great thing, and contains it in rich abundance.

But the evil has come with the good, and much fine gold has been corroded. With riches has come inexcusable waste. We have squandered a great part of what we might have used, and have not stopped to conserve the exceeding bounty of nature, without which our genius for enterprise would have been worthless and impotent, scorning to be careful, shamefully prodigal as well as admirably efficient. We have been proud of our industrial achievements, but we have not hitherto stopped thoughtfully enough to count the human cost, the cost of lives snuffed out, of energies overtaxed and broken, the fearful physical and spiritual cost to the men and women and children upon whom the dead weight and burden of it all has fallen pitilessly the years through. The groans and agony of it all had not yet reached our ears, the solemn, moving undertone of our life, coming up out of the mines and factories, and out of every home where the struggle had its intimate and familiar seat. With the great Government went many deep secret things which we too long delayed to look into and scrutinize with candid, fearless eyes. The great Government we loved has too often been made use of for private and selfish purposes, and those who used it had forgotten the people.

At last a vision has been vouchsafed us of our life as a whole. We see the bad with the good, the debased and decadent with the sound and vital. With this vision we approach new affairs. Our duty is to cleanse, to reconsider, to restore, to correct the evil without impairing the good, to purify and humanize every process of our common life without weakening or sentimentalizing it. There has been something crude and heartless and unfeeling in our haste to succeed and be great. Our thought has been "Let every man look out for himself, let every generation look out for itself," while we reared giant machinery which made it impossible that any but those who stood at the levers of control should have a chance to look out for themselves. We had not forgotten our morals. We remembered well enough that we had set up a policy which was meant to serve the humblest as well as the most powerful, with an eye single to the standards of justice and fair play, and remembered it with pride. But we were very heedless and in a hurry to be great.

We have come now to the sober second thought. The scales of heedlessness have fallen from our eyes. We have made up our minds to square every process of our national life again with the standards we so proudly set up at the beginning and have always carried at our hearts. Our work is a work of restoration.

We have itemized with some degree of particularity the things that ought to be altered and here are some of the chief items: A tariff which cuts us off from our proper part in the commerce of the world, violates the just principles of taxation, and makes the Government a facile instrument in the hands of private interests; a banking and currency system based upon the necessity of the Government to sell its bonds fifty years ago and perfectly adapted to concentrating cash and restricting credits; an industrial system which, take it on all its sides, financial as well as administrative, holds capital in leading strings, restricts the liberties and limits the opportunities of labor, and exploits without renewing or conserving the natural resources of the country; a body of agricultural activities never yet given the efficiency of great business undertakings or served as it should be through the instrumentality of science taken directly to the farm, or afforded the facilities of credit best suited to its practical needs; watercourses undeveloped, waste places unreclaimed, forests untended, fast disappearing without plan or prospect of renewal, unregarded waste heaps at every mine. We have studied as perhaps no other nation has the most effective means of production, but we have not studied cost or economy as we should either as organizers of industry, as statesmen, or as individuals.

Nor have we studied and perfected the means by which government may be put at the service of humanity, in safeguarding the health of the Nation, the health of its men and its women and its children, as well as their rights in the struggle for existence. This is no sentimental duty. The firm basis of government is justice, not pity. These are matters of justice. There can be no equality or opportunity, the first essential of justice in the body politic, if men and women and children be not shielded in their lives, their very vitality, from the consequences of great industrial and social processes which they can not alter, control, or singly cope with. Society must see to it that it does not itself crush or weaken or damage its own constituent parts. The first duty of law is to keep sound the society it serves. Sanitary laws, pure food laws, and laws determining conditions of labor which individuals are powerless to determine for themselves are intimate parts of the very business of justice and legal efficiency.

These are some of the things we ought to do, and not leave the others undone, the old-fashioned, never-to-be-neglected, fundamental safeguarding of property and of individual right. This is the high enterprise of the new day: To lift everything that concerns our life as a Nation to the light that shines from the hearthfire of every man's conscience and vision of the right. It is inconceivable that we should do this as partisans; it is inconceivable we should do it in ignorance of the facts as they are or in blind haste. We shall restore, not destroy. We shall deal with our economic system as it is and as it may be modified, not as it might be if we had a clean sheet of paper to write upon; and step by step we shall make it what it should be, in the spirit of those who question their own wisdom and seek counsel and knowledge, not shallow self-satisfaction or the excitement of excursions whither they can not tell. Justice, and only justice, shall always be our motto.

And yet it will be no cool process of mere science. The Nation has been deeply stirred, stirred by a solemn passion, stirred by the knowledge of wrong, of ideals lost, of government too often debauched and made an instrument of evil. The feelings with which we face this new age of right and opportunity sweep across our heartstrings like some air out of God's own presence, where justice and mercy are reconciled and the judge and the brother are one. We know our task to be no mere task of politics but a task which shall search us through and through, whether we be able to understand our time and the need of our people, whether we be indeed their spokesmen and interpreters, whether we have the pure heart to comprehend and the rectified will to choose our high course of action.

This is not a day of triumph; it is a day of dedication. Here muster, not the forces of party, but the forces of humanity. Men's hearts wait upon us; men's lives hang in the balance; men's hopes call upon us to say what we will do. Who shall live up to the great trust? Who dares fail to try? I summon all honest men, all patriotic, all forward-looking men, to my side. God helping me, I will not fail them, if they will but counsel and sustain me!

Woodrow Wilson: The Fourteen Points 1918

"It would be the irony of fate if my administration had to deal chiefly with foreign affairs," Wilson confided to a friend just before taking office in 1913. A year later war broke out in Europe and despite a determined effort to preserve American neutrality, Wilson found himself driven toward entry into the conflict as German submarines threatened the lives and property of American citizens in the Atlantic. When the German government announced a policy of unrestricted submarine warfare early in 1917, the President knew that he had to take the nation to war, but in doing so he sought a goal that would transcend the mundane issue of neutral rights. The United States, he finally told the Congress, would enter the war "to make the world safe for democracy."

The outbreak of the Bolshevik Revolution in November, 1917, jeopardized Wilson's idealistic crusade. Not only did Lenin and Trotsky threaten to take Russia out of the war against Germany, but they published the texts of secret treaties between the Allies which revealed that England and France were fighting not for noble ideals but for such traditional spoils as territory and colonies. Wilson felt he had to counter the Bolshevik disclosures with a ringing declaration of Allied war aims. He sent Colonel House, his trusted adviser, to Europe to sound out England and France on a joint statement. When House reported that the Allies were not enthusiastic, Wilson decided to speak out on his own. Using a memorandum drafted in part by Walter Lippmann, then an editor of *The New Republic* and an informal presidential adviser, Wilson drew up fourteen specific war aims which he presented to the world in a speech before a joint session of Congress on January 8, 1918. Germany signed the armistice which ended the fighting on the basis of these Fourteen Points, and they formed the agenda for the subsequent peace negotiations which culminated in the Treaty of Versailles.   R.A.D.

Gentlemen of the Congress:

. . . It will be our wish and purpose that the processes of peace, when they are begun, shall be absolutely open and that they shall involve and permit henceforth no secret understandings of any kind. The day of conquest and aggrandizement is gone by; so is also the day of secret covenants entered into in the interest of particular governments and likely at some unlooked-for moment to upset the peace of the world. It is this happy fact, now clear to the view of every public man whose thoughts do not still linger in an age that is dead and gone, which makes it possible for every nation whose purposes are consistent with justice and the peace of the world to avow now or at any other time the objects it has in view.

We entered this war because violations of right had occurred which touched us to the quick and made the life of our own people impossible unless they were corrected and the world secured once for all against their recurrence. What we demand in this war, therefore, is nothing peculiar to ourselves. It is that the world be made fit and safe to live in; and particularly that it be made safe for every peace-loving nation which, like our own, wishes to live its own life, determine its own institutions, be assured of justice and fair dealing by the other peoples of the world as against force and selfish aggression. All the peoples of the world are in effect partners in this interest, and for our own part we see very clearly that unless justice be done to others it will not be done to us. The program of the world's peace, therefore, is our program; and that program, the only possible program, as we see it, is this:

I. Open covenants of peace, openly arrived at, after which there shall be no private international understandings of any kind but diplomacy shall proceed always frankly and in the public view.

II. Absolute freedom of navigation upon the seas, outside territorial waters, alike in peace and in war, except as the seas may be closed in whole or in part by international action for the enforcement of international covenants.

III. The removal, so far as possible, of all economic barriers and the establishment of an equality of trade conditions among all the nations consenting to the peace and associating themselves for its maintenance.

IV. Adequate guarantees given and taken that national armaments will be reduced to the lowest point consistent with domestic safety.

V. A free, open-minded, and absolutely impartial adjustment of all colonial claims, based upon a strict observance of the principle that in determining all such questions of sovereignty the interests of the populations concerned must have equal weight with the equitable claims of the government whose title is to be determined.

VI. The evacuation of all Russian territory and such a settlement of all questions affecting Russia as will secure the best and freest coöperation of the other nations of the world in obtaining for her an unhampered and unembarrassed opportunity for the independent determination of her own political development and national policy and assure her of a sincere welcome into the society of free nations under institutions of her own choosing; and, more than a welcome, assistance also of every kind that she may need and may herself desire. The treatment accorded Russia by her sister nations in the months to come will be the acid test of their good will, of their comprehension of her needs as distinguished from their own interests, and of their intelligent and unselfish sympathy.

VII. Belgium, the whole world will agree, must be evacuated and restored, without any attempt to limit the sovereignty which she enjoys in common with all other free nations. No other single act will serve as this will serve to restore confidence among the nations in the laws which they have themselves set and determined for the government of their relations with one another. Without this healing act the whole structure and validity of international law is forever impaired.

VIII. All French territory should be freed and the invaded portions restored, and the wrong done to France by Prussia in 1871 in the matter of Alsace-Lorraine, which has unsettled the peace of the world for nearly fifty years, should be righted, in order that peace may once more be made secure in the interest of all.

IX. A readjustment of the frontiers of Italy should be effected along clearly recognizable lines of nationality.

X. The peoples of Austria-Hungary, whose place among the nations we wish to see safeguarded and assured, should be accorded the freest opportunity of autonomous development.

XI. Rumania, Serbia, and Montenegro should be evacuated; occupied territories restored; Serbia accorded free and secure access to the sea; and the relations of the several Balkan states to one another determined by friendly counsel along historically established lines of allegiance and nationality; and international guarantees of the political and economic independence and territorial integrity of the several Balkan states should be entered into.

XII. The Turkish portions of the present Ottoman Empire should be assured a secure sovereignty, but the other nationalities which are now under Turkish rule should be assured an undoubted security of life and an absolutely unmolested opportunity of autonomous development, and the Dardanelles should be permanently opened as a free passage to the ships and commerce of all nations under international guarantees.

XIII. An independent Polish state should be erected which should include the territories inhabited by indisputably Polish populations, which should be assured a free and secure access to the sea, and whose political and economic independence and territorial integrity should be guaranteed by international covenant.

XIV. A general association of nations must be formed under specific covenants for the purpose of affording mutual guarantees of political independence and territorial integrity to great and small states alike.

In regard to these essential rectifications of wrong and assertions of right we feel ourselves to be intimate partners of all the governments and peoples associated together against the Imperialists. We cannot be separated in interest or divided in purpose. We stand together until the end.

For such arrangements and covenants we are willing to fight and to continue to fight until they are achieved; but only because we wish the right to prevail and desire a just and stable peace such as can be secured only by removing the chief provocations to war, which this program does not remove. We have no jealousy of German greatness, and there is nothing in this program that impairs it. We grudge her no achievement or distinction of learning or of pacific enterprise such as have made her record very bright and very enviable. We do not wish to injure her or to block in any way her legitimate influence or power. We do not wish to fight her either with arms or with hostile arrangements of trade if she is willing to associate herself with us and the other peace-loving nations of the world in covenants of justice and law and fair dealing. We wish her only to accept a place of equality among the peoples of the world, — the new world in which we now live, — instead of a place of mastery.

Neither do we presume to suggest to her any alteration or modification of her institutions. But it is necessary, we must frankly say, and necessary as a preliminary to any intelligent dealings with her on our part, that we should know whom her spokesmen speak for when they speak to us, whether for the Reichstag majority or for the military party and the men whose creed is imperial domination.

We have spoken now, surely, in terms too concrete to admit of any further doubt or question. An evident principle runs through the whole program I have outlined. It is the principle of justice to all peoples and nationalities, and their right to live on equal terms of liberty and safety with one another, whether they be strong or weak. Unless this principle be made its foundation no part of the structure of international justice can stand. The people of the United States could act upon no other principle; and to the vindication of this principle they are ready to devote their lives, their honor, and everything that they possess. The moral climax of this the culminating and final war for human liberty has come, and they are ready to put their own strength, their own highest purpose, their own integrity and devotion to the test.

Bartolomeo Vanzetti: Statement from Prison 1927

The war to make the world safe for democracy left behind a legacy of fear and hatred that marred the gay exterior of American life in the 1920's. Persecution of German-Americans and the demand for one hundred per cent Americanism created a hostile climate for millions of the foreign born. The Bolshevik Revolution in Russia heightened anxieties and led to a purge of subversives that culminated in the Red Scare of 1919-1920. Attorney General A. Mitchell Palmer conducted a series of raids against suspected radicals which led to the deportation of several thousand aliens without due process of law. Although a few civil libertarians spoke out against this hysteria, most Americans agreed with the patriot who proclaimed, "My motto for the Reds is S.O.S. — ship or shoot."

In April, 1920, at the height of the Red Scare, two men were killed in a payroll robbery in South Braintree, Massachusetts. Three weeks later, police arrested Nicola Sacco and Bartolomeo Vanzetti, recent immigrants from Italy and ardent anarchists. After a speedy trial, under a judge who privately referred to the defendants as "those anarchist bastards," they were found guilty. Radicals quickly claimed that Sacco and Vanzetti's only crime was advocating the overthrow of the government, and intellectuals in America and throughout the world made the case a *cause célèbre*. For six years, appeals spared the lives of Sacco and Vanzetti, but finally in April, 1927, the judge sentenced them to die in the electric chair. Vanzetti, by far the more articulate of the two men, expressed his feelings to reporter Phil Strong in an interview which appeared in the New York *World* in early May. Despite the sympathy this statement won for Vanzetti, the governor of Massachusetts rejected a plea for clemency and the two men were executed on the morning of August 23, 1927.   R.A.D.

If it had not been for these thing, I might have live out my life talking at street corners to scorning men. I might have die, unmarked, unknown, a failure. Now we are not a failure. This is our career and our triumph. Never in our full live could we hope to do such work for tolerance, for joostice, for man's onderstanding of man as now we do by accident. Our words — our lives — our pains — nothing! The taking of our lives — lives of a good shoemaker and a poor fish-peddler — all! That last moment belongs to us — that agony is our triumph.

Herbert Hoover:
Our American System
1928

Few Americans have known the extremes of success and failure that Herbert Clark Hoover experienced. Born to Quaker parents in West Branch, Iowa, and orphaned as a boy, Hoover's early life seemed to be a page out of a Horatio Alger story. He worked his way through Stanford University, amassed a small fortune as a mining engineer and promoter in underdeveloped countries, rose to fame directing overseas relief during the early stages of World War I and as Food Administrator after American entry, and became a leading political figure as Secretary of Commerce under Presidents Harding and Coolidge. Hoover was the logical choice for the Republican nomination in 1928 when Coolidge chose not to run; and most Americans cheered when he declared in his acceptance speech: "We in America today are nearer to the final triumph over poverty than ever before in the history of any land. . . . We shall soon with the help of God be in sight of the day when poverty will be banished from this nation." A year later the great depression undermined this proud boast, and Hoover spent the rest of his life in search of an understanding of what had gone wrong as Democrats made him the scapegoat for economic disaster.

Hoover deserved better. Far from being the reactionary of political caricature, he was a progressive businessman whom Republican conservatives looked upon with considerable misgiving. He embraced the prevailing view of the 1920's that the United States had entered a new economic era of permanent abundance, and he was ready to institutionalize prosperity by initiating bold federal programs. Above all, he expressed a vibrant faith in the free enterprise system and the rugged individualism which had marked his own meteoric career. In a New York City speech ending his 1928 campaign against Alfred E. Smith, the Democratic candidate who was handicapped more by Republican prosperity than by his Catholic faith, Hoover gave a classic statement of his political philosophy.   R.A.D.

This campaign now draws near a close. The platforms of the two parties defining principles and offering solutions of various national problems have been presented and are being earnestly considered by our people. . . .

In my acceptance speech I endeavored to outline the spirit and ideals by which I would be guided in carrying that platform into administration. Tonight I will not deal with the multitude of issues which have been already well canvassed. I intend rather to discuss some of those more fundamental principles and ideals upon which I believe the government of the United States should be conducted. . . .

After the war, when the Republican Party assumed administration of the country, we were faced with the problem of determination of the very nature of our national life. During one hundred and fifty years we have builded up a form of self-government and a social system which is peculiarly our own. It differs essentially from all others in the world. It is the American system. It is just as definite and positive a political and social system as has ever been developed on earth. It is founded upon a particular conception of self-government in which decentralized local responsibility is the very base. Further than this, it is founded upon the conception that only through ordered liberty, freedom, and equal opportunity to the individual will his initiative and enterprise spur on the march of progress. And in our insistence upon equality of opportunity has our system advanced beyond all the world.

During the war we necessarily turned to the government to solve every difficult economic problem. The government having absorbed every energy of our people for war, there was no other solution. For the preservation of the state the Federal Government became a centralized despotism which undertook unprecedented responsibilities, assumed autocratic powers, and took over the business of citizens. To a large degree we regimented our whole people temporarily into a socialistic state. However justified in time of war if continued in peace-time it would destroy not only our American system but with it our progress and freedom as well.

When the war closed, the most vital of all issues both in our own country and throughout the world was whether governments should continue their wartime ownership and operation of many instrumentalities of production and distribution. We were challenged with a peace-time choice between the American system of rugged individualism and a European philosophy of diametrically opposed doctrines—doctrines of paternalism and state socialism. The acceptance of these ideas would have meant the destruction of self-government through centralization of government. It would have meant the undermining of the individual initiative and enterprise through which our people have grown to unparalleled greatness.

The Republican Party from the beginning resolutely turned its face away from these ideas and these war practices. . . . When the Republican Party came into full power it went at once resolutely back to our fundamental conception of the state and the rights and responsibilities of the individual. Thereby it restored confidence and hope in the American people, it freed and stimulated enterprise, it restored the government to its position as an umpire instead of a player in the economic game. For these reasons the American people have gone forward in progress while the rest of the world has halted, and some countries have even gone backwards. If anyone will study the causes of retarded recuperation in Europe, he will find much of it due to stifling of private initiative on one hand, and overloading of the government with business on the other.

There has been revived in this campaign, however, a series of proposals which, if adopted, would be a long step toward the abandonment of our American system and a surrender to the destructive operation of governmental conduct of commercial business. Because the country is faced with difficulty and doubt over certain national problems—that is prohibition, farm relief, and electrical power—our opponents propose that we must thrust government a long way into the businesses which give rise to these problems. In effect, they abandon the tenets of their own party and turn to state socialism as a solution for the difficulties presented by all three. It is proposed that we shall change from prohibition to the state purchase and sale of liquor. If their agricultural relief program means anything, it means that the government shall directly or indirectly buy and sell and fix prices of agricultural products. And we are to go into the hydroelectric power business. In other words, we are confronted with a huge program of government in business.

There is, therefore, submitted to the American people a question of fundamental principle. That is: shall we depart from the principles of our American political and economic system, upon which we have advanced beyond all the rest of the world, in order to adopt methods based on principles destructive of its very foundations? And I wish to emphasize the seriousness of these proposals. I wish to make my position clear; for this goes to the very roots of American life and progress.

I should like to state to you the effect that this projection of government in business would have upon our system of self-government and our economic system. That effect would reach to the daily life of every man and woman. It would impair the very basis of liberty and freedom not only for those left outside the fold of expanded bureaucracy but for those embraced within it.

Let us first see the effect upon self-government. When the Federal Government undertakes to go into commercial business it must at once set up the organization and administration of that business, and it immediately finds itself in a labyrinth, every alley of which leads to the destruction of self-government.

Commercial business requires a concentration of responsibility. Self-government requires decentralization and many checks and balances to safeguard liberty. Our Government to succeed in business would need to become in effect a despotism. There at once begins the destruction of self-government. . . .

It is a false liberalism that interprets itself into the government operation of commercial business. Every step of bureaucratizing of the business of our country poisons the very roots of liberalism — that is, political equality, free speech, free assembly, free press, and equality of opportunity. It is the road not to more liberty, but to less liberty. Liberalism should be found not striving to spread bureaucracy but striving to set bounds to it. True liberalism seeks all legitimate freedom first in the confident belief that without such freedom the pursuit of all other blessings and benefits is vain. That belief is the foundation of all American progress, political as well as economic.

Liberalism is a force truly of the spirit, a force proceeding from the deep realization that economic freedom cannot be sacrificed if political freedom is to be preserved. Even if Governmental conduct of business could give us more efficiency instead of less efficiency, the fundamental objection to it would remain unaltered and unabated. It would destroy political equality. It would increase rather than decrease abuse and corruption. It would stifle initiative and invention. It would undermine the development of leadership. It would cramp and cripple the mental and spiritual energies of our people. It would extinguish equality and opportunity. It would dry up the spirit of liberty and progress. For these reasons primarily it must be resisted. For a hundred and fifty years liberalism has found its true spirit in the American system, not in the European systems.

I do not wish to be misunderstood in this statement. I am defining a general policy. It does not mean that our government is to part with one iota of its national resources without complete protection to the public interest. I have already stated that where the government is engaged in public works for purposes of flood control, of navigation, of irrigation, of scientific research or national defense, or in pioneering a new art, it will at times necessarily produce power or commodities as a by-product. But they must be a by-product of the major purpose, not the major purpose itself.

Nor do I wish to be misinterpreted as believing that the United States is free-for-all and devil-take-the-hindmost. The very essence of equality of opportunity and of American individualism is that there shall be no domination by any group or combination in this republic, whether it be business or political. On the contrary, it demands economic justice as well as political and social justice. It is no system of laissez faire.

I feel deeply on this subject because during the war I had some practical experience with governmental operation and control. I have witnessed not only at home but abroad the many failures of government in business. I have seen its tyrannies, its injustices, its destructions of self-government, its undermining of the very instincts which carry our people forward to progress. I have witnessed the lack of advance, the lowered standards of living, the depressed spirits of people working under such a system. My objection is based not upon theory or upon a failure to recognize wrong or abuse, but I know the adoption of such methods would strike at the very roots of American life and would destroy the very basis of American progress.

Our people have the right to know whether we can continue to solve our great problems without abandonment of our American system. I know we can. . . .

And what have been the results of the American system? Our country has become the land of opportunity to those born without inheritance, not merely because of the wealth of its resources and industry but because of this freedom of initiative and enterprise. Russia has natural resources equal to ours. Her people are equally industrious, but she has not had the blessings of one hundred and fifty years of our form of government and our social system.

By adherence to the principles of decentralized self-government, ordered liberty, equal opportunity, and freedom to the individual, our American experiment in human welfare has yielded a degree of well-being unparalleled in all the world. It has come nearer to the abolition of poverty, to the abolition of fear of want, than humanity has ever reached before. Progress of the past seven years is the proof of it. This alone furnishes the answer to our opponents, who ask us to introduce destructive elements into the system by which this has been accomplished. . . .

I have endeavored to present to you that the greatness of America has grown out of a political and social system and a method of control of economic forces distinctly its own—our American system—which has carried this great experiment in human welfare farther than ever before in all history. We are nearer today to the ideal of the abolition of poverty and fear from the lives of men and women than ever before in any land. And I again repeat that the departure from our American system by injecting principles destructive to it which our opponents propose, will jeopardize the very liberty and freedom of our people, and will destroy equality of opportunity not alone to ourselves but to our children. . . .

Twelve Southern Writers: I'll Take My Stand 1930

Rapid industrialization reached a new peak in the 1920's, threatening to overwhelm the traditional values of an older America. Rural groups tried to strike back in a variety of ways—by upholding Fundamentalism against the theory of evolution, by reviving the Ku Klux Klan, by imposing rigid quotas on immigration from Europe. Intellectuals voiced their dissatisfaction with the new industrial society by rejecting it—either by flight to Europe or by a conscious withdrawal into enclaves like New York's Greenwich Village. The most vigorous and provocative response came from twelve southern writers, members of a literary group centering around Vanderbilt University in Nashville, Tennessee.

Led by poets John Crowe Ransom, Allen Tate, and Donald Davidson, these men indicted the prevailing culture in *I'll Take My Stand: The South and the Agrarian Tradition*, a ringing manifesto published in 1930.

Although the writers formulated their critique of industrialism in the prosperous years of the twenties, their book appeared just after the depression began. The affirmation of the southern agrarian tradition at the very moment modern capitalism seemed to be collapsing gave them a wide audience for their ideas and led the editors of the *Sewanee Review* to describe their work as "the most challenging book published since Henry George's *Progress and Poverty*." R.A.D.

N obody now proposes for the South, or for any other community in this country, an independent political destiny. That idea is thought to have been finished in 1865. But how far shall the South surrender its moral, social, and economic autonomy to the victorious principle of Union? That question remains open. The South is a minority section that has hitherto been jealous of its minority right to live its own kind of life. The South scarcely hopes to determine the other sections, but it does propose to determine itself, within the utmost limits of legal action. Of late, however, there is the melancholy fact that the South itself has wavered a little and shown signs of wanting to join up behind the common or American industrial ideal. It is against that tendency that this book is written. The younger Southerners, who are being converted frequently to the industrial gospel, must come back to the support of the Southern tradition. They must be persuaded to look very critically at the advantages of becoming a "new South" which will be only an undistinguished replica of the usual industrial community.

★   ★   ★

But there are many other minority communities opposed to industrialism, and wanting a much simpler economy to live by. The communities and private persons sharing the agrarian tastes are to be found widely within the Union. Proper living is a matter of the intelligence and the will, does not depend on the local climate or geography, and is capable of a definition which is general and not Southern at all. Southerners have a filial duty to discharge to their own section. But their cause is precarious and they must seek alliances with sympathetic communities everywhere. The members of the present group would be happy to be counted as members of a national agrarian movement.

★   ★   ★

Industrialism is the economic organization of the collective American society. It means the decision of society to invest its economic resources in the applied sciences. But the word science has acquired a certain sanctitude. It is out of order to quarrel with science in the abstract, or even with the applied sciences when their aplications are made subject to criticism and intelligence. The capitalization of the applied sciences has now become extravagant and uncritical; it has enslaved our human energies to a degree now clearly felt to be burdensome. The apologists of industrialism do not like to meet this charge directly; so they often take refuge in saying that they are devoted simply to science! They are really devoted to the applied sciences and to practical production. Therefore it is necessary to employ a certain skepticism even at the expense of the Cult of Science, and to say, It is an Americanism, which looks innocent and disinterested, but really is not either. . . .

★   ★   ★

Religion can hardly expect to flourish in an industrial society. Religion is our submission to the general intention of a nature that is fairly inscrutable; it is the sense of our role as creatures within it. But nature industrialized, transformed into cities and artificial habitations, manufactured into commodities, is no longer nature but a highly simplified picture of nature. We receive the illusion of having power over nature and lose the sense of nature as something mysterious and contingent. The God of nature under these conditions is merely an amiable expression, a superfluity, and the philosophical understanding ordinarily carried in the religious experience is not there for us to have.

★   ★   ★

Nor do the arts have a proper life under industrialism, with the general decay of sensibility which attends it. Art depends, in general, like religion, on a right attitude to nature; and in particular on a free and disinterested observation of nature that occurs only in leisure. Neither the creation nor the understanding of works of art is possible in an industrial age except by some local and unlikely suspension of the industrial drive.

★   ★   ★

The amenities of life also suffer under the curse of a strictly-business or industrial civilization. They consist in such practices as manners, conversation, hospitality, sympathy, family life, romantic love—in the social exchanges which reveal and develop sensibility in human affairs. If religion and the arts are founded on right relations of man-to-nature, these are founded on right relations of man-to-man. . . .

★   ★   ★

The "Humanists" are too abstract. Humanism, properly speaking, is not an abstract system, but a culture, the whole way in which we live, act, think, and feel. It is kind of imaginatively balanced life lived out in a definite social tradition. And, in the concrete, we believe that this, the genuine humanism, was rooted in the agrarian life of the older South and of other parts of the country that shared in such a tradition. It was not an abstract moral "check" derived from the classics—it was not soft material poured in from the top. It was deeply founded in the way of life itself—in its tables, chairs, portraits, festivals, laws, marriage customs. We cannot recover our native humanism by adopting some standard of taste that is critical enough to question the contemporary arts but not critical enough to question the social and economic life which is their ground. . . .

★   ★   ★

Opposed to the industrial society is the agrarian, which does not stand in particular need of definition. An agrarian society is hardly one that has no use at all for industries, for professional vocations, for scholars and artists, and for the life of cities. Technically, perhaps, an agrarian society is one in which agriculture is the leading vocation, whether for wealth, for pleasure, or for prestige—a form of labor that is pursued with intelligence and leisure, and that becomes the model to which the other forms approach as well as they may. But an agrarian regime will be secured readily enough where the superfluous industries are not allowed to rise against it. The theory of agrarianism is that the culture of the soil is the best and most sensitive of vocations, and that therefore it should have the economic preference and enlist the maximum number of workers.

★   ★   ★

These principles do not intend to be very specific in proposing any practical measures. How may the little agrarian community resist the Chamber of Commerce of its county seat, which is always trying to import some foreign industry that cannot be assimilated to the life-pattern of the community? Just what must the Southern leaders do to defend the traditional Southern life? How may the Southern and Western agrarians unite for effective action? Should the agrarian forces try to capture the Democratic party, which historically is so closely affiliated with the defense of individualism, the small community, the state, the South? Or must the agrarians — even the Southern ones — abandon the Democratic party to its fate and try a new one? What legislation could most profitably be championed by the powerful agrarians in the Senate of the United States? What anti-industrial measures might promise to stop the advances of industrialism, or even undo some of them, with the least harm to those concerned? What policy should be pursued by the educators who have a tradition at heart? These and many other questions are of the greatest importance, but they cannot be answered here.

For, in conclusion, this much is clear: If a community, or a section, or a race, or an age, is groaning under industrialism, and well aware that it is an evil dispensation, it must find the way to throw it off. To think that this cannot be done is pusillanimous. And if the whole community, section, race, or age thinks it cannot be done, then it has simply lost its political genius and doomed itself to impotence.

Franklin D. Roosevelt: First Inaugural Address 1933

On March 4, 1933, the nation was closer to collapse than at any time since the Civil War. The great crash in 1929 had been only the beginning of a downward spiral that seemed endless. Fifteen million men, one-third of the nation's labor force, were out of work and nearly all the country's banks were closed, victims of a crisis in public confidence. Herbert Hoover watched the debacle helplessly, unable to stem the downward slide of the economy and utterly incapable of lifting the sagging spirits of the American people.

All eyes were on Franklin D. Roosevelt. In November he had swamped Hoover at the polls, but when the President asked him to cooperate during the four months before the change in administrations took place, Roosevelt declined. Instead he waited, gathering ideas from his "brain trust" of advisers and preparing for the day when he would try to lead the nation out of the depths. Although many Americans dismissed Roosevelt as a charming but superficial man, he had precisely the qualities the nation needed—sunny optimism, shrewd political judgment, an intuitive grasp of public feeling, and, above all, a faith in the future that he was able to communicate through his buoyant manner and electrifying smile.

On the morning of his inauguration, Roosevelt attended services at St. John's Episcopal Church across the street from the White House and then rode to the Capitol through a cold mist, trying to make conversation with a dour and unsmiling Hoover. He had written his speech a week before at his Hyde Park, New York, home; but now he penciled in a new opening sentence as he waited in the Capitol for the ceremonies to begin. Then, moving slowly, his crippled legs encased in steel braces, he walked out to the platform to speak to the huge crowd and to the millions huddled around their radios across the land.

R.A.D.

I am certain that my fellow Americans expect that on my induction into the Presidency I will address them with a candor and a decision which the present situation of our Nation impels.

This is pre-eminently the time to speak the truth, the whole truth, frankly and boldly. Nor need we shrink from honestly facing conditions in our country to-day. This great Nation will endure as it has endured, will revive and will prosper.

So, first of all, let me assert my firm belief that the only thing we have to fear is fear itself—nameless, unreasoning, unjustified terror which paralyzes needed efforts to convert retreat into advance.

In every dark hour of our national life a leadership of frankness and vigor has met with that understanding and support of the people themselves which is essential to victory. I am convinced that you will again give that support to leadership in these critical days.

In such a spirit on my part and on yours we face our common difficulties. They concern, thank God, only material things. Values have shrunken to fantastic levels; taxes have risen; our ability to pay has fallen, government of all kinds is faced by serious curtailment of income; the means of exchange are frozen in the currents of trade; the withered leaves of industrial enterprise lie on every side; farmers find no markets for their produce; the savings of many years in thousands of families are gone.

More important, a host of unemployed citizens face the grim problem of existence, and an equally great number toil with little return. Only a foolish optimist can deny the dark realities of the moment.

Yet our distress comes from no failure of substance. We are stricken by no plague of locusts. Compared with the perils which our forefathers conquered because they believed and were not afraid, we have still much to be thankful for. Nature still offers her bounty and human efforts have multiplied it. Plenty is at our doorstep, but a generous use of it languishes in the very sight of the supply.

Primarily this is because the rulers of the exchange of mankind's goods have failed, through their own stubbornness and their own incompetence, have admitted their failure, and abdicated. Practices of the unscrupulous money changers stand indicted in the court of public opinion, rejected by the hearts and minds of men.

True they have tried, but their efforts have been cast in the pattern of an outworn tradition. Faced by failure of credit they have proposed only the lending of more money.

Stripped of the lure of profit by which to induce our people to follow their false leadership, they have resorted to exhortations, pleading tearfully for restored confidence. They know only the rules of a generation of self-seekers.

They have no vision, and when there is no vision the people perish.

The money changers have fled from their high seats in the temple of our civilization. We may now restore that temple to the ancient truths.

The measure of the restoration lies in the extent to which we apply social values more noble than mere monetary profit.

Happiness lies not in the mere possession of money; it lies in the joy of achievement, in the thrill of creative effort.

The joy and moral stimulation of work no longer must be forgotten in the mad chase of evanescent profits. These dark days will be worth all they cost us if they teach us that our true destiny is not to be ministered unto but to minister to ourselves and to our fellow men.

Recognition of the falsity of material wealth as the standard of success goes hand in hand with the abandonment of the false belief that public office and high political position are to be valued only by the standards of pride of place and personal profit; and there must be an end to a conduct in banking and in business which too often has given to a sacred trust the likeness of callous and selfish wrongdoing.

Small wonder that confidence languishes, for it thrives only on honesty, on honor, on the sacredness of obligations, on faithful protection, on unselfish performance; without them it can not live.

Restoration calls, however, not for changes in ethics alone. This Nation asks for action, and action now.

Our greatest primary task is to put people to work. This is no unsolvable problem if we face it wisely and courageously.

It can be accomplished in part by direct recruiting by the Government itself, treating the task as we would treat the emergency of a war, but at the same time, through this employment, accomplishing greatly needed projects to stimulate and reorganize the use of our natural resources.

Hand in hand with this we must frankly recognize the overbalance of population in our industrial centers and, by engaging on a national scale in a redistribution, endeavor to provide a better use of the land for those best fitted for the land. The task can be helped by definite efforts to raise the values of agricultural products and with this the power to purchase the output of our cities. It can be helped by preventing realistically the tragedy of the growing loss through foreclosure of our small homes and our farms. It can be helped by insistence that the Federal, State, and local governments act forthwith on the demand that their cost be drastically reduced. It can be helped by the unifying of relief activities which to-day are often scattered, uneconomical, and unequal. It can be helped by national planning for and supervision of all forms of transportation and of communications and other utilities which have a definitely public character. There are many ways in which it can be helped, but it can never be helped merely by talking about it. We must act and act quickly.

Finally, in our progress toward a resumption of work we require two safeguards against a return of the evils of the old order; there must be a strict supervision of all banking and credits and investments; there must be an end to speculation with other people's money, and there must be provision for an adequate but sound currency.

There are the lines of attack. I shall presently urge upon a new Congress in special session detailed measures for their fulfillment, and I shall seek the immediate assistance of the several States.

Through this program of action we address ourselves to putting our own national house in order and making income balance outgo.

Our international trade relations, though vastly important, are in point of time and necessity secondary to the establishment of a sound national economy. I favor as a practical policy the putting of first things first. I shall spare no effort to restore world trade by international economic readjustment, but the emergency at home can not wait on that accomplishment.

The basic thought that guides these specific means of national recovery is not narrowly nationalistic. It is the insistence, as a first consideration, upon the interdependence of the various elements in all parts of the United States — a recognition of the old and permanently important manifestation of the American spirit of the pioneer. It is the way to recovery. It is the immediate way. It is the strongest assurance that the recovery will endure.

In the field of world policy I would dedicate this Nation to the policy of the good neighbor—the neighbor who resolutely respects himself and, because he does so, respects the rights of others —the neighbor who respects his obligations and respects the sanctity of his agreements in and with a world of neighbors.

If I read the temper of our people correctly, we now realize as we have never before our interdependence on each other; that we can not merely take but we must give as well; that if we are to go forward, we must move as a trained and loyal army willing to sacrifice for the good of a common discipline, because without such discipline no progress is made, no leadership becomes effective. We are, I know, ready and willing to submit our lives and property to such discipline, because it makes possible a leadership which aims at a larger good. This I propose to offer, pledging that the larger purposes will bind upon us all as a sacred obligation with a unity of duty hitherto evoked only in time of armed strife.

With this pledge taken, I assume unhesitatingly the leadership of *this* great army of our people dedicated to a disciplined attack upon our common problems.

Action in this image and to this end is feasible under the form of government which we have inherited from our ancestors. Our Constitution is so simple and practical that it is possible always to meet extraordinary needs by changes in emphasis and arrangement without loss of essential form. That is why our constitutional system has proved itself the most superbly enduring political mechanism the modern world has produced. It has met every stress of vast expansion of territory, of foreign wars, of bitter internal strife, of world relations.

It is to be hoped that the normal balance of executive and legislative authority may be wholly adequate to meet the unprecedented task before us. But it may be that an unprecedented demand and need for undelayed action may call for temporary departure from that normal balance of public procedure.

I am prepared under my constitutional duty to recommend the measures that a stricken nation in the midst of a stricken world may require. These measures, or such other measures as the Congress may build out of its experience and wisdom, I shall seek, within my constitutional authority, to bring to speedy adoption.

But in the event that the Congress shall fail to take one of these two courses, and in the event that the national emergency is still critical, I shall not evade the clear course of duty that will then confront me. I shall ask the Congress for the one remaining instrument to meet the crisis—broad Executive power to wage a war against the emergency, as great as the power that would be given to me if we were in fact invaded by a foreign foe.

For the trust reposed in me I will return the courage and the devotion that befit the time. I can do no less.

We face the arduous days that lie before us in the warm courage of the national unity; with the clear consciousness of seeking old and precious moral values; with the clean satisfaction that comes from the stern performance of duty by old and young alike. We aim at the assurance of a rounded and permanent national life.

We do not distrust the future of essential democracy. The people of the United States have not failed. In their need they have registered a mandate that they want direct, vigorous action.

They have asked for discipline and direction under leadership. They have made me the present instrument of their wishes. In the spirit of the gift I take it.

In this dedication of a Nation we humbly ask the blessing of God. May He protect each and every one of us. May He guide me in the days to come.

United States v. *One Book Called* Ulysses *1933*

The emergence of a self-conscious group of American intellectuals in the 1920's led to growing tension between the artist and the prevailing business civilization. Condemning Puritanism and the genteel tradition that lingered on from the Victorian era, American writers fled to Europe, where they came to admire the new "stream of consciousness" techniques of Marcel Proust and James Joyce. When Joyce published his novel *Ulysses* in Paris in 1922, American intellectuals hailed it as a stunning achievement; they praised Joyce's ability to use one day in the life of Leopold Bloom, a modern wanderer in the city of Dublin, to reveal the complexity and psychological tension of twentieth-century life. More conventional critics, however, condemned Joyce for his violation of traditional literary standards and especially for his vulgar language and explicit sexual passages. American customs officials banned the importation of the novel, thus preventing its publication and distribution in the United States.

In 1933, Random House decided to test the government's power of censorship by deliberately importing *Ulysses* for sale within the country. The first copy slipped through customs unnoticed, but when the publisher brought it to the attention of federal authorities, they responded by taking the case to court under the Tariff Act of 1930, which provided for prosecution of the book itself rather than of the individual importing it. The government attorneys claimed that the book was obscene, citing both the frequent use of four-letter Anglo-Saxon words and the frank descriptions of the unconscious thought of the book's characters, notably Mollie Bloom. John W. Woolsey, a federal district judge in New York City, heard the case and surprised American intellectuals by ruling in favor of *Ulysses* in a highly literate and sensitive opinion. An appeals court upheld Woolsey by a 2-1 vote, and the government decided not to take the case to the Supreme Court. Random House printed Judge Woolsey's opinion as a Foreword to the American edition of *Ulysses*, which eventually sold nearly a half-million copies. Although the judge did not set forth any sweeping rule of law in finding that *Ulysses* was not obscene, his decision became a landmark in the struggle against literary censorship.   R.A.D.

W

OOLSEY, J. . . . The motion for a decree dismissing the libel herein is granted, and, consequently, of course, the Government's motion for a decree of forfeiture and destruction is denied. . . .

II. I have read "Ulysses" once in its entirety and I have read those passages of which the Government particularly complains several times. In fact, for many weeks, my spare time has been devoted to the consideration of the decision which my duty would require me to make in this matter.

III. The reputation of "Ulysses" in the literary world, however, warranted me taking such time as was necessary to enable me to satisfy myself as to the intent with which the book was written, for, of course, in any case where a book is claimed to be obscene it must first be determined, whether the intent with which it was written was what is called, according to the usual phrase, pornographic — that is, written for the purpose of exploiting obscenity.

If the conclusion is that the book is pornographic that is the end of the inquiry and forfeiture must follow.

But in "Ulysses," in spite of its unusual frankness, I do not detect anywhere the leer of the sensualist. I hold, therefore, that it is not pornographic.

IV. In writing "Ulysses," Joyce sought to make a serious experiment in a new, if not wholly novel, literary genre. He takes persons of the lower middle class living in Dublin in 1904 and seeks not only to describe what they did on a certain day early in June of that year as they went about the City bent on their usual occupation, but also to tell what many of them thought about the while.

Joyce has attempted — it seems to me, with astonishing success — to show how the screen of consciousness with its ever-shifting kaleidoscopic impressions carries, as it were on a plastic palimpsest, not only what is in the focus of each man's observation of the actual things about him, but also in a penumbral zone residua of past impressions, some recent and some drawn up by association from the domain of the subconscious. He shows how each of these impressions affects the life and behavior of the character which he is describing.

What he seeks to get is not unlike the result of a double or, if that is possible, a multiple exposure on a cinema film which would give a clear foreground with a background visible but somewhat blurred and out of focus in varying degrees.

To convey by words an effect which obviously lends itself more appropriately to a graphic technique, accounts, it seems to me, for much of the obscurity which meets a reader of "Ulysses." And it also explains another aspect of the book, which I have further to consider, namely, Joyce's sincerity and his honest effort to show exactly how the minds of his characters operate.

If Joyce did not attempt to be honest in developing the technique which he has adopted in "Ulysses" the result would be psychologically misleading and thus unfaithful to his chosen technique. Such an attitude would be artistically inexcusable.

It is because Joyce has been loyal to his technique and has not funked its necessary implications, but has honestly attempted to tell fully what his characters think about, that he has been the subject of so many attacks and that his purpose has been so often misunderstood and misrepresented. For his attempt sincerely and honestly to realize his objective has required him incidentally to use certain words which are generally considered dirty words and has led at times to what many think is a too poignant preoccupation with sex in the thoughts of his characters.

The words which are criticized as dirty are old Saxon words known to almost all men and, I venture, to many women, and are such words as would be naturally and habitually used, I believe, by the types of folk whose life, physical and mental, Joyce is seeking to describe. In respect of the recurrent emergence of the theme of sex in the minds of his characters, it must always be remembered that his locale was Celtic and his season Spring.

Whether or not one enjoys such a technique as Joyce uses is a matter of taste on which disagreement or argument is futile, but to subject that technique to the standards of some other technique seems to me to be little short of absurd.

Accordingly, I hold that "Ulysses" is a sincere and honest book and I think that the criticisms of it are entirely disposed of by its rationale.

V. Furthermore, "Ulysses" is an amazing *tour de force* when one considers the success which has been in the main achieved with such a difficult objective as Joyce set for himself. As I have stated, "Ulysses" is not an easy book to read. It is brilliant and dull, intelligible and obscure by turns. In many places it seems to me to be disgusting, but although it contains, as I have mentioned above, many words usually considered dirty, I have not found anything that I consider to be dirt for dirt's sake. Each word of the book contributes like a bit of mosaic to the detail of the picture which Joyce is seeking to construct for his readers.

If one does not wish to associate with such folk as Joyce describes, that is one's own choice. In order to avoid indirect contact with them one may not wish to read "Ulysses"; that is quite understandable. But when such a real artist in words, as Joyce undoubtedly is, seeks to draw a true picture of the lower middle class in a European city, ought it to be impossible for the American public legally to see that picture?

To answer this question it is not sufficient merely to find, as I have found above, that Joyce did not write "Ulysses" with what is a commonly called pornographic intent, I must endeavor to apply a more objective standard to his book in order to determine its effect in the result, irrespective of the intent with which it was written.

VI. The statute under which the libel is filed only denounces, in so far as we are here concerned, the importation into the United States from any foreign country of "any obscene book." Section 305 of the Tariff Act of 1930, Title 19 United States Code, Section 1305. It does not marshal against books the spectrum of condemnatory adjectives found, commonly, in laws dealing with matters of this kind. I am therefore, only required to determine whether "Ulysses" is obscene within the legal definition of that word.

The meaning of the word "obscene" as legally defined by the Courts is: tending to stir the sex impulses or to lead to sexually impure and lustful thoughts. . . .

Whether a particular book would tend to excite such impulses and thoughts must be tested by the Court's opinion as to its effect on a person with average sex instincts — what the French would call *l'homme moyen sensuel* — who plays, in this branch of legal inquiry, the same role of hypothetical reagent as does the "reasonable man" in the law of torts and "the man learned in the art" on questions of invention in patent law.

The risk involved in the use of such a reagent arises from the inherent tendency of the trier of facts, however fair he may intend to be, to make his reagent too much subservient to his own idiosyncrasies. Here, I have attempted to avoid this, if possible, and to make my reagent herein more objective than he might otherwise be, by adopting the following course.

After I had made my decision in regard to the aspect of "Ulysses," now under consideration, I checked my impressions with two friends of mine who in my opinion answered to the above stated requirements for my reagent.

These literary assessors—as I might properly describe them—were called on separately, and neither knew that I was consulting the other. They are men whose opinion on literature and on life I value most highly. They had both read "Ulysses," and, of course, were wholly unconnected with this cause.

Without letting either of my assessors know what my decision was, I gave to each of them the legal definition of obscene and asked each whether in his opinion "Ulysses" was obscene within that definition.

I was interested to find that they both agreed with my opinion: that reading "Ulysses" in its entirety, as a book must be read on such a test as this, did not tend to excite sexual impulses or lustful thoughts but that its net effect on them was only that of somewhat tragic and very powerful commentary on the inner lives of men and women.

It is only with the normal person that the law is concerned. Such a test as I have described, therefore, is the only proper test of obscenity in the case of a book like "Ulysses" which is a sincere and serious attempt to devise a new literary method for the observation and description of mankind.

I am quite aware that owing to some of its scenes "Ulysses" is a rather strong draught to ask some sensitive, though normal, persons to take. But my considered opinion, after long reflection, is that whilst in many places the effect of "Ulysses" on the reader undoubtedly is somewhat emetic, nowhere does it tend to be an aphrodisiac.

"Ulysses" may, therefore, be admitted into the United States.

Invalidating the NRA: Schechter Poultry Corp. v. *The United States* 1935

The National Recovery Administration (NRA) was the keystone of Roosevelt's early efforts to overcome the depression. Based on the premise that cooperation was indispensable to recovery, the NRA authorized businessmen to draw up codes of fair competition which had the sanction of law once they were approved by the Roosevelt administration. FDR put the flamboyant Hugh Johnson in charge of the program. Declaring, "It will be red fire at first and dead cats afterwards," Johnson set out to win over industry by holding parades and rallies and publicizing the Blue Eagle as NRA's symbol.

Despite Johnson's fanfare, the NRA was in trouble by 1934 as businessmen began to rebel against the snarl of red tape involved in the codes. Small-scale operators particularly objected to a system dominated by large concerns. As legal challenges mounted, the vital test case came in Brooklyn, where the Schechter brothers, who engaged in the slaughtering of chickens, were found guilty of violating the Code of Fair Competition of the Live Poultry Industry for selling diseased chickens. Both were fined and given brief jail sentences. A distinguished New York law firm, interested in overturning the NRA, came to their rescue and helped the four brothers appeal their case to the Supreme Court.

The justices heard the Schechter case in the spring of 1935, interrupting the lawyers frequently to ask about the unsavory but often comic details of the poultry industry. NRA officials worried over the trend of the judges' questions, but they were unprepared for the verdict. Chief Justice Charles Evans Hughes, speaking for a unanimous Court, ruled the NRA unconstitutional in a sweeping decision that threatened to undermine the entire New Deal by its narrow definition of interstate commerce. In a press conference, Franklin Roosevelt commented on "horse-and-buggy" justice; and two years later, after his overwhelming re-election, he launched an attack on the Court which hurt him politically but led ultimately to more favorable judicial decisions.　　R.A.D.

H

UGHES, C. J. . . . *First.* Two preliminary points are stressed by the Government with respect to the appropriate approach to the important questions presented. We are told that the provision of the statute authorizing the adoption of codes must be viewed in the light of the grave national crisis with which Congress was confronted. Undoubtedly, the conditions to which power is addressed are always to be considered when the exercise of power is challenged. Extraordinary conditions may call for extraordinary remedies. But the argument necessarily stops short of an attempt to justify action which lies outside the sphere of constitutional authority. Extraordinary conditions do not create or enlarge constitutional power. The Constitution established a national government with powers deemed to be adequate, as they have proved to be both in war and peace, but these powers of the national government are limited by the constitutional grants. Those who act under these grants are not at liberty to transcend the imposed limits because they believe that more or different power is necessary. Such assertions of extra-constitutional authority were anticipated and precluded by the explicit terms of the Tenth Amendment,— "The powers not delegated to the United States by the Constitution, nor prohibited by it to the States, are reserved to the States respectively, or to the people."

The further point is urged that the national crisis demanded a broad and intensive cooperative effort by those engaged in trade and industry, and that this necessary cooperation was sought to be fostered by permitting them to initiate the adoption of codes. But the statutory plan is not simply one for voluntary effort. It does not seek merely to endow voluntary trade or industrial associations or groups with privileges or immunities. It involves the coercive exercise of the law-making power. The codes of fair competition, which the statute attempts to authorize, are codes of laws. If valid, they place all persons within their reach under the obligation of positive law, binding equally those who assent and those who do not assent. Violations of the provisions of the codes are punishable as crimes.

Second. The question of the delegation of legislative power. For a statement of the authorized objectives and content of the "codes of fair competition" we are referred repeatedly to the "Declaration of Policy" in section one of Title I of the Recovery Act. Thus, the approval of a code by the President is conditioned on his finding

that it "will tend to effectuate the policy of this title." Sec. 3 (a).
The President is authorized to impose such conditions "for the
protection of consumers, competitors, employees, and others, and
in furtherance of the public interest, and may provide such exceptions to and exemptions from the provisions of such code as
the President in his discretion deems necessary to effectuate the
policy herein declared." *Id.* The "policy herein declared" is mani-
festly that set forth in section one. That declaration embraces a
broad range of objectives. Among them we find the elimination of
"unfair competitive practices." . . .

We think the conclusion is inescapable that the authority sought
to be conferred by section 3 was not merely to deal with "unfair
competitive practices" which offend against existing law, and could
be the subject of judicial condemnation without further legislation,
or to create administrative machinery for the application of established principles of law to particular instances of violation.
Rather, the purpose is clearly disclosed to authorize new and
controlling prohibitions through codes of laws which would embrace what the formulators would propose, and what the President would approve, or prescribe, as wise and beneficent measures
for the government of trades and industries in order to bring
about their rehabilitation, correction and development, according
to the general declaration of policy in section one. Codes of laws
of this sort are styled "codes of fair competition."

We find no real controversy upon this point and we must determine the validity of the Code in question in this aspect.

The question, then, turns upon the authority which section 3 of
the Recovery Act vests in the President to approve or prescribe. If
the codes have standing as penal statutes, this must be due to the
effect of the executive action. But Congress cannot delegate legislative power to the President to exercise an unfettered discretion to
make whatever laws he thinks may be needed or advisable for the
rehabilitation and expansion of trade or industry.

Accordingly we turn to the Recovery Act to ascertain what limits
have been set to the exercise of the President's discretion. *First,*
the President, as a condition of approval, is required to find that
the trade or industrial associations or groups which propose a
code, "impose no inequitable restrictions on admission to membership" and are "truly representative." That condition, however, relates only to the status of the initiators of the new laws and not to

the permissible scope of such laws. *Second,* the President is required to find that the code is not "designed to promote monopolies or to eliminate or oppress small enterprises and will not operate to discriminate against them." And, to this is added a provisio that the code "shall not permit monopolies or monopolistic practices." But these restrictions leave virtually untouched the field of policy envisaged by section one, and, in that wide field of legislative possibilities, the proponents of a code, refraining from monopolistic designs, may roam at will and the President may approve or disapprove their proposals as he may see fit.

Nor is the breadth of the President's discretion left to the necessary implications of this limited requirement as to his findings. As already noted, the President in approving a code may impose his own conditions, adding to or taking from what is proposed, as "in his discretion" he thinks necessary "to effectuate the policy" declared by the Act. Of course, he has no less liberty when he prescribes a code of his own motion or on complaint, and he is free to prescribe one if a code has not been approved. The Act provides for the creation by the President of administrative agencies to assist him, but the action or reports of such agencies, or of his other assistants, — their recommendations and findings in relation to the making of codes — have no sanction beyond the will of the President, who may accept, modify or reject them as he pleases. Such recommendations or findings in no way limit the authority which section 3 undertakes to vest in the President with no other conditions than those there specified. And this authority relates to a host of different trades and industries, thus extending the President's discretion to all the varieties of laws which he may deem to be beneficial in dealing with the vast array of commercial and industrial activities throughout the country.

Such a sweeping delegation of legislative power finds no support in the decisions upon which the Government especially relies.

To summarize and conclude upon this point: Section 3 of the Recovery Act is without precedent. It supplies no standards for any trade, industry or activity. It does not undertake to prescribe rules of conduct to be applied to particular states of fact determined by appropriate administrative procedure. Instead of prescribing rules of conduct, it authorizes the making of codes to prescribe them. For that legislative undertaking, section 3 sets up no standards, aside from the statement of the general aims of rehabilitation, correction and expansion described in section one. In view of the scope of that broad declaration, and of the nature of the few restrictions that are imposed, the discretion of the President in approving or prescribing codes, and thus enacting laws for the government of trade and industry throughout the country, is virtually unfettered. We think that the code-making authority thus conferred is an unconstitutional delegation of legislative power.

Second. The question of the application of the provisions of the Live Poultry Code to intrastate transactions. This aspect of the case presents the question whether the particular provisions of the Live Poultry Code, which the defendants were convicted for violating and for having conspired to violate, were within the regulating power of Congress.

These provisions relate to the hours and wages of those employed by defendants in their slaughterhouses in Brooklyn and to the sales there made to retail dealers and butchers.

(1) Were these transactions *"in"* interstate commerce? Much is made of the fact that almost all the poultry coming to New York is sent there from other States. But the code provisions, as here applied, do not concern the transportation of the poultry from other States to New York, or the transactions of the commission men or others to whom it is consigned, or the sales made by such consignees to defendants. When defendants had made their purchases, whether at the West Washington Market in New York City or at the railroad terminals serving the City, or elsewhere, the poultry was trucked to their slaughterhouses in Brooklyn for local disposition. The interstate transactions in relation to that poultry then ended. Defendants held the poultry at their slaughterhouse markets for slaughter and local sale to retail dealers and butchers who in turn sold directly to consumers. Neither the slaughtering nor the sales by defendants were transactions in interstate commerce.

The undisputed facts thus afford no warrant for the argument that the poultry handled by defendants at their slaughterhouse markets was in a *"current"* or *"flow"* of interstate commerce and was thus subject to congressional regulation. The mere fact that there may be a constant flow of commodities into a State does not mean that the flow continues after the property has arrived and has become commingled with the mass of property within the State and is there held solely for local disposition and use. So far as the poultry here in question is concerned, the flow in interstate commerce had ceased. The poultry had come to a permanent rest within the State. It was not held, used, or sold by defendants in relation to any further transactions in interstate commerce and was not destined for transportation to other states. Hence, decisions which deal with a stream of interstate commerce — where goods come to rest within a State temporarily and are later to go forward in interstate commerce — and with the regulations of transactions involved in that practical continuity of movement, are not applicable here.

(2) Did the defendants' transactions directly "*affect*" interstate commerce so as to be subject to federal regulation? The power of Congress extends not only to the regulation of transactions which are part of interstate commerce, but to the protection of that commerce from injury.

In determining how far the federal government may go in controlling intrastate transactions upon the ground that they "affect" interstate commerce, there is a necessary and well-established distinction between direct and indirect effects. The precise line can be drawn only as individual cases arise, but the distinction is clear in principle. Direct effects are illustrated by the railroad cases we have cited, as *e. g.*, the effect of failure to use prescribed safety appliances on railroads which are the highways of both interstate and intrastate commerce, injury to an employee engaged in interstate transportation by the negligence of an employee engaged in an intrastate movement, the fixing of rates for intrastate transportation which unjustly discriminate against interstate commerce. But where the effect of intrastate transactions upon interstate commerce is merely indirect, such transactions remain within the domain of state power. If the commerce clause were construed to reach all enterprises and transactions which could be said to have an indirect effect upon interstate commerce, the federal authority would embrace practically all the activities of the people and the authority of the State over its domestic concerns would exist only by sufferance of the federal government. Indeed, on such a theory, even the development of the State's commercial facilities would be subject to federal control.

The distinction between direct and indirect effects has been clearly recognized in the application of the Anti-Trust Act. Where a combination or conspiracy is formed, with the intent to restrain interstate commerce or to monopolize any part of it, the violation of the statute is clear. But where that intent is absent, and the objectives are limited to intrastate activities, the fact that there may be an indirect effect upon interstate commerce does not subject the parties to the federal statute, notwithstanding its broad provisions.

While these decisions related to the application of the federal statute, and not to its constitutional validity, the distinction between direct and indirect effects of intrastate transactions upon interstate commerce must be recognized as a fundamental one, essential to the maintenance of our constitutional system. Otherwise as we have said, there would be virtually no limit to the federal power and for all practical purposes we should have a completely centralized government. We must consider the provisions here in question in the light of this distinction.

The question of chief importance relates to the provisions of the Code as to the hours and wages of those employed in defendants' slaughterhouse markets. It is plain that these requirements are imposed in order to govern the details of defendants' management of their local business. The persons employed in slaughtering and selling in local trade are not employed in interstate commerce. Their hours and wages have no direct relation to interstate commerce. The question of how many hours these employees should work and what they should be paid differs in no essential respect from similar questions in other local businesses which handle commodities brought into a State and there dealt in as a part of its internal commerce. This appears from an examination of the considerations urged by the Government with respect to conditions in the poultry trade. Thus, the Government, argues that hours and wages affect prices; that slaughterhouse men sell at a small margin above operating costs; that labor represents 50 to 60 per cent of these costs; that a slaughterhouse operator paying lower wages or reducing his cost by exacting long hours of work, translates his saving into lower prices; that this results in demands for a cheaper grade of goods; and that the cutting of prices brings about demoralization of the price structure. Similar conditions may be adduced in relation to other businesses. The argument of the Government proves too much. If the federal government may determine the wages and hours of employees in the internal commerce of a State, because of their relation to cost and prices and their indirect effect upon interstate commerce, it would seem that a similar control might be exerted over other elements of cost, also affecting prices, such as the number of employees, rents, advertising, methods of doing business, etc. All the processes of production and distribution that enter into cost could likewise be controlled. If the cost of doing an intrastate business is in itself the permitted object of federal control, the extent of the regulation of cost would be a question of discretion and not of power.

The Government also makes the point that efforts to enact state legislation establishing high labor standards have been impeded by the belief that unless similar action is taken generally, commerce will be diverted from the States adopting such standards, and that this fear of diversion has led to demands for federal legislation on the subject of wages and hours. The apparent implication is that the federal authority under the commerce clause should be deemed to extend to the establishment of rules to govern wages and hours in intrastate trade and industry generally throughout the country, thus overriding the authority of the States to deal with domestic problems arising from labor conditions in their internal commerce.

It is not the province of the Court to consider the economic advantages or disadvantages of such a centralized system. It is sufficient to say that the Federal Constitution does not provide for it. Our growth and development have called for wide use of the commerce power of the federal government in its control over the expanded activities of interstate commerce, and in protecting that commerce from burdens, interferences, and conspiracies to restrain and monopolize it. But the authority of the federal government may not be pushed to such an extreme as to destroy the distinction, which the commerce clause itself establishes, between commerce "among the several States" and the internal concerns of a State. The same answer must be made to the contention that is based upon the serious economic situation which led to the passage of the Recovery Act, — the fall in prices, the decline in wages and employment, and the curtailment of the market for commodities. Stress is laid upon the great importance of maintaining wage distributions which would provide the necessary stimulus in starting "the cumulative forces making for expanding commercial activity." Without in any way disparaging this motive, it is enough to say that the recuperative efforts of the federal government must be made in a manner consistent with the authority granted by the

Constitution.

We are of the opinion that the attempt through the provisions of the Code to fix the hours and wages of employees of defendants in their intrastate business was not a valid exercise of federal power.

On both the grounds we have discussed, the attempted delegation of legislative power, and the attempted regulation of intrastate transactions which affect interstate commerce only indirectly, we hold the code provisions here in question to be invalid and that the judgment of conviction must be reversed.

Justice Cardozo delivered a concurring opinion with which Justice Stone concurred.

The Wagner Act 1935

The Supreme Court's invalidation of the NRA served as a catalyst for a much more far-reaching piece of New Deal legislation. At the insistence of Senator Robert F. Wagner of New York, Congress had included the principle of collective bargaining in Section 7a of the original act establishing the NRA in 1933. However, employers soon found ways to get around this provision by using company unions; and President Roosevelt revealed that he was relatively apathetic to the plight of labor by commenting to reporters in 1934 that workers could choose anyone they wanted to represent them whether a union, or the Ahkoond of Swat, or the Royal Geographic Society. Disturbed both by FDR's attitude and prevailing business practices, Senator Wagner introduced a bill in 1934 to create a National Labor Relations Board to insure the right of collective bargaining for labor unions. Roosevelt opposed Wagner's measure; but when the Supreme Court voided the NRA, and thus killed Section 7a, the President shifted his position. The Senate had already voted overwhelmingly for the Wagner bill, and Roosevelt publicly announced his support, placing the measure on his list of "must" legislation. In less than a month, the bill sailed through the House and was signed into law.

Wagner was amazed at the ease with which Congress passed his legislation, which a historian has described as "one of the most drastic legislative innovations of the decade." The Wagner Act revolutionized American labor-management relations by placing the power of the federal government behind collective bargaining and the right of employees to join labor organizations, and by defining unfair labor practices on the employers' part without imposing any corresponding obligations on the unions.   R.A.D.

Section 1: The denial by employers of the right of employees to organize and the refusal by employers to accept the procedure of collective bargaining lead to strikes and other forms of industrial strife or unrest, which have the intent or the necessary effect of burdening or obstructing commerce by (a) impairing the efficiency, safety, or operation of the instrumentalities of commerce; (b) occurring in the current of commerce; (c) materially affecting, re-straining, or controlling the flow of raw materials or manufactured or processed goods from or into the channels of commerce, or the prices of such materials or goods in commerce; or (d) causing diminution of employment and wages in such volume as substan-tially to impair or disrupt the market for goods flowing from or into the channels of commerce.

The inequality of bargaining power between employees who do not possess full freedom of association or actual liberty of contract, and employers who are organized in the corporate or other forms of ownership association substantially burdens and affects the flow of commerce, and tends to aggravate recurrent business de-pressions, by depressing wage rates and the purchasing power of wage earners in industry and by preventing the stabilization of competitive wage rates and working conditions within and between industries.

Experience has proved that protection by law of the right of employees to organize and bargain collectively safeguards com-merce from injury, impairment, or interruption, and promotes the flow of commerce by removing certain recognized sources of industrial strife and unrest, by encouraging practices fundamental to the friendly adjustment of industrial disputes arising out of differences as to wages, hours, or other working conditions, and by restoring equality of bargaining power between employers and employees.

It is hereby declared to be the policy of the United States to eliminate the causes of certain substantial obstructions to the free flow of commerce and to mitigate and eliminate these obstructions when they have occurred by encouraging the practice and pro-cedure of collective bargaining and by protecting the exercise by workers of full freedom of association, self-organization, and de-signation of representatives of their own choosing, for the purpose of negotiating the terms and conditions of their employment or other mutual aid or protection. . . .

SEC. 3. (a) There is hereby created a board, to be known as the "National Labor Relations Board," which shall be composed of three members, who shall be appointed by the President, by and with the advice and consent of the Senate. One of the original members shall be appointed for a term of one year, one for a term of three years, and one for a term of five years, but their successors shall be appointed for terms of five years each, except that any individual chosen to fill a vacancy shall be appointed only for the unexpired term of the member whom he shall succeed. The President shall designate one member to serve as chairman of the Board. Any member of the Board may be removed by the President, upon notice and hearing, for neglect of duty or malfeasance in office, but for no other cause. . . .

SEC. 7. Employees shall have the right of self-organization, to form, join, or assist labor organizations, to bargain collectively through representatives of their own choosing, and to engage in concerted activities, for the purpose of collective bargaining or other mutual aid or protection.

SEC. 8. It shall be an unfair labor practice for an employer—

(1) To interfere with, restrain, or coerce employees in the exercise of the rights guaranteed in Section 7.

(2) To dominate or interfere with the formation or administration of any labor organization or contribute financial or other support to it: *Provided,* That subject to rules and regulations made and published by the Board pursuant to Section 6 (a), an employer shall not be prohibited from permitting employees to confer with him during working hours without loss of time or pay.

(3) By discrimination in regard to hire or tenure of employment or any term or condition of employment to encourage or discourage membership in any labor organization: *Provided,* That nothing in this Act, or in the National Industrial Recovery Act (U.S.C., Supp. VII, title 15, secs. 701–712), as amended from time to time, or in any code or agreement approved or prescribed thereunder, or in any other statute of the United States, shall preclude an employer from making an agreement with a labor organization (not established, maintained, or assisted by any action defined in this Act as an unfair labor practice) to require as a condition of employment membership therein, if such labor organization is the representative of the employees as provided in Section 9 (a), in the appropriate collective bargaining unit cov-

ered by such agreement when made.

(4) To discharge or otherwise discriminate against an employee because he has filed charges or given testimony under this Act.

(5) To refuse to bargain collectively with the representatives of his employees, subject to the provisions of Section 9 (a).

SEC. 9. (a) Representatives designated or selected for the purposes of collective bargaining by the majority of the employees in a unit appropriate for such purposes, shall be the exclusive representatives of all the employees in such unit for the purposes of collective bargaining in respect to rates of pay, wages, hours of employment, or other conditions of employment: *Provided,* That any individual employee or a group of employees shall have the right at any time to present grievances to their employer.

(b) The Board shall decide in each case whether, in order to insure to employees the full benefit of their right to self-organization and to collective bargaining, and otherwise to effectuate the policies of this Act, the unit appropriate for the purposes of collective bargaining shall be the employer unit, craft unit, plant unit, or subdivision thereof.

(c) Whenever a question affecting commerce arises concerning the representation of employees, the Board may investigate such controversy and certify to the parties, in writing, the name or names of the representatives that have been designated or selected. In any such investigation, the Board shall provide for an appropriate hearing upon due notice, either in conjunction with a proceeding under Section 10 or otherwise, and may take a secret ballot of employees, or utilize any other suitable method to ascertain such representatives. . . .

SEC. 10. (a) The Board is empowered, as hereinafter provided, to prevent any person from engaging in any unfair labor practice (listed in Section 8) affecting commerce. This power shall be exclusive, and shall not be affected by any other means of adjustment or prevention that has been or may be established by agreement, code, law, or otherwise.

(b) Whenever it is charged that any person has engaged in or is engaging in any such unfair labor practice, the Board, or any agent or agency designated by the Board for such purposes, shall have power to issue and cause to be served upon such person a complaint stating the charges in that respect, and containing a notice of hearing before the Board or a member thereof, or before a designated agent or agency, at a place therein fixed, not less than five days after the serving of said complaint. Any such complaint may be amended by the member, agent, or agency conducting the hearing for the Board in its discretion at any time prior to the issuance of an order based thereon. The person so complained of shall have the right to file an answer to the original or amended complaint and to appear in person or otherwise and give testimony at the place and time fixed in the complaint. In the discretion of the member, agent or agency conducting the hearing for the Board, any other person may be allowed to intervene in the said proceeding and to present testimony. In any such proceeding the rules of evidence prevailing in courts of law or equity shall not be controlling.

Franklin D. Roosevelt: The Four Freedoms Speech 1941

Franklin Roosevelt, elected originally to save the nation from economic disaster, broke with tradition in 1940 to run for a third term with the world at war. The fall of France, the battle for Britain, and the Japanese invasion of Indo-China all sharpened the sense of peril for the United States, which had tried unsuccessfully to escape from world responsibilities by a policy of isolation in the 1930's. Roosevelt won his third term primarily on the basis of advocating all-out aid to the Allies short of war. A month after the election, Great Britain's Prime Minister Winston Churchill informed him that the British were rapidly running out of funds with which to buy American goods. In a "fireside chat" to the nation on December 29, Roosevelt outlined his remedy — lend-lease aid — which would, as he put it, "eliminate the dollar-sign" and remove all financial restrictions on American aid to Britain.

A week later, FDR was scheduled to deliver his annual message to Congress. On January 1 he sat down with his speechwriters, Harry Hopkins, Samuel Rosenman, and Robert Sherwood, to study the rough draft they had prepared from material he had dictated earlier. Realizing that the speech needed a peroration, Roosevelt recalled a press conference the previous summer in which he had talked to reporters about the long-range peace objectives of the United States. Roosevelt had spoken of a number of freedoms, and a reporter had pointed out that he had omitted freedom from want. Dictating quickly to a stenographer, FDR corrected that oversight by coming up with a new formulation of the four freedoms, thereby providing a fitting climax to his annual message and giving the nation a set of idealistic goals for the war it was soon to enter.   R.A.D.

To the Congress of the United States:

I address you, the Members of the Seventy-Seventh Congress, at a moment unprecedented in the history of the Union. I use the word "unprecedented," because at no previous time has American security been as seriously threatened from without as it is today. . . .

Every realist knows that the democratic way of life is at this moment being directly assailed in every part of the world — assailed either by arms, or by secret spreading of poisonous propaganda by those who seek to destroy unity and promote discord in nations still at peace. During sixteen months this assault has blotted out the whole pattern of democratic life in an appalling number of independent nations, great and small. The assailants are still on the march, threatening other nations, great and small.

Therefore, as your President, performing my constitutional duty to "give to the Congress information of the state of the Union," I find it necessary to report that the future and the safety of our country and of our democracy are overwhelmingly involved in events far beyond our borders.

Armed defense of democratic existence is now being gallantly waged in four continents. If that defense fails, all the population and all the resources of Europe, Asia, Africa and Australasia will be dominated by the conquerors. The total of those populations and their resources greatly exceeds the sum total of the population and resources of the whole of the Western Hemisphere — many times over.

In times like these it is immature — and incidentally untrue — for anybody to brag that an unprepared America, single-handed, and with one hand tied behind its back, can hold off the whole world.

No realistic American can expect from a dictator's peace international generosity, or return of true independence, or world disarmament, or freedom of expression, or freedom of religion — or even good business. Such a peace would bring no security for us or for our neighbors. "Those who would give up essential liberty to purchase a little temporary safety deserve neither liberty nor safety." As a nation we may take pride in the fact that we are soft-hearted; but we cannot afford to be soft-hearted. We must always be wary of those who with sounding brass and a tinkling cymbal preach the "ism" of appeasement. We must especially beware of that small group of selfish men who would clip the wings of the American eagle in order to feather their own nests.

I have recently pointed out how quickly the tempo of modern warfare could bring into our very midst the physical attack which we must expect if the dictator nations win this war.

There is much loose talk of our immunity from immediate and direct invasion from across the seas. Obviously, as long as the British Navy retains its power, no such danger exists. Even if there were no British Navy, it is not probable that any enemy would be stupid enough to attack us by landing troops in the United States from across thousands of miles of ocean, until it had acquired strategic bases from which to operate. But we learn much from the lessons of the past years in Europe—particularly the lesson of Norway, whose essential seaports were captured by treachery and surprise built up over a series of years. The first phase of the invasion of this hemisphere would not be the landing of regular troops. The necessary strategic points would be occupied by secret agents and their dupes—and great numbers of them are already here, and in Latin America.

As long as the aggressor nations maintain the offensive, they—not we—will choose the time and the place and the method of their attack. That is why the future of all American Republics is today in serious danger. That is why this annual message to the Congress is unique in our history. That is why every member of the executive branch of the Government and every Member of the Congress face great responsibility—and great accountability. . . .

Let us say to the democracies: "We Americans are vitally concerned in your defense of freedom. We are putting forth our energies, our resources, and our organizing powers to give you the strength to regain and maintain a free world. We shall send you, in ever-increasing numbers, ships, planes, tanks, guns. This is our purpose and our pledge." In fulfillment of this purpose we will not be intimidated by the threats of dictators that they will regard as a breach of international law and as an act of war our aid to the democracies which dare to resist their aggression. Such aid is not an act of war, even if a dictator should unilaterally proclaim it so to be. When the dictators are ready to make war upon us, they will not wait for an act of war on our part. They did not wait for Norway or Belgium or the Netherlands to commit an act of war. Their only interest is in a new one-way international law, which lacks mutuality in its observance, and, therefore, becomes an instrument of oppression.

The happiness of future generations of Americans may well depend upon how effective and how immediate we can make our aid felt. No one can tell the exact character of the emergency situations that we may be called upon to meet. The Nation's hands must not be tied when the Nation's life is in danger. We must all prepare to make the sacrifices that the emergency—as serious as war itself—demands. Whatever stands in the way of speed and efficiency in defense preparations must give way to the national need.

A free nation has the right to expect full cooperation from all groups. A free nation has the right to look to the leaders of business, of labor, and of agriculture to take the lead in stimulating effort, not among other groups but within their own groups. The best way of dealing with the few slackers or trouble makers in our midst is, first, to shame them by patriotic example, and, if that fails, to use the sovereignty of government to save government.

As men do not live by bread alone, they do not fight by armaments alone. Those who man our defenses, and those behind them who build our defenses, must have the stamina and courage which come from an unshakable belief in the manner of life which they are defending. The mighty action which we are calling for cannot be based on a disregard of all things worth fighting for.

The Nation takes great satisfaction and much strength from the things which have been done to make its people conscious of their individual stake in the preservation of democratic life in America. Those things have toughened the fibre of our people, have renewed their faith and strengthened their devotion to the institutions we make ready to protect. Certainly this is no time to stop thinking about the social and economic problems which are the root cause of the social revolution which is today a supreme factor in the world.

There is nothing mysterious about the foundations of a healthy and strong democracy. The basic things expected by our people of their political and economic systems are simple. They are: equality of opportunity for youth and for others; jobs for those who can work; security for those who need it; the ending of special privilege for the few; the preservation of civil liberties for all; the enjoyment of the fruits of scientific progress in a wider and constantly rising standard of living.

These are the simple and basic things that must never be lost sight of in the turmoil and unbelievable complexity of our modern world. The inner and abiding strength of our economic and political systems is dependent upon the degree to which they fulfill these expectations. . . .

In the future days, which we seek to make secure, we look forward to a world founded upon four essential human freedoms.

The first is freedom of speech and expression—everywhere in the world.

The second is freedom of every person to worship God in his own way—everywhere in the world.

The third is freedom from want—which, translated into world terms, means economic understandings which will secure to every nation a healthy peacetime life for its inhabitants—everywhere in the world.

The fourth is freedom from fear—which, translated into world terms, means a worldwide reduction of armaments to such a point and in such a thorough fashion that no nation will be in a position to commit an act of physical aggression against any neighbor—anywhere in the world.

That is no vision of a distant millennium. It is a definite basis for a kind of world attainable in our own time and generation. That kind of world is the very antithesis of the so-called new order of tyranny which the dictators seek to create with the crash of a bomb.

To that new order we oppose the greater conception—the moral order. A good society is able to face schemes of world domination and foreign revolutions alike without fear.

Since the beginning of our American history we have been engaged in change—in a perpetual peaceful revolution—a revolution which goes on steadily, quietly adjusting itself to changing conditions—without the concentration camp or the quick-lime in the ditch. The world order which we seek is the cooperation of free countries, working together in a friendly, civilized society.

This Nation has placed its destiny in the hands and heads and hearts of its millions of free men and women; and its faith in freedom under the guidance of God. Freedom means the supremacy of human rights everywhere. Our support goes to those who struggle to gain those rights or keep them. Our strength is in our unity of purpose.

To that high concept there can be no end save victory.

Harry S Truman: Statement on the Atomic Bomb 1945

The Second World War brought on an enormous escalation of violence against civilians. The American conscience was outraged by the Japanese bombing of Nanking in 1938 and the needless German aerial assault on such cities as Rotterdam and Coventry in 1940. Yet the casualties in these Axis air raids were relatively small compared to the more than one hundred thousand German civilians who died in the Allied attack on Dresden and the nearly one hundred fifty thousand Japanese who perished during the fire bombings of Tokyo in one week in March, 1945. Viewed against this background, the two atomic bombs dropped by U. S. planes on the Japanese cities of Hiroshima and Nagasaki can be seen as the climax of a wartime trend as well as the beginning of a new era in human affairs.

American development of nuclear weapons began as a result of scientist Albert Einstein's letter to President Roosevelt in 1939 explaining the possibility of an atomic bomb and urging a massive effort to build one before the Germans did. After considerable delay, the secret Manhattan Project got under way in 1942, with major plants to supply fissionable material at Oak Ridge, Tennessee, and Hanford, Washington. By 1944 supplies of the bomb material were arriving at the remote Los Alamos, New Mexico, laboratory where a team of scientists and engineers led by Robert Oppenheimer worked feverishly to make a workable bomb. President Truman, unaware of this vast program upon taking office after Roosevelt's death, accepted the advice of a special committee headed by Secretary of War Henry Stimson to use the bomb without warning against Japanese cities. Oppenheimer's team perfected the bomb and tested it successfully at Alamogordo on July 16, 1945, on the eve of the Potsdam conference, attended by the U. S., Great Britain, and the Soviet Union. President Truman, informed of the successful test just after he arrived at Potsdam, joined with the British in issuing a declaration calling upon the Japanese to surrender or face destruction, but he made no mention of the new weapon. When Japan refused to give in, Truman authorized the use of the bomb. While the President was at sea on his way home from Potsdam, Secretary Stimson released this statement by Truman which gave the American people their first glimpse of the atomic age. R.A.D.

Sixteen hours ago an American airplane dropped one bomb on Hiroshima, an important Japanese Army base. That bomb had more power than 20,000 tons of T.N.T. It had more than two thousand times the blast power of the British "Grand Slam" which is the largest bomb ever yet used in the history of warfare.

The Japanese began the war from the air at Pearl Harbor. They have been repaid many fold. And the end is not yet. With this bomb we have now added a new and revolutionary increase in destruction to supplement the growing power of our armed forces. In their present form these bombs are now in production and ever more powerful forms are in development.

It is an atomic bomb. It is a harnessing of the basic power of the universe. The force from which the sun draws its power has been loosed against those who brought war to the Far East.

Before 1939, it was the accepted belief of scientists that it was theoretically possible to release atomic energy. But no one knew any practical method of doing it. By 1942, however, we knew that the Germans were working feverishly to find a way to add atomic energy to the other engines of war with which they hoped to enslave the world. But they failed. We may be grateful to Providence that the Germans got the V–1's and V–2's late and in limited quantities and even more grateful that they did not get the atomic bomb at all.

The battle of the laboratories held fateful risks for us as well as the battles of the air, land and sea, and we have now won the battle of the laboratories as we have won the other battles.

Beginning in 1940, before Pearl Harbor, scientific knowledge useful in war was pooled between the United States and Great Britain, and many priceless helps to our victories have come from that arrangement. Under that general policy the research on the atomic bomb was begun. With American and British scientists working together we entered the race of discovery against the Germans.

The United States had available the large number of scientists of distinction in the many needed areas of knowledge. It had the tremendous industrial and financial resources necessary for the project and they could be devoted to it without undue impairment of other vital war work. In the United States the laboratory work and the production plants, on which a substantial start had already been made, would be out of reach of enemy bombing, while at that time Britain was exposed to constant air attack and was still threatened with the possibility of invasion. For these reasons Prime Minister Churchill and President Roosevelt agreed that it was wise to carry on the project here. We now have two great plants and many lesser works devoted to the production of atomic power. Employment during peak construction numbered 125,000 and over 65,000 individuals are even now engaged in operating the plants. Many have worked there for two and a half years. Few know what they have been producing. They see great quantities of material going in and they see nothing coming out of these plants, for the physical size of the explosive charge is exceedingly small. We have spent two billion dollars on the greatest scientific gamble in history—and won.

But the greatest marvel is not the size of the enterprise, its secrecy, nor its cost, but the achievement of scientific brains in putting together infinitely complex pieces of knowledge held by many men in different fields of science into a workable plan. And hardly less marvelous has been the capacity of industry to design, and of labor to operate, the machines and methods to do things never done before so that the brain child of many minds came forth in physical shape and performed as it was supposed to do. Both science and industry worked under the direction of the United States Army, which achieved a unique success in managing so diverse a problem in the advancement of knowledge in an amazingly short time. It is doubtful if such another combination could be got together in the world. What has been done is the greatest achievement of organized science in history. It was done under high pressure and without failure.

We are now prepared to obliterate more rapidly and completely every productive enterprise the Japanese have above ground in any city. We shall destroy their docks, their factories, and their communications. Let there be no mistake; we shall completely destroy Japan's power to make war.

It was to spare the Japanese people from utter destruction that the ultimatum of July 26 was issued at Potsdam. Their leaders promptly rejected that ultimatum. If they do not now accept our terms they may expect a rain of ruin from the air, the like of which has never been seen on this earth. Behind this air attack will follow sea and land forces in such numbers and power as they have not yet seen and with the fighting skill of which they are already well aware.

The Secretary of War, who has kept in personal touch with all phases of the project, will immediately make public a statement giving further details.

His statement will give facts concerning the sites at Oak Ridge near Knoxville, Tennessee, and at Richland near Pasco, Washington, and an installation near Santa Fe, New Mexico. Although the workers at the sites have been making materials to be used in producing the greatest destructive force in history they have not themselves been in danger beyond that of many other occupations, for the utmost care has been taken of their safety.

The fact that we can release atomic energy ushers in a new era in man's understanding of nature's forces. Atomic energy may in the future supplement the power that now comes from coal, oil, and falling water, but at present it cannot be produced on a basis to compete with them commercially. Before that comes there must be a long period of intensive research.

It has never been the habit of the scientists of this country or the policy of this Government to withhold from the world scientific knowledge. Normally, therefore, everything about the work with atomic energy would be made public.

But under present circumstances it is not intended to divulge the technical processes of production or all the military applications, pending further examination of possible methods of protecting us and the rest of the world from the danger of sudden destruction.

I shall recommend that the Congress of the United States consider promptly the establishment of an appropriate commission to control the production and use of atomic power within the United States. I shall give further consideration and make further recommendations to the Congress as to how atomic power can become a powerful and forceful influence towards the maintenance of world peace.

The Truman Doctrine 1947

The wartime alliance between the United States and the Soviet Union disintegrated with the defeat of Hitler. Premier Joseph Stalin, pursuing unilateral policies designed to protect Russian security and extend her influence, consolidated the Red Army's control over Eastern Europe, Iran, and Manchuria. The United States, contrary to legend, responded vigorously, cutting off lend-lease aid to Russia abruptly, denying economic assistance it had earlier held out as an inducement to Stalin, and preserving its monopoly over the atomic bomb while challenging the Soviet expansion diplomatically. The Russians withdrew from Iran and Manchuria, but they imposed an even tighter rein on their satellites in Eastern Europe as an "iron curtain" descended across the heart of the Continent. By 1947 mutual fear and suspicion between America and the U.S.S.R. had hardened into what Bernard Baruch so aptly labeled the Cold War.

A sense of crisis developed in Washington in late February, 1947, when the British ambassador informed Under Secretary of State Dean Acheson that England was planning to withdraw from the Eastern Mediterranean, where she had been supporting Turkey against Russian encroachment and helping the Greek government wage a civil war against Communist guerrillas. The State Department, which had been planning a program of economic and military assistance for Greece and Turkey, quickly persuaded President Truman that the United States should take over Britain's role in the Balkans. Congress, however, was controlled by a Republican majority bent on reducing rather than increasing American commitments and expenditures. Truman called a meeting of congressional leaders to discuss the problem, and when he experienced difficulty in convincing the GOP members of the seriousness of the crisis, Dean Acheson took over. Comparing Greece to a rotten apple capable of infecting the whole barrel, Acheson argued that if Greece fell to the Communists, the entire Middle East and ultimately all of Europe would be lost to the Russians. When Acheson finished, an aide noted, "a profound silence ensued that lasted perhaps ten seconds."

Senator Arthur H. Vandenberg, the Republican majority leader, then spoke, saying that he was convinced of the need to act, but added that Truman would have to "scare hell out of the country" in order to get the support of Congress. Accepting this advice, the President went before Congress on March 12, 1947, to request aid for Greece and Turkey and to set forth the Truman Doctrine for the containment of Communism.

R.A.D.

The gravity of the situation which confronts the world today necessitates my appearance before a joint session of the Congress. The foreign policy and the national security of this country are involved.

One aspect of the present situation, which I wish to present to you at this time for your consideration and decision, concerns Greece and Turkey.

The United States has received from the Greek Government an urgent appeal for financial and economic assistance. Preliminary reports from the American Economic Mission now in Greece and reports from the American Ambassador in Greece corroborate the statement of the Greek Government that assistance is imperative if Greece is to survive as a free nation.

I do not believe that the American people and the Congress wish to turn a deaf ear to the appeal of the Greek Government.

The very existence of the Greek state is today threatened by the terrorist activities of several thousand armed men, led by Communists, who defy the Government's authority at a number of points, particularly along the northern boundaries. A commission appointed by the United Nations Security Council is at present investigating disturbed conditions in Northern Greece and alleged border violations along the frontiers between Greece on the one hand and Albania, Bulgaria and Yugoslavia on the other.

Meanwhile, the Greek Government is unable to cope with the situation. The Greek Army is small and poorly equipped. It needs supplies and equipment if it is to restore the authority to the Government throughout Greek territory.

Greece must have assistance if it is to become a self-supporting and self-respecting democracy. The United States must supply this assistance. We have already extended to Greece certain types of relief and economic aid but these are inadequate. There is no other country to which democratic Greece can turn. No other nation is willing and able to provide the necessary support for a democratic Greek Government.

The British Government, which has been helping Greece, can give no further financial or economic aid after March 31. Great Britain finds itself under the necessity of reducing or liquidating its commitments in several parts of the world, including Greece.

We have considered how the United Nations might assist in this crisis. But the situation is an urgent one requiring immediate ac-

The Granger Collection

The Smart Set *reflected the sophisticated and irreverent spirit of the 1920's. Under the capable direction of H. L. Mencken and George Jean Nathan, it introduced such authors as F. Scott Fitzgerald, Eugene O'Neill, and Maxwell Anderson to the reading public.*

New York Convention & Visitors' Bureau

New York's Rockefeller Center, with its bronze figure of Atlas supporting the world, symbolizes the achievements of twentieth-century civilization and of the American free enterprise system eulogized by Herbert Hoover.

UPI/Bettmann Newsphotos

Nicola Sacco (left) and Bartolomeo Vanzetti stand outside the courthouse in Dedham, Massachusetts, shortly after they were sentenced to death in April 1927.

The Bettmann Archive

This World War I veteran selling apples on a Chicago street corner was one of the "host of unemployed citizens" mentioned by Franklin D. Roosevelt in his first inaugural address.

The depression hit both urban and rural areas with equal severity. Here, destitute Oklahoma farm families pause on their way west to look for work in California.

The Bettmann Archive

Crowds gather on Wall Street as news of the stock market crash spreads on October 24, 1929.

The Bettmann Archive

UPI/Bettmann Newsphotos

After taking the oath of office on March 4, 1933, President Roosevelt tells America: "The only thing we have to fear is fear itself."

School children in San Francisco form a Blue Eagle—symbol of the National Recovery Administration— at a rally held to encourage compliance with NRA codes. The Supreme Court's invalidation of the NRA in 1935 was a blow to FDR's New Deal.

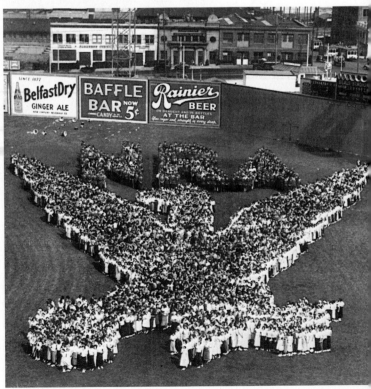

U.S. Air Force Photo

In August 1945, President Harry S Truman decided to complete the Allied victory in World War II by unleashing a terrible new weapon on Japan, the last remaining enemy power. Atomic bombs were dropped on the Japanese cities of Hiroshima and Nagasaki with devastating effect, forcing Japan to surrender. The above photograph shows the nuclear mushroom cloud rising over Nagasaki on August 9. The wing of the U.S. plane that dropped the bomb is visible on the lower right.

The John F. Kennedy Library

John F. Kennedy brought a new sense of idealism and purpose to the presidency.

In September 1957, President Eisenhower sent federal troops to Arkansas to enforce the Supreme Court's ruling on racial integration at Little Rock Central High School.

The Rev. Martin Luther King, Jr., delivers his "I have a dream" speech before a crowd of three hundred thousand civil rights marchers in Washington, D.C., on August 28, 1963.

©Bob Adelman/Magnum

Astronaut Edwin Aldrin, one of the first men to walk on the moon, sets up a seismic detector on the lunar surface. The landing craft Eagle *is in the background.*

NASA

©Susan Meiselas/Magnum

The Vietnam Veterans Memorial in Washington is decorated with mementos left by visitors to honor the American servicemen who died in the Vietnam War.

©Bruce Davidson/Magnum

The nation celebrated its heritage with a spectacular fireworks display marking the one hundredth anniversary of the Statue of Liberty on July 4, 1986.

tion, and the United Nations and its related organizations are not in a position to extend help of the kind that is required. . . .

Greece's neighbor, Turkey, also deserves our attention. The future of Turkey as an independent and economically sound state is clearly no less important to the freedom-loving peoples of the world than the future of Greece. The circumstances in which Turkey finds itself today are considerably different from those of Greece. Turkey has been spared the disasters that have beset Greece. And during the war, the United States and Great Britain furnished Turkey with material aid. Nevertheless, Turkey now needs our support.

Since the war Turkey has sought additional financial assistance from Great Britain and the United States for the purpose of effecting the modernization necessary for the maintenance of its national integrity. That integrity is essential to the preservation of order in the Middle East.

The British Government has informed us that, owing to its own difficulties, it can no longer extend financial or economic aid to Turkey. As in the case of Greece, if Turkey is to have the assistance it needs, the United States must supply it. We are the only country able to provide that help.

I am fully aware of the broad implications involved if the United States extends assistance to Greece and Turkey, and I shall discuss these implications with you at this time.

One of the primary objectives of the foreign policy of the United States is the creation of conditions in which we and other nations will be able to work out a way of life free from coercion. This was a fundamental issue in the war with Germany and Japan. Our victory was won over countries which sought to impose their will, and their way of life, upon other nations.

To ensure the peaceful development of nations, free from coercion, the United States has taken a leading part in establishing the United Nations. The United Nations is designed to make possible lasting freedom and independence for all its members. We shall not realize our objectives, however, unless we are willing to help free peoples to maintain their free institutions and their national integrity against aggressive movements that seek to impose on them totalitarian regimes. This is no more than a frank recognition that totalitarian regimes imposed on free peoples, by direct or indirect aggression, undermine the foundations of international peace and hence the security of the United States.

The peoples of a number of countries of the world have recently had totalitarian regimes forced upon them against their will. The Government of the United States has made frequent protests against coercion and intimidation, in violation of the Yalta Agreement, in Poland, Rumania and Bulgaria. I must also state that in a number of other countries there have been similar developments.

At the present moment in world history nearly every nation must choose between alternative ways of life. The choice is too often not a free one.

One way of life is based upon the will of the majority, and is distinguished by free institutions, representative government, free elections, guarantees of individual liberty, freedom of speech and religion, and freedom from political oppression.

The second way of life is based upon the will of the minority forcibly imposed upon the majority. It relies upon terror and oppression, a controlled press and radio, fixed elections, and the suppression of personal freedoms.

I believe that it must be the policy of the United States to support free peoples who are resisting attempted subjugation by armed minorities or by outside pressures.

I believe that we must assist free peoples to work out their own destinies in their own way.

I believe that our help should be primarily through economic and financial aid which is essential to economic stability and orderly political processes.

The world is not static, and the status quo is not sacred. But we cannot allow changes in the status quo in violation of the charter of the United Nations by such methods as coercion, or by such subterfuges as political infiltration. In helping free and independent nations to maintain their freedom, the United States will be giving effect to the principles of the charter of the United Nations.

It is necessary only to glance at a map to realize that the survival and integrity of the Greek nation are of grave importance in a much wider situation. If Greece should fall under the control of an armed minority, the effect upon its neighbor, Turkey, would be immediate and serious. Confusion and disorder might well spread throughout the entire Middle East.

Moreover, the disappearance of Greece as an independent state would have a profound effect upon those countries in Europe whose peoples are struggling against great difficulties to maintain their freedoms and their independence while they repair the damages of war.

It would be an unspeakable tragedy if these countries, which have struggled so long against overwhelming odds, should lose that victory for which they sacrificed so much. Collapse of free institutions and loss of independence would be disastrous not only for them but for the world. Discouragement and possibly failure would quickly be the lot of neighboring peoples striving to maintain their freedom and independence.

Should we fail to aid Greece and Turkey in this fateful hour, the effect will be far reaching to the west as well as to the east. We must take immediate and resolute action.

I therefore ask the Congress to provide authority for assistance to Greece and Turkey in the amount of $400,000,000 for the period ending June 30, 1948.

In addition to funds, I ask the Congress to authorize the detail of American civilian and military personnel to Greece and Turkey, at the request of those countries, to assist in the tasks of reconstruction, and for the purpose of supervising the use of such financial and material assistance as may be furnished. I recommend that authority also be provided for the instruction and training of selected Greek and Turkish personnel.

Finally, I ask that the Congress provide authority which will permit the speediest and most effective use, in terms of needed commodities, supplies, and equipment, of such funds as may be authorized. . . .

The seeds of totalitarian regimes are nurtured by misery and want. They spread and grow in the evil soil of poverty and strife. They reach their full growth when the hope of a people for a better life has died. We must keep that hope alive. The free peoples of the world look to us for support in maintaining their freedoms.

If we falter in our leadership, we may endanger the peace of the world — and we shall surely endanger the welfare of this nation.

Great responsibilities have been placed upon us by the swift movement of events. I am confident that the Congress will face these responsibilities squarely.

Brown v. Board of Education of Topeka 1954

The movement to elevate the Negro from his status as a second-class citizen into full equality in American life had its roots in the Second World War. The depression had hit hard at black Americans, and the help they received from the New Deal caused many to shift their loyalties from the Republicans, the party of emancipation, to the Democrats. Franklin Roosevelt did little to encourage his new Negro supporters in the 1930's, but just before America entered the war he signed an executive order forbidding racial discrimination in government employment and in defense industries. This step, plus the wartime shortage of labor, greatly accelerated Negro migration out of the rural South into northern industrial cities, where the black man had a better chance for economic advancement and where he secured the right to vote. After the war, Truman was unable to gain congressional approval for a permanent Federal Fair Employment Practices Commission, but he did succeed in desegregating the armed forces and in helping the Democratic Party adopt a strong civil rights plank which contributed to his surprising re-election in 1948.

The greatest push for equality came from Negroes themselves. The National Association for the Advancement of Colored People (NAACP), founded in 1909, began pressing in the 1930's for an end to the segregation of black children in the nation's schools as sanctioned by the Supreme Court's "separate but equal" doctrine set forth in the case of *Plessy* v. *Ferguson* in 1896. The NAACP first sought to secure entry for qualified Negroes in southern law and graduate schools; by 1950 the Court had ruled in its favor in test cases in Missouri, Oklahoma, and Texas. Then, under the leadership of Thurgood Marshall, a brilliant young graduate of the Howard University Law School, the NAACP instituted suit against five local districts across the nation, including Topeka, Kansas, to achieve an end to racial segregation in the schools. Defeated in the lower courts, Marshall and his associates then appealed these cases to the Supreme Court. In a frontal assault on the "separate but equal" doctrine, the NAACP relied upon social scientists who testified to the inherent psychological damage to Negro children in segregated schools, no matter how high the quality of instruction.

Finally, in the spring of 1954, newly-appointed Chief Justice Earl Warren delivered the desegregation decision for a unanimous Court and set forth what a historian has termed "one of the great landmarks in the history of American liberty."   R.A.D.

Warren, C. J. . . . These cases come to us from the States of Kansas, South Carolina, Virginia, and Delaware. They are premised on different facts and different local conditions, but a common legal question justifies their consideration together in this consolidated opinion.

In each of the cases, minors of the Negro race, through their legal representatives, seek the aid of the courts in obtaining admission to the public schools of their community on a nonsegregated basis. In each instance, they have been denied admission to schools attended by white children under laws requiring or permitting segregation according to race. This segregation was alleged to deprive the plaintiffs of the equal protection of the laws under the Fourteenth Amendment. In each of the cases other than the Delaware case, a three-judge federal district court denied relief to the plaintiffs on the so-called "separate but equal" doctrine announced by this Court in Plessy v. Ferguson, 163 U. S. 537. Under that doctrine, equality of treatment is accorded when the races are provided substantially equal facilities, even though these facilities be separate. In the Delaware case, the Supreme Court of Delaware adhered to that doctrine, but ordered that the plaintiffs be admitted to the white schools because of their superiority to the Negro schools.

The plaintiffs contend that segregated public schools are not "equal" and cannot be made "equal," and that hence they are deprived of the equal protection of the laws. Because of the obvious importance of the question presented, the Court took jurisdiction. Argument was heard in the 1952 Term, and reargument was heard this Term on certain questions propounded by the Court.

Reargument was largely devoted to the circumstances surrounding the adoption of the Fourteenth Amendment in 1868. It covered exhaustively consideration of the Amendment in Congress, ratification by the states, then existing practices in racial segregation, and the views of proponents and opponents of the Amendment. This discussion and our own investigation convince us that, although these sources cast some light, it is not enough to resolve the problem with which we are faced. At best, they are inconclusive. The most avid proponents of the post-War Amendments undoubtedly intended them to remove all legal distinctions among "all persons born or naturalized in the United States." Their opponents, just as certainly, were antagonistic to both the letter and the spirit of the Amendments and wished them to have the most limited effect. What others in Congress and the state legislatures had in mind cannot be determined with any degree of certainty.

An additional reason for the inconclusive nature of the Amendment's history, with respect to segregated schools, is the status of public education at that time. In the South, the movement toward free common schools, supported by general taxation, had not yet taken hold. Education of white children was largely in the hands of private groups. Education of Negroes was almost nonexistent, and practically all of the race were illiterate. In fact, any education of Negroes was forbidden by law in some states. Today, in contrast, many Negroes have achieved outstanding success in the arts and sciences as well as in the business and professional world. It is true that public education had already advanced further in the North, but the effect of the Amendment on Northern States was generally ignored in the congressional debates. Even in the North, the conditions of public education did not approximate those existing today. The curriculum was usually rudimentary; ungraded schools were common in rural areas; the school term was but three months a year in many states; and compulsory school attendance was virtually unknown. As a consequence, it is not surprising that there should be so little in the history of the Fourteenth Amendment relating to its intended effect on public education.

In the first cases in this Court construing the Fourteenth Amendment, decided shortly after its adoption, the Court interpreted it as proscribing all state-imposed discriminations against the Negro race. The doctrine of "separate but equal" did not make its appearance in this Court until 1896 in the case of Plessy v. Ferguson, supra, involving not education but transportation. American courts have since labored with the doctrine for over half a century. In this Court, there have been six cases involving the "separate but equal" doctrine in the field of public education. In Cumming v. Board of Education of Richmond County, 175 U. S. 528, and Gong Lum v. Rice, 275 U. S. 78, the validity of the doctrine itself was not challenged. In more recent cases, all on the graduate school level, inequality was found in that specific benefits enjoyed by white students were denied to Negro students of the same educational qualifications. State of Missouri ex rel. Gaines v. Canada, 305 U. S. 337; Sipuel v. Board of Regents of University of Oklahoma, 332 U. S. 631; Sweatt v. Painter, 339 U. S. 629; McLaurin v. Oklahoma State Regents, 339 U. S. 637. In none of these cases was it necessary to reexamine the doctrine to grant relief to the Negro plaintiff. And in Sweatt v. Painter, supra, the Court expressly reserved decision on the question whether Plessy v. Ferguson should be held inapplicable to public education.

In the instant cases, that question is directly presented. Here, unlike Sweatt v. Painter, there are findings below that the Negro and white schools involved have been equalized, or are being equalized, with respect to buildings, curricula, qualifications and salaries of teachers, and other "tangible" factors. Our decision, therefore, cannot turn on merely a comparison of these tangible factors in the Negro and white schools involved in each of the cases. We must look instead to the effect of segregation itself on public education.

In approaching this problem, we cannot turn the clock back to 1868 when the Amendment was adopted, or even to 1896 when Plessy v. Ferguson was written. We must consider public education in the light of its full development and its present place in American life throughout the Nation. Only in this way can it be determined if segregation in public schools deprives these plaintiffs of the equal protection of the laws.

Today, education is perhaps the most important function of state and local governments. Compulsory school attendance laws and the great expenditures for education both demonstrate our recognition of the importance of education to our democratic society. It is required in the performance of our most basic public responsibilities, even service in the armed forces. It is the very foundation of good citizenship. Today it is a principal instrument in awakening the child to cultural values, in preparing him for later professional training, and in helping him to adjust normally to his environment. In these days, it is doubtful that any child may reasonably be expected to succeed in life if he is denied the opportunity of an education. Such an opportunity, where the state has undertaken to provide it, is a right which must be made available to all on equal terms.

We come then to the question presented: Does segregation of children in public schools solely on the basis of race, even though the physical facilities and other "tangible" factors may be equal, deprive the children of the minority group of equal educational opportunities? We believe that it does.

In Sweatt v. Painter, supra [339 U. S. 629, 70 S.Ct. 850], in find-ing that a segregated law school for Negroes could not provide them equal educational opportunities, this Court relied in large part on "those qualities which are incapable of objective measure-ment but which make for greatness in a law school." In McLaurin v. Oklahoma State Regents, supra [339 U. S. 637, 70 S.Ct. 853], the Court, in requiring that a Negro admitted to a white graduate school be treated like all other students, again resorted to in-tangible considerations: ". . . his ability to study, to engage in dis-cussions and exchange views with other students, and, in general, to learn his profession." Such considerations apply with added force to children in grade and high schools. To separate them from others of similar age and qualifications solely because of their race generates a feeling of inferiority as to their status in the community that may affect their hearts and minds in a way unlikely ever to be undone. The effect of this separation on their educational oppor-tunities was well stated by a finding in the Kansas case by a court which nevertheless felt compelled to rule against the Negro plaintiffs:

> "Segregation of white and colored children in public schools has a detrimental effect upon the colored children. The impact is greater when it has the sanction of the law; for the policy of separating the races is usually interpreted as denoting the inferiority of the Negro group. A sense of inferiority affects the motivation of a child to learn. Segre-gation with the sanction of law, therefore, has a tendency to retard the educational and mental development of Negro children and to deprive them of some of the benefits they would receive in a racially integrated school system."

Whatever may have been the extent of psychological knowledge at the time of Plessy v. Ferguson, this finding is amply supported by modern authority. Any language in Plessy v. Ferguson contrary to this finding is rejected.

We conclude that in the field of public education the doctrine of "separate but equal" has no place. Separate educational facilities are inherently unequal. Therefore, we hold that the plaintiffs and others similarly situated for whom the actions have been brought are, by reason of the segregation complained of, deprived of the equal protection of the laws guaranteed by the Fourteenth Amendment. This deposition makes unnecessary any discussion whether such segregation also violates the Due Process Clause of the Fourteenth Amendment.

Because these are class actions, because of the wide applicability of this decision, and because of the great variety of local conditions, the formulation of decrees in these cases presents problems of considerable complexity. On reargument, the consideration of appropriate relief was necessarily subordinated to the primary question — the constitutionality of segregation in public education. We have now announced that such segregation is a denial of the equal protection of the laws. In order that we may have the full assistance of the parties in formulating decrees, the cases will be restored to the docket, and the parties are requested to present further argument. . . . The Attorney General of the United States is again invited to participate. The Attorneys General of the states requiring or permitting segregation in public education will also be permitted to appear as *amici curiae* upon request to do so by September 15, 1954, and submission of briefs by October 1, 1954.

It is so ordered.

Dwight D. Eisenhower: Farewell Address 1961

The Cold War had a profound impact on the U. S. economy and the role of the military in American society. Traditionally, the United States had maintained a very small standing army; when war threatened, the nation would mobilize its military strength rapidly, and when peace returned, it would quickly allow the armed forces to deteriorate. The same pattern followed World War II; by 1950 the 11 million men and women who were in service at the time of victory had dwindled to less than 2 million, and the defense budget had fallen to $12 billion. But peace had not really returned and the threat of Soviet expansion and the fact of the Korean War led to a frantic build-up in the armed services and a rise in defense spending to a level of $50 billion annually.

When Dwight D. Eisenhower, the former Supreme Commander of Allied Forces in Europe, entered the White House in 1953, he brought with him a healthy skepticism toward the military and a determination to bring the federal budget into balance. Once the Korean conflict was over, he sought to hold down defense spending by relying on a policy of massive retaliation to check Soviet aggression; this resulted in sharp cutbacks in the Army and Navy and an expanded role for the Air Force. When the Soviets launched Sputnik I, the world's first artificial satellite, it created intense pressures for heavy American spending in missile and space programs. Despite Eisenhower's reluctance, Congress appropriated huge sums for defense that led in 1959 to the largest deficit since World War II. Dismayed by this trend, Eisenhower decided to warn his countrymen of the dangerous consequences they faced. The phrase "military-industrial complex" came from his speechwriter Malcolm Moos; but the speech, which the President later termed "the most challenging message I could leave with the American people," expressed Eisenhower's own deeply-held convictions.   R.A.D.

M

y fellow Americans:

Three days from now, after half a century in the service of our country, I shall lay down the responsibilities of office as, in traditional and solemn ceremony, the authority of the Presidency is vested in my successor. . . .

We now stand ten years past the midpoint of a century that has witnessed four major wars among great nations. Three of them involved our own country. Despite these holocausts America is today the strongest, the most influential and most productive nation in the world. Understandably proud of this pre-eminence we yet realize that America's leadership and prestige depend, not merely upon our unmatched material progress, riches and military strength, but on how we use our power in the interests of world peace and human betterment.

Throughout America's adventure in free government, our basic purposes have been to keep the peace; to foster progress in human achievement, and to enhance liberty, dignity and integrity among people and among nations. To strive for less would be unworthy of a free and religious people. Any failure traceable to arrogance, or our lack of comprehension or readiness to sacrifice would inflict upon us grievous hurt both at home and abroad.

Progress toward these noble goals is persistently threatened by the conflict now engulfing the world. It commands our whole attention, absorbs our very beings. We face a hostile ideology — global in scope, atheistic in character, ruthless in purpose, and insidious in method. Unhappily the danger it poses promises to be of indefinite duration. To meet it successfully, there is called for, not so much the emotional and transitory sacrifices of crisis, but rather those which enable us to carry forward steadily, surely, and without complaint the burdens of a prolonged and complex struggle — with liberty the stake. Only thus shall we remain, despite every provocation, on our charted course toward permanent peace and human betterment. . . .

A vital element in keeping the peace is our military establishment. Our arms must be mighty, ready for instant action, so that no potential aggressor may be tempted to risk his own destruction.

Our military organization today bears little relation to that known by any of my predecessors in peacetime, or indeed by the fighting men of World War II or Korea.

Until the latest of our world conflicts, the United States had no armaments industry. American makers of plowshares could, with time and as required, make swords as well. But now we can no longer risk emergency improvisation of national defense; we have been compelled to create a permanent armaments industry of vast proportions. Added to this, three and a half million men and women are directly engaged in the defense establishment. We annually spend on military security more than the net income of all United States corporations.

This conjunction of an immense military establishment and a large arms industry is new in the American experience. The total influence—economic, political, even spiritual—is felt in every city, every statehouse, every office of the federal government. We recognize the imperative need for this development. Yet we must not fail to comprehend its grave implications. Our toil, resources, and livelihood are all involved; so is the very structure of our society.

In the councils of government, we must guard against the acquisition of unwarranted influence, whether sought or unsought, by the military-industrial complex. The potential for the disastrous rise of misplaced power exists and will persist.

We must never let the weight of this combination endanger our liberties or democratic processes. We should take nothing for granted. Only an alert and knowledgeable citizenry can compel the proper meshing of the huge industrial and military machinery of defense with our peaceful methods and goals, so that security and liberty may prosper together.

Akin to, and largely responsible for the sweeping changes in our industrial-military posture, has been the technological revolution during recent decades.

In this revolution, research has become central; it also becomes more formalized, complex, and costly. A steadily increasing share is conducted for, by, or at the direction of, the federal government. . . .

The prospect of domination of the nation's scholars by federal employment, project allocations, and the power of money is ever present—and is gravely to be regarded.

Yet, in holding scientific research and discovery in respect, as we should, we must also be alert to the equal and opposite danger that public policy could itself become the captive of a scientific-technological elite.

It is the task of statesmanship to mold, to balance, and to integrate these and other forces, new and old, within the principles of our democratic system—ever aiming toward the supreme goals of our free society.

Another factor in maintaining balance involves the element of time. As we peer into society's future, we—you and I, and our government—must avoid the impulse to live only for today, plundering, for our own ease and convenience, the precious resources of tomorrow. We cannot mortgage the material assets of our grandchildren without risking the loss also of their political and spiritual heritage. We want democracy to survive for all generations to come, not to become the insolvent phantom of tomorrow.

Down the long lane of the history yet to be written America knows that this world of ours, ever growing smaller, must avoid becoming a community of dreadful fear and hate, and be, instead, a proud confederation of mutual trust and respect.

Such a confederation must be one of equals. The weakest must come to the conference table with the same confidence as do we, protected as we are by our moral, economic, and military strength. That table, though scarred by many past frustrations, cannot be abandoned for the certain agony of the battlefield.

Disarmament, with mutual honor and confidence, is a continuing imperative. Together we must learn how to compose differences, not with arms, but with intellect and decent purpose. Because this need is so sharp and apparent I confess that I lay down my official responsibilities in this field with a definite sense of disappointment. As one who has witnessed the horror and the lingering sadness of war—as one who knows that another war could utterly destroy this civilization which has been so slowly and painfully built over thousands of years—I wish I could say tonight that a lasting peace is in sight.

Happily, I can say that war has been avoided. Steady progress toward our ultimate goal has been made. But, so much remains to be done. As a private citizen, I shall never cease to do what little I can to help the world advance along that road. . . .

John F. Kennedy: Inaugural Address 1961

John F. Kennedy's election in 1960 appeared to mark the beginning of a new era in American life. In two terms as President, Dwight Eisenhower had succeeded in quieting the fears and anxieties that had plagued the nation when he took office in 1953. Ike had ended the Korean War; he had contributed to the demise of Senator Joseph McCarthy by treating the Wisconsin demagogue with silent contempt. But new problems arose in the 1950's which seemed to cry out for bolder presidential leadership—the growing deterioration of American cities, the slowing rate of economic growth, punctuated by three recessions in eight years, and the rising tide of Negro unrest against the continued pattern of segregation in the North as well as the South. In the campaign against Richard M. Nixon, Kennedy accentuated his own youth and vigor and promised to get the nation moving again after a decade of stagnation. Using television debates to reveal his personal charm, shrewd intelligence, and keen wit, Kennedy achieved a narrow victory.

Although JFK had stressed domestic issues under his slogan of a "New Frontier," he decided to devote his inaugural address exclusively to foreign policy. Relying primarily on Theodore Sorensen, his close adviser and speechwriter, Kennedy worked on the final draft in his father's oceanfront home in Palm Beach in mid-January. Striving for a short, poetic speech, Kennedy and Sorensen completed the text on a patio overlooking the Atlantic. They flew back to Washington and made a few slight changes at the suggestion of John Kenneth Galbraith, Dean Rusk, and Walter Lippmann.

On January 19, the day before the inauguration, a heavy snow fell on Washington, but the next morning dawned bright and clear, with the temperature in the low twenties. The ceremonies, planned personally by the President-elect, began ominously when a short-circuit in the public address system caused smoke to rise from the lectern; a few minutes later, the aged Robert Frost, trying to read a poem written especially for the occasion, was blinded by the combination of bright sun and snow and had to recite an old favorite from memory. But Kennedy remained buoyant. Removing his overcoat, he stepped forward to take the oath from Chief Justice Warren and then began speaking in his clear, strident voice.   R.A.D.

W
e observe today not a victory of party, but a celebration of freedom—symbolizing an end, as well as a beginning—signifying renewal, as well as change. For I have sworn before you and Almighty God the same solemn oath our forebearers prescribed nearly a century and three quarters ago.

The world is very different now. For man holds in his mortal hands the power to abolish all forms of human poverty and all forms of human life. And yet the same revolutionary beliefs for which our forebearers fought are still at issue around the globe— the belief that the rights of man come not from the generosity of the state but from the hand of God.

We dare not forget today that we are the heirs of that first revolution. Let the word go forth from this time and place, to friend and foe alike, that the torch has been passed to a new generation of Americans—born in this century, tempered by war, disciplined by a hard and bitter peace, proud of our ancient heritage—and unwilling to witness or permit the slow undoing of those human rights to which this Nation has always been committed, and to which we are committed today at home and around the world.

Let every nation know, whether it wishes us well or ill, that we shall pay any price, bear any burden, meet any hardship, support any friend, oppose any foe, in order to assure the survival and the success of liberty.

This much we pledge—and more.

To those old allies whose cultural and spiritual origins we share, we pledge the loyalty of faithful friends. United, there is little we cannot do in a host of cooperative ventures. Divided, there is little we can do—for we dare not meet a powerful challenge at odds and split asunder.

To those new States whom we welcome to the ranks of the free, we pledge our words that one form of colonial control shall not have passed away merely to be replaced by a far greater iron tyranny. We shall not always expect to find them supporting our view. But we shall always hope to find them strongly supporting their own freedom—and to remember that, in the past, those who foolishly sought power by riding the back of the tiger ended up inside.

To those peoples in the huts and villages across the globe struggling to break the bonds of mass misery, we pledge our best efforts to help them help themselves, for whatever period is required —not because the Communists may be doing it, not because we seek their votes, but because it is right. If a free society cannot

239

help the many who are poor, it cannot save the few who are rich.

To our sister republics south of our border, we offer a special pledge — to convert our good words into good deeds, in a new alliance for progress, to assist free men and free governments in casting off the chains of poverty. But this peaceful revolution of hope cannot become the prey of hostile powers. Let all our neighbors know that we shall join with them to oppose aggression or subversion anywhere in the Americas. And let every other power know that this hemisphere intends to remain the master of its own house.

To that world assembly of sovereign states, the United Nations, our last best hope in an age where the instruments of war have far outpaced the instruments of peace, we renew our pledge of support — to prevent it from becoming merely a forum for invective — to strengthen its shield of the new and the weak — and to enlarge the area in which its writ may run.

Finally, to those nations who would make themselves our adversary, we offer not a pledge but a request: that both sides begin anew the quest for peace, before the dark powers of destruction unleashed by science engulf all humanity in planned or accidental self-destruction.

We dare not tempt them with weakness. For only when our arms are sufficient beyond doubt can we be certain beyond doubt that they will never be employed.

But neither can two great and powerful groups of nations take comfort from our present course — both sides overburdened by the cost of modern weapons, both rightly alarmed by the steady spread of the deadly atom, yet both racing to alter that uncertain balance of terror that stays the hand of mankind's final war.

So let us begin anew — remembering on both sides that civility is not a sign of weakness, and sincerity is always subject to proof. *Let us never negotiate out of fear. But let us never fear to negotiate.*

Let both sides explore what problems unite us instead of laboring those problems which divide us.

Let both sides, for the first time, formulate serious and precise proposals for the inspection and control of arms — and bring the absolute power to destroy other nations under the absolute control of all nations.

Let both sides seek to invoke the wonders of science instead of its terrors. Together let us explore the stars, conquer the deserts, eradicate disease, tap the ocean depths, and encourage the arts and commerce.

Let both sides unite to heed in all corners of the earth the command of Isaiah — to "undo the heavy burdens and let the oppressed go free."

And if a beachhead of cooperation may push back the jungle of suspicion, let both sides join in creating a new endeavor, not a new balance of power, but a new world of law, where the strong are just and the weak secure and the peace preserved.

All this will not be finished in the first 100 days. Nor will it be finished in the first 1,000 days, nor in the life of this administration, nor even perhaps in our lifetime on this planet. But let us begin.

In your hands, my fellow citizens, more than mine, will rest the final success or failure of our course. Since this country was founded, each generation of Americans has been summoned to give testimony to its national loyalty. The graves of young Americans who answered the call to service surround the globe.

Now the trumpet summons us again — not as a call to bear arms, though arms we need; not as a call to battle, though embattled we are; but a call to bear the burden of a long twilight struggle, year in, and year out, "rejoicing in hope, patient in tribulation" — a struggle against the common enemies of man: tyranny, poverty, disease, and war itself.

Can we forge against these enemies a grand and global alliance, North and South, East and West, that can assure a more fruitful life for all mankind? Will you join in that historic effort?

In the long history of the world, only a few generations have been granted the role of defending freedom in its hour of maximum danger. I do not shrink from this responsibility — I welcome it. I do not believe that any of us would exchange places with any other people or any other generation. The energy, the faith, the devotion which we bring to this endeavor will light our country and all who serve it — and the glow from that fire can truly light the world.

And so, my fellow Americans, ask not what your country can do for you: Ask what you can do for your country.

My fellow citizens of the world: Ask not what America will do for you, but what together we can do for the freedom of man.

Finally, whether you are citizens of America or citizens of the world, ask of us the same high standards of strength and sacrifice which we ask of you. With a good conscience our only sure reward, with history the final judge of our deeds, let us go forth to lead the land we love, asking His blessing and His help, but knowing that here on earth God's work must truly be our own.

Martin Luther King: I Have A Dream 1963

The movement for Negro rights, sparked by the Supreme Court's desegregation decision, took on a new vitality in the early 1960's. The first signs of black activism came in Montgomery, Alabama, in 1955 when Martin Luther King, Jr., led a yearlong boycott of the city's buses that transformed the young Baptist minister into a national figure and gave millions of southern Negroes a new sense of purpose. In February, 1960, black youths in Greensboro, North Carolina, began a sit-in at a local lunch counter that touched off a spontaneous movement across the South to force the desegregation of public facilities. Despite frequent acts of violence by whites, the Negroes accepted the technique of passive civil disobedience advocated by King as a means of achieving their goals peacefully.

This new activism of the previously downtrodden southern Negroes spread to the ghettoes of the North and created demands for economic as well as social equality. In the summer of 1963, Negro labor and civil rights leaders, headed by A. Philip Randolph, issued a call for a March on Washington for Jobs and Freedom to take place on August 28. In part, Randolph and his associates wanted to bring pressure to bear on Congress, which was then debating a voting rights act, but even more the black leaders hoped to convince the Kennedy administration of the need for a more sweeping and dynamic civil rights program.

Displaying remarkable discipline and self-control, a crowd of nearly three hundred thousand, mostly black but sprinkled with white faces, marched from the Washington Monument to the mall in front of the Lincoln Memorial. There they listened to speeches by such celebrities as Dr. Ralph Bunche, Sammy Davis, Jr., and Jackie Robinson and heard singers Peter, Paul and Mary ask "How Many Times Must a Man Look Up Before He Can See the Sky?" and Joan Baez sing the movement's anthem, "We Shall Overcome." As the afternoon wore on, the crowd grew restless waiting for Martin Luther King to speak. Mahalia Jackson won their attention with a stirring solo, and then Randolph introduced King as the band struck up "The Battle Hymn of the Republic." In a rich baritone voice, Martin Luther King began a speech he had spent two days preparing and which was destined to become, in the words of a Negro journalist, "the rallying cry for 20 million black Americans, delivered by a twentieth-century Messiah."

R.A.D.

I am happy to join with you today in what will go down in history as the greatest demonstration for freedom in the history of our nation.

Five score years ago, a great American, in whose symbolic shadow we stand today, signed the Emancipation Proclamation. This momentous decree came as a great beacon of hope to millions of slaves, who had been seared in the flames of withering injustice. It came as a joyous daybreak to end the long night of their captivity.

But one hundred years later the colored American is still not free. One hundred years later the life of the colored American is still sadly crippled by the manacle of segregation and the chains of discrimination.

One hundred years later the colored American lives on a lonely island of poverty in the midst of a vast ocean of material prosperity. One hundred years later, the colored American is still languishing in the corners of American society and finds himself an exile in his own land. So we have come here today to dramatize a shameful condition.

In a sense we have come to our Nation's Capital to cash a check. When the architects of our great republic wrote the magnificent words of the Constitution and the Declaration of Independence, they were signing a promissory note to which every American was to fall heir.

This note was a promise that all men, yes, black men as well as white men, would be guaranteed the inalienable rights of life, liberty, and the pursuit of happiness.

It is obvious today that America has defaulted on this promissory note insofar as her citizens of color are concerned. Instead of honoring this sacred obligation, America has given its colored people a bad check, a check that has come back marked "insufficient funds."

But we refuse to believe that the bank of justice is bankrupt. We refuse to believe that there are insufficient funds in the great vaults of opportunity of this nation. So we have come to cash this check, a check that will give us upon demand the riches of freedom and security of justice.

We have also come to this hallowed spot to remind America of the fierce urgency of *Now*. This is no time to engage in the luxury of cooling off or to take the tranquilizing drug of gradualism.

Now is the time to make real the promise of democracy.

243

Now is the time to rise from the dark and desolate valley of segregation to the sunlit path of racial justice.

Now is the time to lift our nation from the quicksands of racial injustice to the solid rock of brotherhood.

Now is the time to make justice a reality to all of God's children.

It would be fatal for the nation to overlook the urgency of the moment and to underestimate the determination of its colored citizens. This sweltering summer of the colored people's legitimate discontent will not pass until there is an invigorating autumn of freedom and equality. Nineteen sixty-three is not an end but a beginning. Those who hope that the colored Americans needed to blow off steam and will now be content, will have a rude awakening if the nation returns to business as usual.

There will be neither rest nor tranquility in America until the colored citizen is granted his citizenship rights. The whirlwinds of revolt will continue to shake the foundations of our nation until the bright day of justice emerges.

But there is something that I must say to my people who stand on the threshold which leads into the palace of justice. In the process of gaining our rightful place we must not be guilty of wrongful deeds.

Let us not seek to satisfy our thirst for freedom by drinking from the cup of bitterness and hatred.

We must forever conduct our struggle on the high plane of dignity and discipline. We must not allow our creative protest to degenerate into physical violence.

Again and again we must rise to the majestic heights of meeting physical force with soul force. The marvelous new militancy which has engulfed the colored community must not lead us to a distrust of all white people, for many of our white brothers, evidenced by their presence here today, have come to realize that their destiny is tied up with our destiny and their freedom is inextricably bound to our freedom.

We cannot walk alone.

As we walk, we must make the pledge that we shall always march ahead. We cannot turn back. There are those who are asking the devotees of civil rights, "When will you be satisfied?"

We can never be satisfied as long as the colored person is the victim of the unspeakable horrors of police brutality.

We can never be satisfied as long as our bodies, heavy with the fatigue of travel, cannot gain lodging in the motels of the high-ways and the hotels of the cities.

We cannot be satisfied as long as the colored person's basic mobility is from a smaller ghetto to a larger one.

We can never be satisfied as long as our children are stripped of their selfhood and robbed of their dignity by signs stating "for white only."

We cannot be satisfied as long as a colored person in Mississippi cannot vote and a colored person in New York believes he has nothing for which to vote.

No, no we are not satisfied and we will not be satisfied until justice rolls down like waters and righteousness like a mighty stream.

I am not unmindful that some of you have come here out of your trials and tribulations. Some of you have come straight from narrow jail cells. Some of you have come from areas where your quest for freedom left you battered by storms of persecutions and staggered by the winds of police brutality.

You have been the veterans of creative suffering. Continue to work with the faith that unearned suffering is redemptive.

Go back to Mississippi, go back to Alabama, go back to South Carolina, go back to Georgia, go back to Louisiana, go back to the slums and ghettos of our modern cities, knowing that somehow this situation can and will be changed.

Let us not wallow in the valley of despair. I say to you, my friends, we face the difficulties of today and tomorrow.

I still have a dream. It is a dream deeply rooted in the American dream.

I have a dream that one day this nation will rise up and live out the true meaning of its creed. We hold these truths to be self-evident that all men are created equal.

I have a dream that one day out in the red hills of Georgia the sons of former slaves and the sons of former slaveowners will be able to sit down together at the table of brotherhood.

I have a dream that one day even the state of Mississippi, a state sweltering with the heat of oppression, will be transformed into an oasis of freedom and justice.

I have a dream that my four little children will one day live in a nation where they will not be judged by the color of their skin but by their character.

I have a dream today.

I have a dream that one day down in Alabama, with its vicious racists, with its governor having his lips dripping with the words of interposition and nullification; that one day right down in Alabama little black boys and black girls will be able to join hands with little white boys and white girls as sisters and brothers.

I have a dream today.

I have a dream that one day every valley shall be ungulfed, every hill shall be exalted, and every mountain shall be made low, the rough places will be made plains, and the crooked places will be made straight, and the glory of the Lord shall be revealed and all flesh shall see it together.

This is our hope. This is the faith that I will go back to the South with. With this faith we will be able to hew out of the mountain of despair a stone of hope.

With this faith we will be able to transform the jangling discords of our nation into a beautiful symphony of brotherhood.

With this faith we will be able to work together, to pray together, to struggle together, to go to jail together, to climb up for freedom together, knowing that we will be free one day.

This will be the day when all of God's children will be able to sing with new meaning "My country 'tis of thee, sweet land of liberty, of thee I sing. Land where my fathers died, land of the Pilgrim's pride, from every mountainside, let freedom ring!"

And if America is to be a great nation, this must become true. So, let freedom ring from the hilltops of New Hampshire. Let freedom ring from the mighty mountains of New York.

Let freedom ring from the heightening Alleghenies of Pennsylvania.

Let freedom ring from the snow-capped Rockies of Colorado.

Let freedom ring from the curvacious slopes of California.

But not only that, let freedom ring from the Stone Mountain of Georgia.

Let freedom ring from every hill and molehill of Mississippi and every mountainside.

When we let freedom ring, when we let it ring from every tenement and every hamlet, from every state and every city, we will be able to speed up that day when all of God's children, black men and white men, Jews and Gentiles, Protestants and Catholics, will be able to join hands and sing in the words of the old spiritual, "Free at last, free at last? Thank God Almighty, we are free at last."

The Civil Rights Act 1964

The pressure and enthusiasm generated by the 1963 March On Washington helped ensure the passage of a comprehensive civil rights act by Congress the following year. President Lyndon B. Johnson, who took office after the assassination of John F. Kennedy in November 1963, quickly submitted a bill to the House, which approved it on February 10, 1964. Months of debate ensued in the Senate, with the Republican minority leader, Everett M. Dirksen of Illinois, working to arrange the compromises necessary for passage over fierce opposition from segregationist southern senators.

The amended measure was approved by the Senate on June 19, and by the House on July 2, when President Johnson also signed it into law. It forbade discrimination in education, employment, and public facilities on the basis of "race, color, religion, or national origin," and also outlawed discrimination against women in the workplace. Provision for "affirmative action," or preferential treatment for disadvantaged minority groups, was added to the law in 1972.

The 1964 Civil Rights Act, the first major piece of legislation in Johnson's liberal "Great Society" program, marked an important victory in the struggle to win equality for black Americans.   J.R.

T

o enforce the constitutional right to vote, to confer jurisdiction upon the district courts of the United States to provide injunctive relief against discrimination in public accommodations, to authorize the Attorney General to institute suits to protect constitutional rights in public facilities and public education, to extend the Commission on Civil Rights, to prevent discrimination in federally assisted programs, to establish a Commission on Equal Employment Opportunity, and for other purposes.

TITLE I—VOTING RIGHTS

. . . No person acting under color of law shall (A) in determining whether any individual is qualified under State law or laws to vote in any Federal election, apply any standard, practice, or procedure different from the standards, practices, or procedures applied under such law or laws to other individuals within the same county, parish, or similar political subdivision who have been found by State officials to be qualified to vote; (B) deny the right of any individual to vote in any Federal election because of an error or omission on any record or paper relating to any application, registration, or other act requisite to voting, if such error or omission is not material in determining whether such individual is qualified under State law to vote in such election; or (C) employ any literacy test as a qualification for voting in any Federal election unless (i) such test is administered to each individual and is conducted wholly in writing, and (ii) a certified copy of the test and of the answers given by the individual is furnished to him within twenty-five days of the submission of his request. . . .

TITLE II—INJUNCTIVE RELIEF AGAINST DISCRIMINATION IN PLACES OF PUBLIC ACCOMMODATION

All persons shall be entitled to the full and equal enjoyment of the goods, services, facilities, privileges, advantages, and accommodations of any place of public accommodation, without discrimination or segregation on the ground of race, color, religion, or national origin. . . .

Whenever the Attorney General has reasonable cause to believe that any person or group of persons is engaged in a pattern or practice of resistance to the full enjoyment of any of the rights secured by this title, and that the pattern or practice is of such a nature and is intended to deny the full exercise of the rights herein described, the Attorney General may bring a civil action in the appropriate district court of the United States by filing it with a complaint (1) signed by him (or in his absence the Acting Attorney General), (2) setting forth facts pertaining to such pattern or practice, and (3) requesting such preventive relief, including an application for a permanent or temporary injunction, restraining order or other order against the person or persons responsible for such pattern or practice, as he deems necessary to insure the full enjoyment of the rights herein described. . . .

TITLE III—DESEGREGATION OF PUBLIC FACILITIES

Whenever the Attorney General receives a complaint in writing signed by an individual to the effect that he is being deprived of or threatened with the loss of his right to the equal protection of the laws, on account of his race, color, religion, or national origin, by being denied equal utilization of any public facility which is owned, operated, or managed by or on behalf of any State or subdivision thereof . . . and the Attorney General believes the complaint is meritorious and certifies that the signer or signers of such complaint are unable, in his judgment, to initiate and maintain appropriate legal proceedings for relief and that the institution of an action will materially further the orderly progress of desegregation in public facilities, the Attorney General is authorized to institute for or in the name of the United States a civil action in any appropriate district court of the United States against such parties and for such relief as may be appropriate, and such court shall have and shall exercise jurisdiction or proceedings instituted pursuant to this section. The Attorney General may implead as defendants such additional parties as are or become necessary to the grant of effective relief hereunder.

The Attorney General may deem a person or persons unable to initiate and maintain appropriate legal proceedings within the meaning of subsection (a) of this section when such person or persons are unable, either directly or through other interested persons or organizations, to bear the expense of the litigation or to obtain effective legal representation; or whenever he is satisfied that the institution of such litigation would jeopardize the personal safety, employment, or economic standing of such person or persons, their families or their property. . . .

TITLE IV—DESEGREGATION OF PUBLIC EDUCATION

. . . Whenever the Attorney General receives a complaint in writing (1) signed by a parent or group of parents to the effect that his or their minor children, as members of a class of persons similarly situated, are being deprived by a school board of the equal protection of the laws, or (2) signed by an individual, or his parent, to the effect that he has been denied admission to or not permitted to continue in attendance at a public college by reason of race, color, religion, or national origin, and the Attorney General believes the complaint is meritorious and certifies that the signer or signers of such complaint are unable, in his judgment, to initiate and maintain appropriate legal proceedings for relief and that the institution of an action will materially further the orderly achievement of desegregation in public education, the Attorney General is authorized, after giving notice of such complaint to the appropriate school board or college authority and after certifying that he is satisfied that such board or authority has had a reasonable time to adjust the conditions alleged in such complaint, to institute for or in the name of the United States a civil action in any appropriate district court of the United States against such parties. . . .

TITLE V—COMMISSION ON CIVIL RIGHTS

. . . Section 104(a) of the Civil Rights Act of 1957 . . . as amended, is further amended to read as follows:
. . . The Commission shall—
(1) investigate allegations in writing under oath or affirmation that certain citizens of the United States are being deprived of their right to vote and have that vote counted by reason of their color, race, religion, or national origin; which writing, under oath or affirmation, shall set forth the facts upon which such belief or beliefs are based;
(2) study and collect information concerning legal developments constituting a denial of equal protection of the laws under the

Constitution because of race, color, religion or national origin or in the administration of justice;

(3) appraise laws and policies of the Federal Government with respect to denials of equal protection of the laws under the Constitution because of race, color, religion or national origin or in the administration of justice;

(4) serve as a national clearinghouse for information in respect to denials of equal protection of the laws because of race, color, religion or national origin, including but not limited to the fields of voting, education, housing, employment, the use of public facilities, and transportation, or in the administration of justice. . . .

TITLE VI—NONDISCRIMINATION IN FEDERALLY ASSISTED PROGRAMS

No person in the United States shall, on the ground of race, color, or national origin, be excluded from participation in, be denied the benefits of, or be subjected to discrimination under any program or activity receiving Federal financial assistance. . . .

TITLE VII—EQUAL EMPLOYMENT OPPORTUNITY

. . . It shall be an unlawful employment practice for an employer (1) to fail or refuse to hire or discharge any individual, or otherwise to discriminate against any individual with respect to his compensation, terms, conditions, or privileges of employment, because of such individual's race, color, religion, sex, or national origin; or (2) to limit, segregate, or classify his employees in any way which would deprive or tend to deprive any individual of employment opportunities or otherwise adversely affect his status as an employee, because of such individual's race, color, religion, sex, or national origin. . . .

The Eagle Has Landed:
The First Men on the Moon
1969

In a speech before a joint session of Congress on May 25, 1961, President Kennedy announced his goal for the U.S. space program: to land a man on the moon and return him safely to earth before the end of the decade. The Apollo project, begun in 1964, accomplished that goal, although Kennedy did not live to see it.

The main elements of Apollo were a three-man spacecraft and a two-man lunar module, which detached from the spacecraft and made the actual landing on the surface of the moon. After a manned spacecraft had or-bited the moon and reconnoitered a landing site in the Apollo 8 flight (1968) and the lunar module had been tested in flights 9 and 10 (March and May 1969), historic Apollo 11 was launched on July 16, 1969.

Four days later, on July 20, two astronauts, Neil Armstrong and Edwin E. (Buzz) Aldrin, Jr., aboard the lunar module *Eagle,* touched down on the portion of the lunar surface known as the Sea of Tranquility. Tens of millions listened by radio and television to their conversations with the NASA Manned Spacecraft Center.   J.R.

H OUSTON: Eagle, you're looking great, coming up 9 minutes.

CONTROL: We're now in the approach phase of it, looking good. Altitude 5,200 feet.

HOUSTON: You're go for landing.

EAGLE: Roger, understand. Go for landing. 3,000 feet. . . .

CONTROL: Altitude 1,600. 1,400 feet. Still looking very good.

EAGLE: (Aldrin, calling out altitude readings to Armstrong): 35 degrees. 750, coming down at 23. 700 feet, 21 down. 33 degrees. 600 feet, down at 19. 540 feet, down at 30—down at 15. 400 feet, down at 9. 8 forward. 350, down at 4. 330, 3½ down. We're pegged on horizontal velocity. 300 feet, down 3½. 47 forward . . . down 1 a minute. 1½ down. 70. Got the shadow out there. 50, down at 2½. 19 forward. Altitude-velocity lights. 3½ down, 220 feet. 13 forward, 11 forward, coming down nicely. 200 feet, 4½ down. 5½ down, 9 forward. 5 percent. Quantity light. 75 feet, things looking good.

HOUSTON: 60 seconds.

EAGLE: Lights on. Down 2½. Forward. Forward. Good. 40 feet, down 2½. Picking up some dust. 30 feet, 2½ down. Faint shadow. 4 forward, drifting to the right a little.

HOUSTON: 30 seconds.

EAGLE: Drifting right, contact light. OK, engine stop. . . .

HOUSTON: We copy you down, Eagle.

EAGLE: (Armstrong): Houston, Tranquility Base here. The Eagle has landed.

HOUSTON: Roger, Tranquility, we copy you on the ground. You've got a bunch of guys about to turn blue. We're breathing again. Thanks a lot.

Immediately after landing at 4:18 P.M. (EDT), Armstrong and Aldrin began putting the craft in readiness for the Eagle's eventual ascent back to the Columbia spacecraft, still orbiting the moon. With that and other chores out of the way, Armstrong was ready, 6 hours and 21 minutes later (and 5 hours ahead of schedule), to open the hatch and start down the 9-step, 10-foot ladder. On the second step, he pulled a D-ring that deployed a TV camera on the spacecraft to depict his progress down the ladder.

HOUSTON: Man, we're getting a picture on the TV. OK, Neil, we can see you coming down the ladder now. . . .

ARMSTRONG: I'm at the foot of the ladder. The LM footpads

are only depressed in the surface about 1 or 2 inches. Although the surface appears to be very, very fine grained, as you get close to it it's almost like a powder. Now and then, it's very fine.

[at 10:56 P.M.] I'm going to step off the LM now. That's one small step for a man, one giant leap for mankind.

The surface is fine and powdery. I can kick it up loosely with my toe. It does adhere in fine layers like powdered charcoal to the sole and sides of my boots. I go in only a small fraction of an inch, maybe an eighth of an inch, but I can see the footprints of my boots and the treads in the fine, sandy particles.

There seems to be no difficulty in moving around as we suspected. It's even perhaps easier than the simulations at one-sixth G that we performed on the ground.

It's quite dark here in the shadow and a little hard for me to see if I have good footing. I'll work my way over into the sunlight here without looking directly into the sun. . . .

ARMSTRONG: . . . This is very interesting. It's a very soft surface but here and there where I plug with a contingency sample collector I run into a very hard surface, but it appears to be very cohesive material of the same sort.

ALDRIN (from within Eagle): That looks beautiful from here, Neil.

ARMSTRONG: It has a stark beauty all its own. It's like much of the high desert in the United States. It's different, but it's very pretty out here.

At 11:11 P.M., Aldrin squeezes out of the hatch—a task made difficult by the bulk of his Portable Life Support System—and prepares to back down the ladder as Armstrong photographs him.

ARMSTRONG: The shoes are about to come over the sill. . . . There you go—you're clear.

ALDRIN: Now I want to back up and partially close the hatch, making sure not to lock it on my way out.

ARMSTRONG: A good thought.

ALDRIN: That's our home for the next couple of hours and I want to take good care of it. . . .

ALDRIN: (on lunar surface): Beautiful, beautiful!

ARMSTRONG: Isn't that something? Magnificent sight down here!

ALDRIN: Magnificent desolation!

ALDRIN: . . . The rocks are rather slippery. . . . Very powdery surface when the sun hits. . . . We will attempt to slide over it rather easily. . . .

COLUMBIA: (Michael Collins, orbiting the moon): . . . How's it going?

HOUSTON: The Eva [extravehicular activity] is progressing beautifully. I believe they are setting up the flag now.

COLUMBIA: Great.

HOUSTON: I guess you're about the only person around that doesn't have TV coverage of the scene.

COLUMBIA: That's right. That's all right, I don't mind a bit. How is the quality of the TV?

HOUSTON: Oh, it's beautiful, Mike. Really is. . . . They've got the flag up and you can see the Stars and Stripes on the lunar surface.

COLUMBIA: Beautiful, just beautiful!

ALDRIN: . . . You do have to be rather careful to keep track of where your center of mass is. Sometimes, it takes two or three paces to make sure you've got your feet underneath you. About two to three or maybe four easy paces can bring you to a nearly smooth stop. Next direction, like a football player, you have to split out to the side and cut a little bit. A kangaroo hop does work but it seems that your forward ability is not as good as it is in the conventional one foot after another. . . .

HOUSTON: Tranquility Base, this is Houston. Could we get both of you on the camera for a minute, please?

ARMSTRONG: Say again, Houston.

HOUSTON: Roger. We'd like to get both of you in the field of view of the camera for a minute. Neil and Buzz, the President of the United States is in his office now and would like to say a few words to you. . . .

PRESIDENT NIXON: Neil and Buzz, I am talking to you by telephone from the Oval Room at the White House. And this certainly has to be the most historic telephone call ever made. . . . For every American, this has to be the proudest day of their lives. And for people all over the world, I am sure they, too, join with Americans in recognizing what a feat this is. Because of what you have done, the heavens have become a part of man's world. And as you talk to us from the Sea of Tranquility, it inspires us to double our efforts to bring peace and tranquility to earth. For one priceless moment . . . in the whole history of man, all the people on earth are truly one.

The Watergate Case: United States v. Richard Nixon 1974

The Watergate case provoked a political crisis that convulsed the U.S. government and brought about the downfall of Republican President Richard M. Nixon less than two years after his 1972 landslide reelection victory over Democratic challenger George S. McGovern.

It began before that victory, when five men were caught burglarizing the Democratic National Headquarters at the Watergate office building in Washington, D.C., on June 17, 1972. The burglary investigation, which went on for months, revealed that the men had ties with the Nixon White House. After probing by U.S. District Court Judge John J. Sirica, top presidential aides admitted to knowledge of the break-in, which had been intended to gather political intelligence. Testifying in June 1973 before a Senate committee headed by Sen. Sam Ervin, Nixon's former counsel John W. Dean accused the president of involvement in an attempt to cover up the affair. Between the summer of 1973 and the summer of 1974, Sirica, the Ervin Committee, and special prosecutors Archibald Cox and Leon Jaworski struggled to get the White House to hand over tape recordings of conversations relevant to the case. Nixon resisted, claiming the "absolute privilege" to protect the confidentiality of his communications. The matter was referred to the Supreme Court, and in a unanimous decision (July 24, 1974) written by Chief Justice Warren Burger, the court directed the president to surrender the tapes; Nixon complied. Then, discredited by the scandal and threatened with impeachment, he resigned on August 9.   J.R.

In support of his claim of absolute privilege, the President's counsel urges two grounds, one of which is common to all governments and one of which is peculiar to our system of separation of powers. The first ground is the valid need for protection of communications between high government officials and those who advise and assist them in the performance of their manifold duties; the importance of this confidentiality is too plain to require further discussion. Human experience teaches that those who expect public dissemination of their remarks may well temper candor with a concern for appearances and for their own interests to the detriment of the decision-making process. Whatever the nature of the privilege of confidentiality of Presidential communications in the exercise of Art. II powers, the privilege can be said to derive from the supremacy of each branch within its own assigned area of constitutional duties. Certain powers and privileges flow from the nature of enumerated powers; the protection of the confidentiality of Presidential communications has similar constitutional underpinnings.

The second ground asserted by the President's counsel in support of the claim of absolute privilege rests on the doctrine of separation of powers. Here it is argued that the independence of the executive branch within its own sphere insulates a President from a judicial subpoena in an ongoing criminal prosecution, and thereby protects confidential Presidential communications.

However, neither the doctrine of separation of powers, nor the need for confidentiality of high level communications, without more, can sustain an absolute unqualified Presidential privilege of immunity from judicial process under all circumstances. The President's need for complete candor and objectivity from advisers calls for great deference from the courts. However, when the privilege depends solely on the broad, undifferentiated claim of public interest in the confidentiality of such conversations, a confrontation with other values arises. Absent a claim of need to protect military, diplomatic, or sensitive national security secrets, we find it difficult to accept the argument that even the very important interest in confidentiality of Presidential communications is significantly diminished by production of such material for in camera inspection with all the protection that a District Court will be obliged to provide.

The impediment that an absolute, unqualified privilege would place in the way of primary constitutional duty of the judicial branch to do justice in criminal prosecutions would plainly conflict with the function of the courts under Art. III. In designing the structure of our Government and dividing and allocating the sovereign power among three coequal branches, the framers of the Constitution sought to provide a comprehensive system, but the separate powers were not intended to operate with absolute independence. . . .

To read the Art. II powers of the President as providing an absolute privilege as against a subpoena essential to enforcement of criminal statutes on no more than a generalized claim of the public interest in confidentiality of nonmilitary and nondiplomatic discussions would upset the constitutional balance of "a workable government" and gravely impair the role of the courts under Art. III. . . .

Since we conclude that the legitimate needs of the judicial process may outweigh Presidential privilege, it is necessary to resolve those competing interests in a manner that preserves the essential functions of each branch. The right and indeed the duty to resolve that question does not free the judiciary from according high respect to the representations made on behalf of the President.

The expectation of a President to the confidentiality of his conversations and correspondence, like the claim of confidentiality of judicial deliberations, for example, has all the values to which we accord deference for the privacy of all citizens and added to those values the necessity for protection of the public interest in candid, objective, and even blunt or harsh opinions in Presidential decision-making.

A president and those who assist him must be free to explore alternatives in the process of shaping policies and making decisions and to do so in a way many would be unwilling to express except privately. These are the considerations justifying a presumptive privilege for Presidential communications. . . .

But this presumptive privilege must be considered in light of our historic commitment to the rule of law. . . . We have elected to employ an adversary system of criminal justice in which the parties contest all issues before a court of law. The need to develop all relevant facts in the adversary system is both fundamental and comprehensive. The ends of criminal justice would be defeated if judgments were to be founded on a partial or speculative presentation of the facts. The very integrity of the judicial system and public confidence in the system depend on full disclosure of all the facts, within the framework of the rules of evidence.

To ensure that justice is done, it is imperative to the function of courts that compulsory process be available for the production of evidence needed either by the prosecution or by the defense.

Only recently the Court restated the ancient proposition of law . . . that the public has a right to every man's evidence, except for those persons protected by a constitutional, common law, or statutory privilege. The privileges referred to by the Court are designed to protect weighty and legitimate competing interests. Thus, the Fifth Amendment to the Constitution provides that no man "shall be compelled in any criminal case to be a witness against himself."

And, generally, an attorney or a priest may not be required to disclose what has been revealed in professional confidence. These and other interests are recognized in law by privileges against forced disclosure, established in the Constitution, by statute, or at common law. Whatever their origins, these exceptions to the demand for every man's evidence are not lightly created nor expansively construed, for they are in derogation of the search for the truth.

In this case the President challenges a subpoena served on him as a third party requiring the production of materials for use in a criminal prosecution on the claim that he has a privilege against disclosure of confidential communications. He does not place his claim of privilege on the ground that they are military or diplomatic secrets. As to these areas of Art. II duties the courts have traditionally shown the utmost deference to Presidential responsibilities.

No case of the Court, however, had extended this high degree of deference to a President's generalized interest in confidentiality. Nowhere in the Constitution, as we have noted earlier, is there any explicit reference to a privilege of confidentiality, yet to the extent this interest relates to the effective discharge of a President's powers, it is constitutionally based.

The right to the production of all evidence at a criminal trial similarly has constitutional dimensions. The Sixth Amendment explicitly confers upon every defendant in a criminal trial the right "to be confronted with the witnesses against him" and "to have compulsory process for obtaining witnesses in his favor." Moreover, the Fifth Amendment also guarantees that no person shall be deprived of liberty without due process of law. It is the manifest duty of the courts to vindicate those guarantees and to accomplish that it is essential that all relevant and admissible evidence be produced.

In this case we must weigh the importance of the general privilege of confidentiality of Presidential communications in performance of his responsibilities against the inroads of such a privilege on the fair administration of criminal justice. The interest in preserving confidentiality is weighty indeed and entitled to great respect. However, we cannot conclude that advisers will be moved to temper the candor of their remarks by the infrequent occasions of disclosure because of the possibility that such conversations will be called for in the context of a criminal prosecution.

On the other hand, the allowance of the privilege to withhold evidence that is demonstrably relevant in a criminal trial would cut deeply into the guarantee of due process of law and gravely impair the basic function of the courts. A President's acknowledged need for confidentiality in the communications of his office is general in nature, whereas the constitutional need for production of relevant evidence in a criminal proceeding is specific and central to the fair adjudication of a particular criminal case in the administration of justice.

Without access to specific facts a criminal prosecution may be totally frustrated. The President's broad interest in confidentiality of communications will not be vitiated by disclosure of a limited number of conversations preliminarily shown to have some bearing on the pending criminal cases.

We conclude that when the ground for asserting privilege as to subpoenaed materials sought for use in a criminal trial is based only on the generalized interest in confidentiality, it cannot prevail over the fundamental demands of due process of law in the fair administration of criminal justice. . . .

Ronald W. Reagan: Dedication of the Vietnam Veterans Memorial 1984

The involvement of the United States in the effort to prevent a Communist takeover of South Vietnam during the Johnson and Nixon administrations caused tremendous controversy among the American people. Student protests, which had been focused on the civil rights struggle in the early sixties, shifted to the antiwar movement after 1965, when President Johnson began committing more and more American troops to the fight against South Vietnamese Communist insurgents and their North Vietnamese allies. Opposition to the war in Johnson's own Democratic Party became so strong that he decided not to run for reelection in 1968. His successor, Richard Nixon, began withdrawing U.S. ground forces and initiated peace talks with the North Vietnamese, but the war dragged on into the early 1970s, with the fighting spreading into Laos and Cambodia, and U.S. bombing raids continuing unabated.

At home, bitterness between pro-war and anti-war factions increased. When the U.S. finally withdrew from the conflict in 1973 and a Communist victory followed in the South, people wanted to forget about Vietnam. The returning servicemen who had fought there, many of whom felt demoralized and let down by their country, were largely ignored as public attention was diverted to the sensational Watergate crisis.

In 1982, almost ten years after the end of the war, the Vietnam Veterans Memorial was erected in Washington, D.C. A V-shaped wall designed by a Yale architecture student, it is inscribed with the names of the more than 58,000 Americans killed or missing in action in Vietnam. When a bronze sculpture of three soldiers was added to it in November 1984, President Ronald Reagan spoke of the Memorial's significance at the dedication ceremony.   J.R.

Ladies and gentlemen, honored guests, my remarks today will be brief because so much has been said over the years and said so well about the loyalty and the valor of those who served us in Vietnam. It has occurred to me that only one very important thing has been left unsaid, and I will try to speak of it today.

It is almost 10 years now since U.S. military involvement in Vietnam came to a close. Two years ago, our government dedicated the memorial bearing the names of those who died or are still missing. Every day, the families and friends of those brave men and women come to the wall and search out a name and touch it.

The memorial reflects as a mirror reflects, so that when you find the name you are searching for you find it in your own reflection. And as you touch it, from certain angles, you are touching, too, the reflection of the Washington Monument or the chair in which great Abe Lincoln sits.

Those who fought in Vietnam are part of us, part of our history. They reflected the best in us. No number of wreaths, no amount of music and memorializing will ever do them justice. But it is good for us that we honor them and their sacrifice. And it is good that we do it in the reflected glow of the enduring symbols of our Republic.

The fighting men depicted in the statue we dedicate today, the three young American servicemen, are individual only in times of —or in terms of their battle dress. All are as one, with eyes fixed upon the memorial bearing the names of their brothers in arms. On their youthful faces, faces too young to have experienced war, we see expressions of loneliness and profound love and a fierce determination never to forget.

The men of Vietnam answered the call of their country. Some of them died in the arms of many of you here today, asking you to look after a newly born child or care for a loved one. They died uncomplaining. The tears staining their mud-caked faces were not for self-pity but for the sorrow they knew the news of their death would cause their families and friends.

As you knelt alongside his litter and held him one last time, you heard his silent message—he asked you not to forget.

Today we pay homage not only to those who gave their lives but to their comrades present today and all across the country. You did not forget. You kept the faith. You walked from the litter, wiped away your tears, and returned to the battle. You fought on, sustained by one another and deaf to the voices of those who did not comprehend. You performed with a steadfastness and valor that veterans of other wars salute, and you are forever in the ranks of that special number of Americans in every generation that the Nation records as true patriots. . . .

The war in Vietnam threatened to tear our society apart. And the political and philosophical disagreements that animated each side continue to some extent.

It has been said that these memorials reflect a hunger for healing. Well, I do not know if perfect healing ever occurs, but I know that sometimes when a bone is broken, if it's knit together well, it will in the end be stronger than if it had not been broken. I believe that in the decade since Vietnam the healing has begun. And I hope that before my days as Commander in Chief are over the process will be completed.

There were great moral and philosophical disagreements about the rightness of the war, and we cannot forget them because there is no wisdom to be gained in forgetting. But we can forgive each other and ourselves for those things that we now recognize may have been wrong—and I think it's time we did.

There has been much rethinking by those who did not serve and those who held strong views on the war and by those who did not know which view was right. There has been rethinking on all sides, and this is good. And it is time we moved on in unity and with resolve—with the resolve to always stand for freedom, as those who fought did, and to always try to protect and preserve the peace.

And we must in unity work to account for those still missing and aid those returned who still suffer from the pain and memory of Vietnam. We must, as a society, take guidance from the fighting men memorialized by this statue. The three servicemen are watchful, ready, and challenged, but they are also standing forever together.

And let me say to the Vietnam veterans gathered here today: When you returned home, you brought solace to the loved ones of those who fell, but little solace was given to you. Some of your countrymen were unable to distinguish between our native distaste for war and the stainless patriotism of those who suffered its scars. But there has been a rethinking there, too. And now we can say to you, and say as a nation: Thank you for your courage. Thank you for being patient with your countrymen. Thank you for continuing to stand with us together.

The men and women of Vietnam fought for freedom in a place where liberty was in danger. They put their lives in danger to help a people in a land far away from their own. Many sacrificed their lives in the name of duty, honor, and country. All were patriots who lit the world with their fidelity and courage.

They were both our children and our heroes. We will never ever forget them. We will never forget their devotion and their sacrifice. They stand before us, marching into time and into shared memory, forever. May God bless their souls.

Amendments to the Constitution

When delegates to the Constitutional Convention of 1787 considered the question of future amendments to the body of laws they had created, they concluded that changes might be desirable with the passage of time, and Article V of the Constitution established the means of bringing this about. An amendment, they decided, could be proposed by a two-thirds vote of both Houses of Congress or by a convention called at the request of two-thirds of the state legislatures; when and if ratified by three-fourths of the states, it would take effect.

In the course of more than eighteen decades, some twenty-six amendments have been added to the Constitution. Since the first ten of these—the Bill of Rights—were added almost immediately after the original document was ratified, they may fairly be regarded as part of the original. So it is all the more remarkable that after 1791 only the so-called Civil War amendments—the Thirteenth, Fourteenth [see page 135], and Fifteenth, which were addressed to the rights of Negroes—effected any basic changes in the Constitution. All the others were intended to correct certain ambiguities which emerged as a result of experience and hindsight.

The Eleventh and Sixteenth came about because of a desire to alter the Supreme Court's interpretation of the Constitution. The Eighteenth—which was the nation's "noble experiment" to legislate morality by prohibiting commerce in intoxicating liquors—was repealed by the Twenty-first. And all the others have to do with the mechanics of the governing process. Thus, the Twelfth, Twentieth, Twenty-second, and Twenty-fifth define and clarify the procedures to be followed in presidential elections and provide for the succession to the Presidency in the event of the incumbent's disability. The Seventeenth, Nineteenth, Twenty-third, Twenty-fourth, and Twenty-sixth make possible the popular election of senators, women's suffrage, voting by citizens of the District of Columbia in presidential elections, elimination of the poll tax as a requirement for voting in national elections, and the lowering of the voting age. How few changes have been considered necessary is the ultimate tribute to the wisdom and durability of that extraordinary document. R.A.D.

ART. XI
Jan. 8, 1798

The judicial power of the United States shall not be construed to extend to any suit in law or equity, commenced or prosecuted against one of the United States by Citizens of another State, or by Citizens or Subjects of any Foreign State.

ART. XII
Sept. 25, 1804

The Electors shall meet in their respective states, and vote by ballot for President and Vice-President, one of whom, at least, shall not be an inhabitant of the same state with themselves; they shall name in their ballots the person voted for as President, and in distinct ballots the person voted for as Vice-President, and they shall make distinct lists of all persons voted for as President, and of all persons voted for as Vice-President, and of the number of votes for each, which lists they shall sign and certify, and transmit sealed to the seat of the government of the United States, directed to the President of the Senate;—The President of the Senate shall, in the presence of the Senate and House of Representatives, open all the certificates and the votes shall then be counted;—The person having the greatest number of votes for President, shall be the President, if such number be a majority of the whole number of Electors appointed; and if no person have such majority, then from the persons having the highest numbers not exceeding three on the list of those voted for as President, the House of Representatives shall choose immediately, by ballot, the President. But in choosing the President, the votes shall be taken by states, the representation from each state having one vote; a quorum for this purpose shall consist of a member or members from two-thirds of the states, and a majority of all the states shall be necessary to a choice. And if the House of Representatives shall not choose a President whenever the right of choice shall devolve upon them, before the fourth day of March next following, then the Vice-President shall act as President, as in the case of the death or other constitutional disability of the President.—The person having the greatest number of votes as Vice-President, shall be the Vice-President, if such number be a majority of the whole number of Electors appointed, and if no person have a majority, then from the two highest numbers on the list, the Senate shall choose the Vice-President; a quorum for the purpose shall consist of two-thirds of the whole number of Senators, and a majority of the whole number shall be necessary to a choice. But no person constitutionally ineligible to the office of President shall be eligible to that of Vice-President of the United States.

Art. XIII
Dec. 18, 1865

Sec. 1. Neither slavery nor involuntary servitude, except as a punishment for crime whereof the party shall have been duly convicted, shall exist within the United States, or any place subject to their jurisdiction.
Sec. 2. Congress shall have power to enforce this article by appropriate legislation.

The text of the Fourteenth Amendment appears on page 136.

Art. XV
March 30, 1870

Sec. 1. The right of citizens of the United States to vote shall not be denied or abridged by the United States or by any State on account of race, color, or previous condition of servitude —
Sec. 2. The Congress shall have power to enforce this article by appropriate legislation —

Art. XVI
February 25, 1913

The Congress shall have power to lay and collect taxes on incomes, from whatever source derived, without apportionment among the several States and without regard to any census or enumeration.

Art. XVII
May 31, 1913

The Senate of the United States shall be composed of two senators from each State, elected by the people thereof, for six years; and each Senator shall have one vote. The electors in each State shall have the qualifications requisite for electors of the most numerous branch of the State legislature.

When vacancies happen in the representation of any State in the Senate, the executive authority of such State shall issue writs of election to fill such vacancies: *Provided,* That the legislature of any

State may empower the executive thereof to make temporary appointments until the people fill the vacancies by election as the legislature may direct.

This amendment shall not be so construed as to affect the election or term of any senator chosen before it becomes valid as part of the Constitution.

ART. XVIII
January 29, 1919

After one year from the ratification of this article, the manufacture, sale, or transportation of intoxicating liquors within, the importation thereof into, or the exportation thereof from the United States and all territory subject to the jurisdiction thereof for beverage purposes is hereby prohibited.

The Congress and the several States shall have concurrent power to enforce this article by appropriate legislation.

This article shall be inoperative unless it shall have been ratified as an amendment to the Constitution by the legislatures of the several States, as provided in the Constitution, within seven years from the date of the submission hereof to the States by Congress.

ART. XIX
August 26, 1920

The right of citizens of the United States to vote shall not be denied or abridged by the United States or by any States on account of sex.

The Congress shall have power by appropriate legislation to enforce the provisions of this article.

ART. XX
February 6, 1933

Sec. 1. The terms of the President and Vice-President shall end at noon on the twentieth day of January, and the terms of Senators and Representatives at noon on the third day of January, of the years in which such terms would have ended if this article had not been ratified; and the terms of their successors shall then begin. Sec. 2. The Congress shall assemble at least once in every year, and such meeting shall begin at noon on the third day of January, unless they shall by law appoint a different day. Sec. 3. If, at the time fixed for the beginning of the term of the

President, the President-elect shall have died, the Vice-President-elect shall become President. If a President shall not have been chosen before the time fixed for the beginning of his term, or if the President-elect shall have failed to qualify, then the Vice-President-elect shall act as President until a President shall have qualified; and the Congress may by law provide for the case wherein neither a President-elect nor a Vice-President-elect shall have qualified, declaring who shall then act as President, or the manner in which one who is to act shall be selected, and such person shall act accordingly until a President or Vice-President shall have qualified. Sec. 4. The Congress may by law provide for the case of the death of any of the persons from whom the House of Representatives may choose a President whenever the right of choice shall have devolved upon them, and for the case of the death of any of the persons from whom the Senate may choose a Vice-President whenever the right of choice shall have devolved upon them. Sec. 5. Sections 1 and 2 shall take effect on the 15th day of October following the ratification of this article. Sec. 6. This article shall be inoperative unless it shall have been ratified as an amendment to the Constitution by the legislatures of three-fourths of the several States within seven years from the date of its submission.

Art. XXI
December 5, 1933

Sec. 1. The eighteenth article of amendment to the Constitution of the United States is hereby repealed. . . .

Art. XXII
February 26, 1951

Sec. 1. No person shall be elected to the office of the President more than twice, and no person who has held the office of President, or acted as President for more than two years of a term to which some other person was elected President shall be elected to the office of the President more than once. But this Article shall not apply to any person holding the office of President when this Article was proposed by the Congress, and shall not prevent any person who may be holding the office of President, or acting as President, during the term within which this Article becomes operative from holding the office of President or acting as President during the remainder of such term.

ART. XXIII
March 29, 1961

SEC. 1.   The District constituting the seat of Government of the United States shall appoint in such manner as the Congress may direct:

A number of electors of President and Vice-President equal to the whole number of Senators and Representatives in Congress to which the District would be entitled if it were a State, but in no event more than the least populous state; they shall be in addition to those appointed by the states, but they shall be considered, for the purposes of the election of President and Vice-President, to be electors appointed by a state; and they shall meet in the District and perform such duties as provided by the twelfth article of amendment.

SEC. 2.   The Congress shall have power to enforce this article by appropriate legislation.

ART. XXIV
January 24, 1964

SEC. 1.   The right of citizens of the United States to vote in any primary or other election for President or Vice-President, for electors for President or Vice-President, or for Senator or Representative in Congress, shall not be denied or abridged by the United States or any state by reason of failure to pay any poll tax or other tax.

SEC. 2.   The Congress shall have power to enforce this article by appropriate legislation.

ART. XXV
February 10, 1967

SEC. 1.   In case of the removal of the President from office or his death or resignation, the Vice-President shall become President.

SEC. 2.   Whenever there is a vacancy in the office of the Vice-President, the President shall nominate a Vice-President who shall take the office upon confirmation by a majority vote of both houses of Congress.

SEC. 3.   Whenever the President transmits to the President pro tempore of the Senate and the Speaker of the House of Representatives his written declaration that he is unable to discharge the powers and duties of his office, and until he transmits to them a written declaration to the contrary, such powers and duties shall be discharged by the Vice-President as Acting President.

SEC. 4. Whenever the Vice-President and a majority of either the principal officers of the executive departments, or of such other body as Congress may by law provide, transmit to the President pro tempore of the Senate and the Speaker of the House of Representatives their written declaration that the President is unable to discharge the powers and duties of his office, the Vice-President shall immediately assume the powers and duties of the office as Acting President.

Thereafter, when the President transmits to the President pro tempore of the Senate and the Speaker of the House of Representatives his written declaration that no inability exists, he shall resume the powers and duties of his office unless the Vice-President and a majority of either the principal officers of the executive department, or of such other body as Congress may by law provide, transmit within four days to the President pro tempore of the Senate and the Speaker of the House of Representatives their written declaration that the President is unable to discharge the powers and duties of his office. Thereupon Congress shall decide the issue, assembling within 48 hours for that purpose if not in session. If the Congress, within 21 days after receipt of the latter written declaration, or, if Congress is not in session, within 21 days after Congress is required to assemble, determines by two-thirds vote of both houses that the President is unable to discharge the powers and duties of his office, the Vice-President shall continue to discharge the same as Acting President; otherwise, the President shall resume the powers and duties of his office.

ART. XXVI
June 30, 1971

SEC. 1. The right of citizens of the United States, who are 18 years of age or older, to vote shall not be denied or abridged by the United States or any state on account of age.

SEC. 2. The Congress shall have the power to enforce this article by appropriate legislation.